TRACING YOUR PRISONER OF WAR ANCESTORS: THE FIRST WORLD WAR

TRACING YOUR PRISONER OF WAR ANCESTORS: THE FIRST WORLD WAR

A Guide for Family Historians

Sarah Paterson

Pen & Sword
FAMILY HISTORY

IMPERIAL WAR MUSEUMS

In association with Imperial War Museums

DEDICATION

In memory of my father, Eifion Wyn Roberts, 1937–2010

First published in Great Britain in 2012 by
PEN & SWORD FAMILY HISTORY
an imprint of
Pen & Sword Books Ltd
47 Church Street
Barnsley
South Yorkshire
S70 2AS

ISBN 978 1 84884 501 5

Typeset in Palatino and Optima by
Phoenix Typesetting, Auldgirth, Dumfriesshire

Printed and bound in England by
CPI Group (UK) Ltd, Croydon, CR0 4YY

Pen & Sword Books Ltd incorporates the imprints of
Pen & Sword Aviation, Pen & Sword Family History, Pen & Sword Maritime,
Pen & Sword Military, Pen & Sword Discovery, Wharncliffe Local History,
Wharncliffe True Crime, Wharncliffe Transport, Pen & Sword Select, Pen &
Sword Military Classics, Leo Cooper, The Praetorian Press, Remember When,
Seaforth Publishing and Frontline Publishing

Cover illustrations, clockwise from top left: *Waiting for Dinner in the Huts* by
George Kenner (© Kenner Bedford/photo: IWM, ART 17089), *Panoramic View of
Ruhleben Prison Camp* by Nico Jungman (© IWM, ART 522), Private Charles
Kirby (© the author), Ruhleben ox bone (© IWM, EPH 3802), Isle of Man stamp
featuring Second Lieutenant R F Corlett (© Isle of Man Post Office)

CONTENTS

Chapter 1

INTRODUCTION

Founded in 1917, Imperial War Museums (IWM) has always helped people to discover the wartime or military experiences of family members. For nearly a quarter of a century I have been at the core of the team active in this type of work, and the demand continues to grow. Some aspects of this military genealogy are more difficult and complex than others, and the prisoner of war (POW) experience in the First World War is one of these. There has been a long-felt need for a guide to assist people researching this subject: many records simply have not survived, and it is not as well documented as captivity in the Second World War. I know from experience the type of questions that are frequently asked, and also where people are likely to get stuck. In this book I have concentrated on areas where information is sparse, rather than on other subjects such as escapes, which are well covered in records and literature (but directions to these are given for furthering this research). The book is aimed at those who know little about the subject, but the lists of camps and other information contained in these pages should appeal to anyone interested in POWs and internees in the First World War.

This book deals mainly with the experiences of British POWs and internees held by the Germans and Turks during the First World War. It also covers prisoners and internees held in the United Kingdom. The Quick Guide to Key Resources in Appendix 1 provides an instant overview of where records are to be found, with the different chapters going into more detail about what the records contain, and providing useful context through case studies.

Personal experiences assume an enormous importance in the absence of other records, and IWM is a vast repository of these. Most of the case studies in this book are drawn from IWM Collections, and there is a wealth of material available to those who are able to visit the museum's research facilities in London. Increasing amounts of material can also be found on the website – www.iwm.org.uk – and readers are welcome to make enquiries by post, telephone or email.

Many of my colleagues at IWM have been immensely helpful in the writing of this book, and it has resulted in several animated discussions about different aspects of First World War captivity. I am also very grateful for assistance from other experts in this field outside IWM, and to the archives and libraries where I have conducted research. A great pleasure resulting from this has been the contact with the families of the men whose papers and stories are held at IWM, and their permission to include these. Needless to say, any mistakes contained here are mine alone.

Here, the term 'prisoner of war' is taken to mean members of the armed forces captured and imprisoned by an enemy power during conflict, while the term 'civilian internee' is taken to mean a civilian who has been imprisoned by an enemy power. During this period these terms were often used interchangeably, which can sometimes cause confusion. Very few women were interned in the First World War and here all POWs and internees are referred to as men.

The POW experience is almost one of the hidden histories of the First World War. Statistically speaking, few men of the fighting forces were taken captive – fewer than 3 per cent of British service personnel serving on the Western Front (the theatre of war with the largest number of British POWs). For most, it would have been a completely alien situation; servicemen may have thought about being killed or wounded on active service, but being captured was probably not a possibility they even considered. There was no training or advice about what to do in the event of being taken prisoner by the enemy (this was one of the lessons learned for the Second World War). This also applied to civilians interned in enemy countries. Approximately 192,000 British and Commonwealth servicemen became POWs. Over 16,000 did not return, and those that did were often reluctant to talk. Their experiences, usually painful, were frequently beyond the comprehension of family or friends, and their own desire to forge a new life – or to retreat into the comfort of a former routine – has meant that surprisingly little is known about an aspect of the war that had a profound effect on those unfortunate few.

The public perception of the POW experience relates almost exclusively to what happened in the Second World War. Film and television representations such as *The Great Escape, Colditz, Bridge Over the River Kwai* and *Tenko* come instantly to mind, and although there are some similarities, overall the situation in the First World War was quite different. The issue of POWs did not make much of an impact on the British public at large during the war, except for those whose family or friends were incarcerated. However, fundraising initiatives specifically to aid and support POWs and internees were established, usually by regimental or local organizations, and did marvellous work. These faced competition from a multitude of other good causes for which money was sought between 1914 and 1918. Public support groups for those affected also came into effect during these years – particularly for the families of the officers imprisoned after the Fall of Kut el Amara.

A spate of books were written during and after the First World War, but most of the literary output relating to the prison camp experience concentrated almost entirely on escapes and successful 'home runs'. This was evidently seen as being the area of most interest to the reading public. The relatively mundane existence of boredom, deprivation and daily struggle for survival was clearly not regarded as a subject that would sell. Comparatively few men escaped, although many would have dreamt of doing so. Escaping from German territory was easier than in the Second World War simply because there was greater access to neutral countries. One could escape south-west through Switzerland, north-west through the Netherlands or due north through Denmark. Escaping from Turkey offered greater challenges, but some men did manage to get away. In the camps there was also a conflict of opinion about escaping. There were those who felt it was the duty of a prisoner to try and escape to fight again. In doing so they could make life as difficult as possible for the enemy and tie up enemy resources as much as possible. Others felt the chance of success was so slight that it was not worth the risk to themselves, or the inevitable (often severe) retribution that would be meted out on those who remained.

Dejected and exhausted POWs lie and rest on the bare ground in their cage. These are German troops at Acheux in July 1916, taken at the Battle of Albert, but this scene would have been universal for men in their situation (© IWM, Q 732).

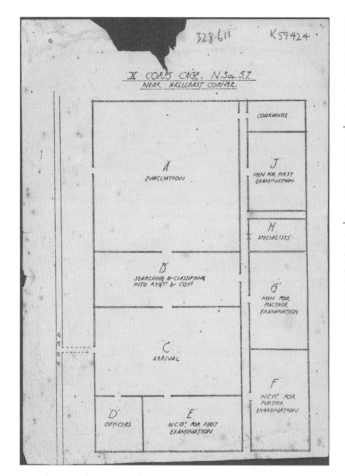

328.611   K 59424

X CORPS CAGE. N.3a. 57.
NEAR HALLEBAST CORNER.

COOKHOUSE

A
EVACUATION

J
MEN FOR FIRST
EXAMINATION

H
SPECIALISTS

B
SEARCHING & CLASSIFYING
INTO REG.TS & COYS

G
MEN FOR
FURTHER
EXAMINATION

C
ARRIVAL

F
N.C.O.s FOR
FURTHER
EXAMINATION

D
OFFICERS

E
N.C.O.s FOR FIRST
EXAMINATION

Holding places became more sophisticated as experience enabled an efficient system for handling large numbers of men. This plan of the X Corps Cage near Halleblast Corner dates from 1917 and shows a logical progression for processing and extracting information (© IWM, K 59424).

It is difficult to generalize about the POW experience. The situation was a fluid one, which developed as the war progressed. Immediately after the outbreak of war conditions for POWs were likely to be poor. They were something of a logistical nuisance and had to be dealt with among other more pressing concerns. New camps had to be built and original locations expanded (or closed down) according to operational needs. Inspections might result in improvements, but reprisals often took place when an enemy government punished prisoners as a result of a perceived breach of an agreed convention.

Prisoners may have been captured individually – perhaps in a trench raid or as a result of a plane being shot down – or *en masse* as happened at Kut el Amara in 1916 and the German spring offensive of 1918. Fear, anger, shame and bewilderment were all feelings that would have been experienced. The moment of capture could have been a traumatic experience, with fierce fighting and horrific scenes causing considerable psychological distress. An initial feeling of relief at not being shot out of hand may also have been common – a serviceman's own experiences, as well as his own side's propaganda, might have led him to expect the worst from his enemy. Instant despatch would certainly have made the captor's life easier, especially in a situation where heavy fighting was taking place. A POW would need to be fed, housed, guarded, recorded and debriefed, all of which would take up manpower and other resources. However, there would also have been kudos involved in capturing prisoners who might yield useful information, and it would serve as a morale boost both for the troops who witnessed them being taken behind the lines and for the civilians who saw them travelling to their camps. Many prisoners were wounded and not in a position to evade capture, and their experience would have been different again, as they were exposed early on to their enemy's medical facilities. POWs were often initially held in makeshift accommodation or a 'cage' not far behind the front line, where there was

Francis Dodd's painting is entitled Interrogation *and shows a German POW being examined by two British officers (© IWM, ART 2234).*

5

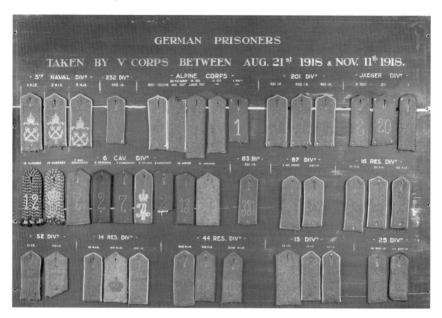

Trophy and intelligence: British V Corps produced a board showing the shoulder straps of German POWs taken between 21 August and 11 November 1918. The shoulder straps provided evidence of the unit that a POW came from, and put together in this way give an order of battle (© IWM, EPH 9319).

the constant threat of coming under fire from their own side. There would usually be an attempt to debrief the prisoner before moving him to a permanent camp.

It was common for POWs to be moved around, often to fulfil the labour needs of their captors. The journey from one location to another could be an extremely grim physical experience – whether route marching on foot, crammed sardine-like into cattle trucks or submerged in a filthy hold on a ship, itself vulnerable to submarine attack – made more difficult by the uncertainty of travelling to the unknown. Hunger, thirst, exhaustion, fear, extreme temperatures, inadequate accommodation, shocking sanitation and disease stalked many of the prison camps, with the ever-present psychological distress of not knowing how long imprisonment would last and worry about relatives back home. Lack of communication was a major issue, not only with home, but also with the people who were now ruling the prisoners' lives. To many prisoners their captors' language would be incomprehensible, while cultural differences would also cause problems and lead to a sense of dislocation. 'Barbed Wire Disease', a term coined by the Swiss physician Dr Adolf Vischer based on his experience of visiting POW camps during the First World War, was a recognized complaint afflicting those who had been in captivity for a long time. (The sufferer sank into a depressive malaise that was made worse by prison camp privations and monotony.) Officers were more prone to this than men of lower rank, despite generally having better conditions, since they were not obliged to work and had more time to dwell on their situation. Boredom exacerbated this problem and enormous efforts were made by various benevolent organizations to provide reading matter, educational and recreational facilities.

As well as the different nationalities in a camp, it was likely that men from different services would be mixed up together. During the Second World War Nazi Germany had separate camps for army, navy and air force POWs, but this was not the case in 1914–1918. Although sometimes factions would form, this lack of distinction provided an opportunity to mix in a way that would have been unlikely in ordinary life. Similarly, the possibility of getting to know people of a different nationality would broaden horizons. A positive aspect of captivity was that strong bonds of friendship with fellow prisoners were formed, which sometimes continued long after release, either individually or through ex-prisoner of war associations. A camp would have represented security and a regular (however inadequate) food supply, and there may also have been the chance to take advantage of educational opportunities that would not have been available at home.

Members of the armed forces were also held in internment camps in neutral countries. In the First World War, thousands of POWs from both sides were transferred to Switzerland and the Netherlands, where they were forced to remain so that they did not contribute to their country's war effort. These prisoners enjoyed a freer lifestyle and more comfortable existence, and there were also provisions for repatriations and prisoner exchanges that enabled some of them to return home.

Civilians had similar experiences in their own camps. Every nation wanted to safeguard its security by ensuring that there would be no opportunity for enemy nationals to pass on information or to conduct sabotage. Often, just registering those who were not suspected of being a real threat and restricting their movements would be sufficient, but frequently there would be a general internment of civilians, although women were not usually interned in the First World War. There were many reasons why foreign nationals might be living in a country: they may have been long-term residents who had been working there for many years (and may even have been naturalized citizens, with sons fighting in that country's armed forces), or they may have been studying, or were simply on holiday when the war broke out. Merchant seamen were always well represented in internment camps. Inter-marriage also brought difficulties when the respective nations of husband and wife were at war. Families living outside the wire, with their breadwinner no longer capable of supporting them, faced great hardship. Letters written for assistance or the records of organizations set up to ameliorate this distress may prove useful for research purposes, but are also potent reminders that suffering was not just experienced by those in the camps.

The growth of interest in local history has meant that people are often fascinated to learn more about what was happening in their own area during the war years. Camps littered the British landscape, and many people had contact with, or knew about, prisoners in their locality, especially those in the countryside. The situation was not as pronounced as it would be between 1939 and 1948 because there was an initial desire to keep POWs out of the public eye and to prevent them from mixing with the British. However, between 1916 and 1919 POW labour was increasingly used on the land, and some parts of the country would have been familiar with German workers.

The First World War was the first total war; virtually every family had an active role of some sort. Most of these experiences are relatively simple to find out, but this is not the case when it comes to researching POWs. For example, when tracing soldiers one can use sources such as service records and unit war diaries. Although the International Committee of the Red Cross (ICRC) at Geneva in Switzerland has records of POWs, the holdings are incomplete. Information had to be filtered through enemy and neutral countries, with attendant language problems, time delays and the ever-present possibility of mistakes. Events over the past century have also meant that names of places may have changed (Constantinople is now Istanbul, for example). Locations are referred to here as they were named at the time as this is how they will appear in contemporary records. Non-European languages with a completely different alphabet present another difficulty – these have been transliterated in different ways, and one can encounter names spelt phonetically.

There are no complete listings of POWs or internees for either of the world wars, but the problem is particularly acute for the First World War. Many family historians are aware of the 1940 bombing of Arnside Street in south-east London which destroyed large numbers of First World War army service records. Less well known is the fact that a card index of officers and men taken prisoner, together with other POW information, also went up in flames. POW camps do not usually have histories along the lines of a unit war diary, although one can find documentation about them in inspection reports, official correspondence, camp magazines, etc. Personal accounts can prove extremely useful, and they assume an extra significance because of the paucity of other materials. Published autobiographies are important sources and some helpful titles can be found in the Select Bibliography in Appendix 5. These books may be available through the inter-library loan scheme, while one of the many benefits of the internet is that the full text of many long out-of-print First World War titles may be found by this means through sites such as www.archive.org.

There are a number of other sources for finding information. This book provides guidance on the resources that are available officially through the ICRC and The National Archives (TNA), drawing on a wide variety of record classes. As well as the Air Ministry (AIR), Admiralty (ADM) and War Office (WO) files for those who served in the Royal Air Force, Royal Navy and Army respectively, the Foreign Office (FO) has many useful records, while the Home Office (HO) has material relating to prisoners and internees in this country. The Colonial Office (CO) and the Ministry of Transport (MT) are also possible sources.

The IWM – established in 1917 to provide a memorial and place of record for the First World War, and whose terms of reference were extended to cover later conflicts – has a wealth of collections that may help place people and provide a useful context for their experiences, as well as some name sources. Regimental museums and other institutions often have excellent collections and knowledgeable staff. Museums, libraries and archives are always gaining new acquisitions, with the result that you can never consider the topic fully covered or exhausted. If a POW died in captivity the Commonwealth War Graves Commission (CWGC) should be the starting point (though not for civilian internees in the First World War since they did not come under the Commission's remit).

Each individual will usually have two stories to research: the experience leading up to captivity, and what happened afterwards. The former is outside the scope of this publication and has been covered well elsewhere, but it is important to be aware that knowing about this may suggest other lines of research for finding out about a relative's imprisonment, and how it might have come about.

It is also worth making the point that, in exactly the same way that the Second World War has tended to overshadow the First in publications and film, there is more material on the POWs of the latter conflict on the web. Many of the same locations were used as prison camps in both world wars, but it will usually be the 1939–1945 era that will be covered on internet sites.

The internet offers exciting new possibilities which particularly lend themselves to POW research, especially as it transcends national boundaries. POW camps were 'melting pots' holding men of many nationalities. Civilian internment camps were similarly varied. One has to remember that there were two sides to the POW experience. On one side the prisoners, and on the other their guards. Relatives of each will be interested in looking at the same subject from different angles. There is thus potential international family history interest that could be instantly accessible. Internet translation services such as Google Translate make it much easier to communicate with people even if one doesn't speak foreign languages. The internet allows contact with people all over the world, and there are many websites established by enthusiasts – often inspired by a relative's experience with the aim of ensuring their story is not forgotten. This may not be exactly the same as the experience of the person one is tracing, but if they spent time at the same camp there will be something of relevance that can further one's understanding of what life would have been like for them there. All the websites mentioned in this book were live at the time of writing, but sites can appear and disappear without warning and are more transient than a good old-fashioned book! At the time of going to press I have learnt that the new Discovery catalogue on The National Archives website will be replacing the Documents Online and Your Archive facilities.

Organizations such as the Anglo-German Family History Society and Isle of Man National Heritage have done excellent work in marking the sites of some camps and locations significant to the First World War and POW story. In most places it is difficult to establish exactly where these sites would have been. Even at the National Memorial Arboretum in Staffordshire – not far from the German military cemetery at Cannock Chase – there is currently nothing that marks the First World War prisoner experience. The arboretum is growing at a rapid rate, and delights in unveiling new memorials; the Second World War POW experience is well represented, especially for the Far East, and it is a pity that the experience of a generation earlier is almost forgotten. It may be that with the 2014 centenary of the outbreak of the First World War this omission will be rectified.

It may be challenging to find out about an individual POW or internee, because many records simply do not exist, but this publication sets out to be the definitive guide to the type of material that is available. It will also suggest ideas for lateral thinking and less obvious resources, such as looking at Princess Mary's Gift Box records for men taken prisoner before Christmas 1914, and camp magazines. I hope that readers will finish this book with a clearer basic idea of what life in a prison camp was like, and with the enthusiasm and direction to further this knowledge.

Chapter 2

THE INTERNATIONAL COMMITTEE OF THE RED CROSS

Prisoners of war have always been a by-product of conflict. In the Crusades captured wealthy knights were released in return for payment of a ransom. Although ordinary soldiers were of no intrinsic financial value, they could be used as forced labour. There may also have been some benefit to keeping them alive, in that they were bargaining chips. Good or bad treatment was likely to be replicated by the other side.

The International Committee of the Red Cross had its origins in February 1863, when a small group of Swiss citizens met in Geneva. Henry Dunant, one of their number, had published a book, *A Souvenir of Solferino*, the previous year. This was based on his experiences as an unexpected participant in the Battle of Solferino on 24 June 1859. He was not a combatant – Austrians fought French and Sardinian troops – but found himself, together with some local women volunteers, caring for the wounded, and witnessing at first hand the human suffering that accompanied armies in action.

Dunant's aim was to establish an organization that would provide assistance to those wounded in war. It would be the impartial hub through which national societies (which would provide medical training for their members) operated. The first national society was a German one – that of the state of Württemberg – founded in November 1863. The Red Cross symbol (a red cross on a white background, the inverse of Switzerland's national flag) became immediately identified with the provision of medical assistance. The cross symbol had Christian connotations, and so when Turkey became associated with the movement it formed the Turkish Red Crescent.

The first Geneva Convention quickly followed in 1864, with another in 1906, after the Russo-Japanese War of 1904–1905. These concentrated more on the plight of the wounded than those taken prisoner, but the 1864

Convention emphasized the impartiality of those wearing the red cross, and Article 6 declared:

> Wounded and sick combatants, to whatever nation they may belong, shall be collected and cared for. Commanders-in-Chief may hand over immediately to the enemy combatants wounded during an engagement, when circumstances allow and subject to the agreement of both parties. Those who, after their recovery, are recognized as being unfit for further service, shall be repatriated. The others may likewise be sent back, on condition that they shall not again, for the duration of hostilities, take up arms. Evacuation parties, and the personnel conducting them, shall be considered as being absolutely neutral.

A third Geneva Convention came into effect in 1929. This would regulate treatment in the Second World War (addressing some of the issues that had occurred in the First World War). A revision followed in 1949 and is still in force today.

It was the Hague Conventions of 1899 and 1907 that provided international law relating to POWs in the First World War. In Britain this was codified into the *Manual of Military Law* produced by the War Office. The government holding POWs was responsible for their maintenance, and they should be given 'the same scale and quality of rations, quarters and clothing as the troops of the Government which captured them'. Britain was the only country to recognize that a 'difference of habits' might make food unpalatable. It suggested that allowance should be made for this, and that 'captured supplies should be used if they are available.' It stipulated that POWs were in the power of the captor government, not the individuals who captured them, and that they must be treated humanely. They should retain all their belongings with the exceptions of arms, military papers and horses. POW labour could be utilized by the captor government, but the work should not directly assist the war effort. Money should be paid 'to purchase comforts and small luxuries' – this usually took the form of vouchers or tokens unique to the camp (common souvenirs brought home) as the currency of the country would have been a useful escape aid. POWs would also have free postage, though the mail would be heavily censored. The only information POWs were obliged to provide was their name and rank. It also stipulated that on the outbreak of hostilities an information bureau should be set up in each country to maintain records of enemy POWs held.

The British office was established at 49 Wellington Street, off the Strand in London, within days of the outbreak of the war. TNA has a *Report on the Prisoners of War Information Bureau* which can be found in WO 162/341. It contains the following description of its role:

A bureau for information relative to prisoners of war is instituted at the commencement of hostilities in each of the belligerent states, and, when necessary, in neutral countries which have received belligerents in their territory. The business of this bureau is to reply to all enquiries about the prisoners, to receive from the various services concerned full information respecting internments and transfers, releases on parole, exchanges, escapes, admissions into hospital, deaths, as well as other information necessary to enable it to make out and keep up to date an individual return of each prisoner of war. The bureau must state in their return the regimental number, name and surname, age, place of origin, rank, unit, wounds, dates and place of capture, internment, wounding, and death, as well as any observations of a special character. The individual return shall be sent to the Government of the other belligerent after the conclusion of peace.

It is also the business of the information bureau to gather and keep together all personal effects, valuables, letters, etc, found on the field of battle, or left by prisoners who have been released on parole, or exchanged, or who have escaped, or died in hospitals or ambulances, and to forward them to those concerned.

Weekly lists of POWs in Britain and the empire would eventually be sent to the Red Cross offices in Frankfurt-am-Main, Vienna and Sofia, and to the Red Crescent in Constantinople.

Geneva set up the International Prisoner of War Agency (IPOWA) on 21 August 1914. It received data from the various information bureaux, and the names of POWs were contained in a huge card index, which ran to almost six million cards (though it appears that these only cover two million POWs). Although there was no provision or precedent for work with civilian internees, a civilian section of the IPOWA was established. It eventually employed more than 1,200 people. The impartiality of the ICRC enabled it to conduct inspection visits to the camps in different countries to check on the conditions in which the POWs were living. These began in December 1914, and were a very important way of enabling information about the different camps to be made public. There was no obligation on the part of the detaining power to act on any of the criticisms or suggested improvements, but some moral pressure was applied. In addition, the ICRC was involved in the repatriation of POWs after the war. The IPOWA closed on 31 December 1919.

The ICRC was also instrumental in launching such initiatives as the exchanging of seriously wounded or sick POWs who would be unable to fight again. These arrangements were usually made on a basis of equal numbers, not only of men, but preferably also of ranks. From the late spring of 1916, contingents of incapacitated men were transferred from

Lazarett-Stat. ....

Lfde. Nr. ....   Krankenbuch Nr. ....
                                              Aachen

Austausch-Station ~~Konstanz~~

1. Familienname *Wagstaff*   Religion: *engl. Kirche*

2. Vorname: *William*   Nation: *engl.*

3. Dienstgrad: *Hauptmann*

   Aktiver Diensteintritt: *20. IX. 1908.*

   Nr. des aktiven Regiments: *The Bedfordshire ~~XXX~~ Regiment.*

4. Nr. des gegenwärtigen Regiments: *The Bedfordshire Regt.*

   Kompagnie: *D*

5. Geburtstag: *23. 6. 88*

   Geburtsort: *London*

   Kreis: *London*

6. Aufenthaltsort vor Ankunft in ~~Konstanz~~: *Aachen*
   Holzminden

7. Verwundung oder Krankheit: *Born ...*

   Tag der Verwundung: *26. 8. '14*

8. Beruf: *Offizier*

9. Wohnort vor dem Kriege:
   Mullingar. Co West Meath. Ireland.

10. Wohnort der Eltern, (oder wenn verheiratet) der Frau:
    Mr. Wagstaff, Leighton Buzzard Bedfordshire

   Aerztliche Bemerkung:

Zugang am:	Abgang am: ....
....	nach: ....

Form. Nr 6.

Sample paperwork that would accompany a POW exchanged on medical grounds. As well as personal details it includes the name of their previous camp and date and details of injury (leg). The heading means Exchange-Station, and the fact that Aachen has been handwritten indicates that the POW is being exchanged to Holland and not Switzerland soon after the scheme was established. The Times reported Captain Wagstaff as one of 40 officers and 252 NCOs exchanged to Scheveningen on 23 January 1918 (© IWM, K 07/347).

14

Germany to Switzerland, with equal numbers of Germans sent to Switzerland from Britain. The scheme was extended to the Netherlands late in 1917 – and as well as invalids, officers and non-commissioned officers (NCOs) who had been POWs for over eighteen months were released (the Germans refused to allow the release of British rank and file because, unlike the more senior ranks, they were a work resource). In January 1917 an agreement came into effect, after protracted negotiations, to exchange all civilian men over the age of 45. The talks involved in these arrangements were always difficult, with POWs and families aware that they were going on and frustrated at the slow progress. Even when something had been agreed, there were usually delays in implemention, and the initial numbers that could be facilitated were always small.

Medical staff and chaplains should have been recognized as Protected Personnel – as non-combatants they should not have been held as POWs, although their duties may have required them to remain with the wounded. Diaries, letters and accounts by chaplains and medics can be especially useful, since they were often concerned to record their work, and these may contain important facts relating to the people in their care, including details of deaths while in captivity.

Visits to camps were also made by representatives of the Protecting Powers – neutral nations that were designated to look after the interests of a country at war. For Britain, the United States of America filled that role until the American entry into the war in 1917, when the Netherlands took over this function.

The First World War ICRC records are known to be incomplete, and it appears to be more difficult to find a record for a POW in Turkey than in Germany. There are plans to make the First World War POW records accessible on the internet from 2014. However, because of the preservation and digitization work that is taking place, the records are currently inaccessible, and the ICRC archives service is unable to conduct a paid search in the way that it could prior to August 2011. Information about the records can be found on the website at www.icrc.org/eng. The postal address is: Archives Division and Research Service, International Committee of the Red Cross, 19 Avenue de la Paix, CH-1202 Geneva, Switzerland.

The ICRC has an informative website: www.icrc.org/eng.

ICRC links to various international humanitarian law databases with full text of the many and various treaties and documents: http://www.icrc.org/eng/resources/ihl-databases/index.jsp.

Chapter 3

THE BRITISH RED CROSS SOCIETY AND THE CENTRAL PRISONERS OF WAR COMMITTEE

The national Red Cross societies supported and cared for their own countrymen and women. Although it is probably fair to say that the bulk of the British Red Cross effort (or more properly Joint War Committee of the British Red Cross Society and the Order of St John of Jerusalem in England – here shortened for convenience to Red Cross) was geared towards medical aid and assisting the sick and wounded, an enormous amount of work was done for POWs, and their supply of food to the camps helped to keep many of the prisoners alive.

In September 1916 the Central Prisoners of War Committee (CPWC) was established as a branch of the Red Cross. As soon as the first prisoners were taken, a raft of organizations slowly grew up to provide assistance to them. These were mainly either regimental or local associations, but there were inconsistencies as not every area or unit was covered. There was great variation in the parcels that were being sent out to the prisoners, with prohibited items sometimes being included as well as information useful to the enemy being inadvertently sent. There were also some complaints about too much – or more often, too little – food being received by POWs.

The CPWC was set up to expand and standardize the aid given to POWs. It defined its functions as:

1. Authorization of Committees, Associations and approved Shops, engaged in the packing and despatch of parcels to Prisoners of War.
2. The control and co-ordination of the work of all such Committees, Associations and Shops.
3. The grant of financial assistance to those Regimental Care Committees, and later to local Associations, which might require it.

This Machine Gun Corps Prisoners of War Fund poster shows the dejection and suffering of a captured soldier. The fund was an example of one of the many organizations that were appealing for money to send food and comforts to POWs (© the artist/photo: IWM, PST 7952).

"MACHINE GUN CORPS
PRISONERS OF WAR FUND"

4. The acting as Care Committee for all Prisoners of Regiments or Units who for any reason were without a Care Committee; for all Civilian Prisoners and, after October, 1917, for all Officer Prisoners of War.

5. The packing and despatching of the prescribed amount of food-stuff and bread to all prisoners included in the last paragraph, not otherwise provided for, and similar duties, on payment, in the case of all prisoners entrusted to the Central Prisoner of War Committee's care by the Care Committees concerned.

6. The administration, as required by the War Office in the Military Intelligence Department, of the requirements of the Censorship

and of the Blockade in so far as despatches to Prisoners of War were concerned and could be dealt with by an unofficial body.

7. The transport to enemy countries of consignments to or for prisoners not covered by parcel post.

8. The provision in consultation with, and with the help of the Food and other Controlling Authorities and the War Office, of the supplies of food, packing material, clothing etc., for all Prisoners of War in enemy countries.

9. Last, but not least, the Committee became soon after its inception, an immense enquiry office, on all conceivable subjects connected with Prisoners of War in enemy and neutral countries.

This new development was not popular with everyone. The Women's Work Collection (WWC) at IWM has a wealth of information in the Prisoners section about the different funds and organizations, both those which continued to operate as part of the CPWC, and those which ceased to function. An example of this was the *Weekly Tale Teller* Fund for Prisoners of War (Prisoners 9/24A). This originated just before Christmas

Model made by Helen Frazer Rock in 1919 to demonstrate one aspect of the war work undertaken by women. This shows the CPWC Depot Packing Department in action. Kate Elizabeth Oliver, who worked on the model in an advisory capacity, had been in charge of the unit (© IWM, MOD 364).

1914 when the editor of the magazine received two postcards from POWs. One was from a contributor to the paper now incarcerated at Göttingen, while the second was sent by a regular reader held at Döberitz. An appeal was made for funds, food and clothing, and copies of the magazine, containing messages for POWs, were also sent to Germany. The fund was, however, unable to enlist under the banner of the CPWC in 1916 because it received irregular donations and its income was subject to fluctuation.

There were problems for such a rigid and large organization as it set about its mammoth task. Nothing could be sent to POWs that did not pass through the CPWC or its approved agents (there were 181 Care Committees, 81 local associations, 40 authorized London shops, and 27 in the provinces). There were also 215 Clothing Associations, which packed and sent items provided twice a year by the War Office. The Post Office would not accept any package that did not carry the relevant Red Cross label and conform to CPWC requirements. The staff of the CPWC expanded as the numbers of POWs grew. Based at 3 and 4 Thurloe Place in London, they took over numbers 1 and 2 in January 1917 to accommodate the growing number of personnel.

The Packing Department was immensely important since the aim was to send three parcels fortnightly, each weighing about 10lb, to every other rank POW (officers had a separate arrangement). The food was specially selected to provide a broad range of vitamins and the necessary sustenance for men who were engaged in heavy work. Bread was sent separately. The cost of a parcel in 1916 was 6s, but costs rose (despite the extensive buying power of the CPWC and well-negotiated prices) to 10s by July 1918. The packers were all approved, and in possession of a censorship certificate. They had to commit to working a minimum of three half days a week, and over 1,000 people, mainly women, worked in this capacity. Categories of workers included writers (putting labels in boxes and writing names and addresses on the side of the box), stickers (attaching labels to lids of boxes), fillers (putting standard items in boxes – as many as 1,000 boxes an hour could be filled by the most proficient staff), packers (packing the boxes neatly and ensuring everything was inserted – the average was 30 boxes an hour), stringers (tying the boxes securely – they had a bottom and a lid and were not wrapped in paper, so effective knots were essential – the average stringer could secure 80 parcels an hour, while the best managed 150). There could be as many as 200 workers at any one time, and the system was a semi-automated one, with the boxes passing along a number of chutes. A post office was established at Thurloe Place in December 1916, and the parcels were put straight into mail bags and sent directly to the docks.

There was also provision for 'special parcels', which were packed in a completely different room. The Turkish and Bulgarian parcels came under this category (because they had to be sewn up in hemp canvas,

Humorous CPWC Christmas card for 1918. The packers can be seen ensuring the strings on the Germany-bound parcels are pulled tight, after the dreadful accusation 'The stringing of this table is too loose!'(© IWM, WWC Prisoners 2/5).

rather than the cardboard boxes that went to Germany). Other parcels included Invalid, Vegetarian, Indian and No Tins, and there was also provision for enclosures from relatives to be packed.

Clothing was despatched from the Packing Department. This was greatly needed as a POW's uniform would be filthy and probably verminous by the time he reached his camp, and all he had was the clothes he was wearing when captured. Bitterly cold winters and hard labour rapidly wore out clothes and meant these parcels were always appreciated. They could be despatched twice a year, wrapped in paper. Clothing was packed around boots to avoid them ripping the packaging, with the clothing contained in towels or handkerchiefs pinned together before being wrapped in paper. It was necessary for POW clothing to be marked to render it easily identifiable in the event of an escape. Brown canvas strips of material were added to clothing – usually on the arm – if the POW did not agree to this, the dark suit would be stored away to be handed over on his release. Yellow edges were also added to clothing.

The addresses for the parcels came from the Records Department. This maintained three series of index cards which included the name, regiment, battalion, number and address of every prisoner in Germany or Austria-Hungary. Officers had their own department, as did other theatres of war. There were three distinct indexes: a regimental index, a camp list and an alphabetical list (for when a man's regiment was not known). Information came from various sources, including telegrams from the Red Cross Bureau in Copenhagen (this information came via the Frankfurt Red Cross – this source of communication was usually the swiftest because the others came mainly by post), official lists from Berlin came through the ICRC in Geneva, postcards from POWs, letters from family and friends and official information from the War Office. British Help Committees in the different POW camps also sent information about what was needed, and details about new arrivals, etc. These were set up in some camps from the end of winter 1914–1915, but they varied enormously. Unfortunately, these records are now lost, and the only information of this nature that survives are the documents at the ICRC in Geneva.

Parcels were addressed to individual POWs during the First World War, so it was vitally important that the news of a man's whereabouts got back to the UK as soon as possible. One problem was knowing where a man was physically located – Bert Munyard's experiences when he was sent to the Courland as a reprisal in the summer of 1916 are recorded in Chapter 5 and demonstrate this. For the 2,000 men in the same situation it was a major problem since no one knew where they were; their address was simply EKI, Friedrichsfeld. The initials stood for Englander Kommando I – the men were scattered in various locations across quite a wide area – with Friedrichsfeld being the parent camp. The parcels took an extremely long time to get through to the men who desperately needed them. Many parcels went astray and never arrived.

'First Capture' postcards were introduced in November 1917. POWs could send these home to inform their next of kin they had been captured, and that their address would follow later. These cards were headed Limburg, and, although it was clearly stated that neither parcels nor post should be sent there, enormous confusion was caused by this, with people in Britain assuming that this was where the POW was physically located. The situation was further complicated because Limburg might have been given as the parent camp (*Stammlager*) or as the name of a working camp (*Filialager*) attached to Limburg. Further complications arose from the middle of 1918, when POWs who had a nominal postal address at a location such as Stendal or Giessen were actually working behind the German lines on the Western Front. The parcels stacked up at the camp named in their address, but these camps usually had no idea where the men were, and could not forward them. This happened to Sergeant Herbert Holmes of 8th Battalion North Staffordshire Regiment, who was captured and sent home a card 'from' Limburg on 18 November 1916. Nothing more was heard from him, and he was lamenting the fact that he had received no post, when after nineteen months he sent a card home saying he had received his first mail, including a grand total of fifty-two parcels that week! Although it would not have helped in this situation, it is worth commenting that during the Second World War POW parcels were sent to different camps according to the number of men who were there, rather than to named individuals. From early 1917 bulk supplies were sent out to the larger camps for the benefit of newly arrived POWs and as a stock-pile in case of future distribution problems. However, the War Office forbad this from the spring of that year, since it felt that the personal parcels should be providing enough food and it was not prepared to relieve the Germans of their responsibility to feed and clothe their POWs. A compromise was reached in the summer 1917 in the shape of 20,000 emergency parcels sent to a depot in Rotterdam. German POW camps kept 12,000 of these, administered by the British Help Committees, but this was not sufficient following the influx of POWS after the Battle of Cambrai in 1917, and the number of emergency parcels was increased. A further 488,200 of these were issued, at a cost of £333,000. An emergency parcel was made up of three tins of beef, ¼lb of tea, ¼lb of cocoa, 2lb of biscuits, two tins of cheese or loaf goods, one tin of dripping, two tins of milk and fifty cigarettes.

In October 1917 the Germans issued an edict that parcels could not be distributed to British POWs in *Lazarets* (hospitals) because they caused discontent among the German patients witnessing the superior food the British were receiving. It would seem, though, that this was a central German Government ruling that was not necessarily closely applied by the military authorities on the ground.

Food became increasingly scarce in Germany as the blockade instituted by the UK took hold. The Royal Navy prevented food or raw materials that might assist the war effort reaching Germany. German black bread was not popular with the British POWs. It was an alien taste in the first place, and, increasingly adulterated by sawdust and potatoes as the blockade took hold, it became even less palatable. There was also not enough of it. The white bread supplied separately by the CPWC (13lb per fortnight per POW) was very much appreciated. It came mainly from two different locations; the Bureau de Secours in Berne (generally supplying the camps nearer to Switzerland) and Copenhagen (generally supplying the North German and East Prussian camps). Some bread was despatched from England – the Irish Women's Association, the largest Care Committee outside the CPWC, used the bakers Dudeney and Johnson of Bedford to supply their POWs. Bread supply was fraught with difficulty: the quality of flour deteriorated owing to the wartime conditions, and transport was a constant problem, with fast delivery being essential to ensure the bread arrived in good condition. This was a special problem during the

You can sometimes (very occasionally) find named individuals in the IWM extensive photograph collection. This image shows wounded Lewis Gunner Sergeant Sponder demonstrating his daily ration of the disliked 'German sawdust war bread' and a piece of German soap made mainly from sand (© IWM, Q 64086).

summer, when the heat encouraged the growth of mould. From the summer of 1917, Canadian flour was used, with that in Denmark coming from America, and Switzerland being supplied by army provisions in France.

Rusks could also be substituted for bread – these were frequently used in the summer months, and were routinely sent to the men in *Kommandos*, as the delays involved in sending bread on to the working parties from the parent camps meant it was inedible when it arrived. Although the rusks could be eaten instantly, they were designed to be baked for a few minutes after the addition of a little water through a hole made for this purpose. Because the rusks could be kept for at least six months with no deterioration in quality they could be stockpiled for use in an emergency. For example, in March 1918 when the numbers of POWs escalated, the bread supply had to be reduced and rusks were increasingly used as a substitute. Copenhagen could not supply rusks on the same scale, so Huntley and Palmer biscuits had to be sent out from England.

The situation for officers was different. In May 1917 a deeply unpopular move was made to bring their parcels into line with those of the men. The scheme allowed for 60lb of food to be sent to an officer every four weeks – through the CPWC, an authorized packing association or through an authorized shop. An extra 22lb per month (or two parcels a fortnight) could be sent through the latter two channels. This was due to come into effect at the beginning of October 1917 but the public outcry was such that the amount of food was raised from 60 to 100lb, and relatives were allowed to pack their own parcels – which were subjected to censorship examination. A complicated system of coupons came into use for those parcels not packed by the CPWC or packing associations, with food rationing adding a further layer of complexity. Officers were also allowed to receive wine, but this needed to be done under the permit system. Authorized shops could supply twenty-four half-bottles of wine (under 30 per cent proof) every twelve weeks. Spirits were not permissible. An

This ox-tongue tin was sent to inveterate escaper Captain Shaw at Holzminden. The Armistice caused it to be returned to sender unopened. The maps, wire-cutters and compasses would have been invaluable escape aids and the tin could only have been issued to Shaw after bribing the German guards. Tins were routinely opened to prevent them being stored for escape attempts and to ascertain they did not contain forbidden materials (© IWM, EPH 810).

officer or his family also had the choice of bread supply from Berne, Copenhagen or from England. From September 1918 bread was no longer addressed individually but was sent to the different camps, the amount being determined by the number of officers, with most of it coming from Copenhagen. Officers' parcels were paid for by their family, or by the officers themselves, though if this proved difficult they could be placed on the 'Committee List', whereby they received the same 60lb of parcels as the men received, and they were also put on the bread list.

All POWs could be sent an 11lb (maximum weight) 'personal parcel', which was packed by friends or relations. These were sent by the Post Office and had blue labels rather than a Red Cross label, and were subject to postal censorship. The items these could contain were listed as:

> Pipes, sponge, pencils, tooth powder, badges of rank, numerals and shoulder titles, shaving brush, safety razor, boot-laces (mohair), pipe lights, medal ribbons, brass polish, housewife, handkerchiefs (one a quarter), shaving soap (one stick a quarter), health salts, insecticide powder, braces and belts (provided they are made of webbing and include no rubber or leather), combs, hair brushes, tooth brushes, buttons, chess, draughts, dominoes, dubbin, hob-nails, sweets or chocolate (8oz only), one pair mittens every quarter, one muffler every quarter, one pair of socks instead of mittens or muffler.

From February 1918 these parcels could be sent to men interned in neutral countries (who did not receive the other parcels, which were only sent to men held on enemy territory).

Civilian prisoners had their own department at the CPWC. Ruhleben was the largest civilian camp to which supplies were sent. As well as food, disinfectants, cleansing agents and foods for invalids were despatched. Raw materials for the Handicraft Committee were also provided. These included leather for bookbinding, mahogany and sycamore wood for the boat-building class, etc. Clothing was a particular problem: there was no official clothing provision as there was with military POWs, and there were restrictions on what could be sent to the internees. Some towns, such as Hull and Grimsby, had committees for their own inhabitants or crews. An attractive testimonial certificate signed by all the Ruhleben beneficiaries of the Hull Voluntary Aid Committee was sent to Honorary Secretary Miss Marjorie M Harris in March 1918. This is now held in the Art Department of IWM (ART 6514).There were also a variety of organizations that could supply merchant seamen – for example the Merchant Seamen's Help Society, which looked after 800 mariners, as did the British and Foreign Sailor's Society. Some relatives also supplied their men under the permit system, whereby parcels were sent from authorized shops.

The Civilians and Special Department also dealt with the supply of games and items for entertainment. Footballs and tennis balls were restricted because of the materials they were made of, while gramophone records and games had to meet censorship regulations. This department also arranged for embroidery and carpet-making classes in Switzerland to be held for the interned prisoners there. In addition, it facilitated the supply of false teeth, and helped prepare the lists of prisoners to be examined for internment in a neutral country.

The Mediterranean Department looked after POWs in Turkey and Bulgaria. It faced great challenges because of distance and communication problems. Many parcels were pilfered, or simply didn't arrive at all. It took between five and ten months for a parcel to reach Turkey from the UK, with nine being the average, and eighteen not unknown. The delay principally came from transport through Austria, and the unreliability and length of the journey meant that the same quantity of parcels could not be despatched to POWs in the east. Two weekly 10lb parcels were sent to each man from January 1917 until March 1918, and from June 1917 these were supplemented with a monetary remittance of 10s per fortnight. From November 1917 advice was given that there was no point in sending parcels or money to camps east of Aleppo as they could not be got to the men, and there was no food available to be purchased with the money. From December 1917 opium pills and chalk were included in parcels to help combat the effects of malaria. In May 1918 parcel mail through Austria was abandoned, and parcels were packed into large wooden crates which were sent by railway directly through to Constantinople. This speeded up the process considerably – delivery took about ten weeks – but after the Armistice over 10,000 cases were discovered in Vienna. These were later used for the relief of British subjects and suffering Austrian women and children. The parcels were sewn in hessian material rather than wrapped in paper or cardboard, and you can see a sample of this on the internet at www.kingsownmuseum .plus.com/pwcc.htm.

Expenditure on supplies to POWs came to approximately £6,500,000, and nearly 9,000,000 food and 800,000 clothing parcels were sent.

Unfortunately, most of the many records that were produced for operational reasons during the First World War no longer exist. The ICRC at Geneva has the most complete set of records, and although the British Red Cross Society has a good archive, there is very little relating to the First World War POW experience. They have a run of the magazine *The British Prisoner of War* (also held at IWM) edited by Mrs Una Pope-Hennessy, but this was published only in the last year of the war. This type of illustrated publication, which circulated news about the camps and general POW information, was of great value to relatives at home – and to the family historian of the future – and was to be widespread during the next war. The idea probably sprang from the rather primitive newsletters produced by the families of POWs held by the Turks and also from the magazines produced in the camps themselves, which were often sent home to Britain. It had a circulation of about 12,000, and although it only ran for a year, netted nearly £1,200 profit for the funds. Mrs Pope-Hennessy was also responsible for the *Map and Gazetteer of POW Camps in Germany and Austria* – see the map on page 150 and the list of camps in Appendix 6. Two editions of this were made: the first with the names of the camps on the cover and the second featuring details on the camps on pages inside. Some documents relating to her POW work, including a run of the magazine and material relating to the 1919 Ruhleben exhibition, can be found at the IWM Department of Documents in the papers of her husband Major General L H R Pope-Hennessy CB, DSO (03/35/1).

Another regular publication, *The British Red Cross Society: Summary of Work for the Week Ending . . .* contains a paragraph about the work for 'Wounded and Prisoners' or 'British Prisoners of War Fund'. From 29 May 1915 it features some postcard responses as thanks for parcels sent. Initially no names are given – just the camp, the date and the message – and later these are usually signed with initials. Very occasionally full names are given. There are also sometimes notes of thanks from grateful

Typical example of an acknowledgement card sent to reassure the senders that a parcel had arrived safely. This one was sent by Private Harry Hawksworth in Bulgaria to Lady Dodds at the BRCS (© IWM, K 80/3304).

wives and mothers, writing on behalf of their POW relatives. This was produced weekly until 16 October 1915, when it became fortnightly, and then monthly from October 1916. These publications are also very useful for finding out about Red Cross activities generally, and about the arrangements, and facts and figures, for repatriation at the end of the war. These documents can be found at IWM in the British Red Cross Society Ephemera Collection, Box B (Eph.C. BRCS).

An acknowledgement card was contained in each parcel to enable the POW to return it and show it had arrived safely. Some of these may have survived, either from before the CPWC took over the supply of parcels in 1916 or from the associations that continued to provide for their own men. Check regimental collections or local archives for this. Prisoners 3/1-/62 in the WWC at IWM contains sixty-two cards or letters mainly sent by POWs in Bulgaria thanking Lady Dodds for the parcels that were received from the Red Cross. Some of them are the pre-printed postcards that were put in each parcel, and one is a letter from Lieutenant Gilliland, who took over the distribution of items from the parcels at Philippolis. He provided interesting feedback about goods that did not travel well, and what was really needed by the men.

The very detailed publication *The Work of the Central Prisoners of War Committee, 1916–1919* (London: Charles Cull, 1919?) contains a complete list of the Care Committees and associations. It can be found in the WWC (Prisoners 2/8) and also in hard copy at IWM. This makes interesting reading in its own right, because it provides the numbers of POWs from each regiment (correct up to mid-October 1918), the address of the Care Committee (where records were kept) and the address to which private parcels should be sent for onward transmission (the packing organization). For example, the eleven POWs of the 2nd Life Guards were catered for by the Hon. Mrs Montgomerie, CO's House, Cavalry Barracks, Windsor – following the tradition of the commanding officer's wife looking after the welfare of her husband's men. The twenty-two POWs of the Welsh Guards had their parcels packed by the Civil Service Co-Operative Stores, 28 Haymarket, London. There are also separate appendices for Clothing Committees and authorized local associations. These date from 1916 only – there will have been other bodies working for POWs before the establishment of the CPWC.

Care Committee albums or lists may be found in regimental or local county/borough collections, and are always worth looking for, even though many may no longer exist. The National Army Museum has a splendid leather-bound example for the 4th Dragoon Guards compiled by Mrs C A Rickards (1956-10-50). There is also a handwritten ledger with a list of camps, together with details of the men in each of these. It includes alphabetical lists of men, with details of their parcels (the dates sent and contents, and a column for date of acknowledgement).

Another example is the Queen's Royal Regiment collection at the Surrey History Centre, which has excellent POW material in the shape of a POW Relief Fund scrapbook kept by Lieutenant Colonel Elias Morgan and his wife (QRWS/30/ELIAA), and a hand-written continually updated register of POWs (QRWS/1/5/1).

The WWC at IWM has some material relating to the Royal Flying Corps (and Royal Air Force) Aid Committee in Prisoners 4. This includes acknowledgement cards and letters, and also items such as an exercise book listing parcels and men, in Prisoners 4/143. This contains surnames (presumably mainly officers), together with some lists of what was sent, and prices and contents of parcels.

IWM also has some correspondence relating to the Nottingham and Nottinghamshire Comforts for the Troops Fund in the collection of Miss B Whitby (95/38/1).

Local newspapers and regimental magazines may also yield information about these – subscriptions to the funds were often published in the local newspapers, as a way of thanking people, raising awareness and encouraging more donations. Newspapers were sometimes instrumental in running funds for POWs. Publications may also have been produced about particular funds. An example is *War Prisoners' Fund for Oxfordshire and Buckinghamshire Regiments: March, 1915, to April, 1919: Final Report and Statement of Accounts* in the WWC (Prisoners 11/1). It is extremely detailed and, although names are not included, it contains a very informative breakdown of numbers of POWs from each unit, where they were captured, and how many survived and died. It also gives a very clear indication of the amount of work involved in tracing and caring for these men.

Another fascinating publication is *Memories Grave and Gay: Of Burton Prisoners of War and the Local Work with Allusions to War-time Legislation* by Lily Thomas (Derby: Bemrose, 1919?). It is an excellent account of work done locally, and also makes the point of how supportive local organizations could be to family and friends who lived in the community. The association prided itself on sending 'mystery packets' to its 'Godsons': unusual items such as jugged hare, dried codlings, parsnips, tinned beetroots or 'cokernuts' might be unwrapped. It also took the trouble to find out what items were particularly needed, and for men working in salt mines, coloured glasses were much appreciated – blindness, frozen finger tips as well as boils and sores were frequent hazards in this type of work. Sample letters of thanks with names and camps are also included.

Some information about the King's Own Royal Lancaster Regiment Care Committee can be found at www.kingsownmuseum.plus.com/pwcc.htm.

Chapter 4

THE COMMONWEALTH
WAR GRAVES COMMISSION

The Commonwealth War Graves Commission (CWGC), originally known as the Imperial War Graves Commission, should be the first place to start looking for British prisoners of war who died in captivity. The original graves and cemeteries were in enemy territory, and the British obviously had no control over where burials took place, although information that a death had occurred was relayed to the UK.

Consequently, after the conclusion of hostilities, decisions had to be taken about building and maintaining the POW cemeteries. There was considerable public concern at bodies remaining in enemy territory, but the Commission stuck to its principles of uniformity in death, and no bodies were repatriated. The German burial tradition dictated that a grave would be occupied for only thirty years; for the CWGC it was important that the burial sites would last in perpetuity. It was easier to care for the graves in larger cemeteries, although that usually meant re-interring bodies. Ease of access for potential visitors was also a consideration. Cemeteries tended to be built where large prisoner burial grounds had already been established or in cemeteries for large towns or cities, where there was a good transport infrastructure.

The situation regarding civilian internees was always different as the CWGC had no remit to bury or record their deaths. After the First World War civilian bodies could be repatriated, and their deaths were not recorded by the Commission. Merchant seamen who died as prisoners were not recorded either, unless they were deemed to have died as a result of direct enemy action. This situation evolved during the Second World War as the CWGC expanded its terms of reference. In autumn 1940, as a result of mounting casualties in the Blitz, Second World War civilians were included in the CWGC records.

The 'Debt of Honour' database on the Commission website at www.cwgc.org is very easy to look up, and useful information can also be gleaned from the cemetery details. Many graves were concentrated into larger cemeteries in the years after the wars. You should also be aware that burials may have taken place near a hospital rather than a place of internment. Prisoners may have been transferred to a hospital and subsequently died. For example, one of the early prison camps in Germany was at Döberitz, just outside Berlin, but ill patients from there may have been transferred to, and subsequently died at, the Alexandrinenstrasse Hospital in the centre of the city. Berlin Hasenheide Garrison Cemetery was the cemetery where POWs at this hospital were originally buried.

It is possible that the CWGC may have information about an original burial place. This is definitely not always the case and each chapter provides details about where the Commission may be able to help. Contact can be through its website, or by post at Commonwealth War Graves Commission, 2 Marlow Road, Maidenhead, Berkshire SL6 7DX.

It is also worth mentioning that, although there is a central cemetery for German prisoners of war at Cannock Chase, if a German prisoner was originally buried in a CWGC cemetery, his grave remained there. The Commission has details of all those buried in its cemeteries, though you will need to contact it directly to enquire about these.

Chapter 5

BRITISH PRISONERS OF WAR IN GERMANY

More British prisoners of war (168,846 British and Commonwealth other ranks and 6,778 officers) were taken on the Western Front than in any other theatre. The initial months of the war featured more mobile action than would later be the case once trench warfare took hold, and large numbers of men were captured at the Battles of Mons, Marne and Ypres. Nearly 17,000 Britons were imprisoned by the end of 1914. In the more static years that followed, prisoners were often picked up in trench raids, some of which were substantial operations lasting several hours. Although major offensives such as the Somme resulted in large numbers of captives, numbers escalated when the war became mobile again in 1918. The greatest number of prisoners was caught during the German spring offensive of 1918, with 21,000 on 21 March alone. Many of these 1918 prisoners did not travel to Germany, but remained just behind the German lines on the Western Front, where they were forced to work. It has been estimated that this was the case for one-sixth of British prisoners in November 1918.

Some POWs were captured by Austria-Hungary, but the numbers were comparatively tiny. The Central Prisoners of War Committee gave the figures for the duration of the war as 40 officers and 325 other ranks. The names of the camps can be found in the list of camps in Germany and Austria in Appendix 6.

For those seeking to visit the site of a POW camp or to establish exactly where it was located, there is a fascinating little file at TNA in AIR 1/2154/209/3/312, entitled 'Bomb Targets: Prisoners of War Camps in Germany'. This contains aerial photographs and marked printed and hand-drawn maps showing where the camps were located (although only a few are featured). It also shows how information about the POW camps was acquired (repatriated/escaped POWs, aerial observation, informants, etc) and put together. A list stamped July 1918 provides a breakdown of the numbers of 'British Army, Colonial, Indian Army and Naval men' in each camp. The file is concerned with air raids; the Germans allegedly left the lights on in the POW camps to encourage British pilots to drop their bombs on them. A poignant letter from 'A very anxious British mother' to the 'Commanding Officer of the Independent Air Service' reads: 'My one and only son is a British prisoner of war along with many other British Officers at Saarbrucken. After enduring all the horrors of the battlefield, it is terrible to think he may be killed by our own airmen. Can anything be done to save their lives?'

An Other Rank's Experience

Herbert Munyard joined the East Surrey Regiment at the end of 1904 or the beginning of 1905. As a regular soldier he had served in India, and was based in Ireland at the outbreak of war. His service record was amongst those destroyed in 1940, but some information can be gleaned from his Medal Index Card. This can be viewed digitally at TNA, or can be seen online either through TNA's Documents Online facility at www.nationalarchives.gov.uk/documentsonline (pay per view) or through the subscription website www.ancestry.co.uk. Munyard's card contains the hand-written notation 'PoW', indicating that a man has been a prisoner of war, often but not invariably seen on cards where this is the case. It can usually be found on the cards of men who were captured in 1914, but there are a few occurrences of this happening for 1915 and 1916 as well.

Unusually, Munyard's card gives both his battalion and regiment – 1st

Herbert Munyard shortly after he joined the army. He is wearing the rather Germanic-looking Broderick cap introduced in 1902. It was extremely unpopular and short lived as it was no longer issued after 1905 – hence photographs of soldiers wearing it can be quite precisely dated (courtesy Mrs Molly Ford).

Battalion East Surrey Regiment – as well as his regimental number L/8429 and rank. He is listed as lance corporal, but private has been written underneath this. The reason for this apparent demotion is that lance corporal is not a rank but an appointment – he was a corporal-in-waiting, ready to be promoted when a vacancy arose – but in some circumstances a lance corporal (and the same would apply to a lance sergeant) would revert to his actual substantive rank. This related to his pay; captured lance corporals or lance sergeants retained their appointments (physically depicted by the stripes on their uniforms) but did not receive the extra money to which the appointment entitled them (Munyard would have been paid as a private throughout his captivity). He was awarded the three First World War campaign medals: the 1914 Star, British War and Victory Medals. The card also provides the date that Munyard first entered a theatre of war – 16-8-14 – which confirms, as one would expect with a regular soldier, that he was with his battalion when it arrived in France as part of the British Expeditionary Force. Checking whether the dates on a Medal Index Card coincide with the whole unit first going abroad, or otherwise if they represent a reinforcement draft, can be done through several sources, such as orders of battle or The Long, Long Trail website at www.1914-1918.net, etc.

There is a good chance that regimental museums or archives will have some useful records. The East Surrey Regiment collection is held at the Surrey History Centre, and has an excellent collection of material, including '1st Battalion East Surrey Regiment List of Warrant Officers, Non Commissioned Officers and Men who Landed in France 16/8/14' (ESR/2/3/28), which confirms that Munyard was there. There are also two detailed 1st Battalion nominal rolls, the first covering the period 1916–1919 (which contains useful POW information) and the second 1917–1919, but Munyard is not listed in these because they seem to apply only to men who joined during the war. It is reasonably common for regimental archives to have lists of POWs, though these might be in a more generic list such as the Casualty and Sickness Ledger for the 1st, 2nd, 7th, 8th and 9th Battalions of the Norfolk Regiment. Over 15,000 soldiers are listed in this unique document compiled at the regimental depot. It covers those who were wounded, sick and POWs, containing useful details such as the hospitals they were in and dates of repatriation or death. This is a key document for the regiment in the First World War, and can be seen at the Royal Norfolk Regimental Museum. It has been digitized and indexed (though it is not available online).

Munyard's collection at IWM (01/25/1) contains a series of postcards that he sent to his future wife, and the first of these – a delightful Russian-designed Easter card from Döberitz POW camp – dates from Easter 1915. There is anecdotal evidence to suggest that he was taken captive at the Battle of Mons, but there are ways to check this. The official war diary for the 1st Battalion of the East Surrey Regiment is a particularly detailed one. The numbers of other ranks killed, wounded and missing are given respectively as 3, 43 and 182 between 24 and 29 August 1914, and these men are all named. Held at TNA, many of the war diaries are available via the Documents Online facility, although this one does not yet appear. However, it has been transcribed and made available via the website www.queensroyalsurreys.org.uk. Munyard's name has been transcribed incorrectly, though – it is given as 'L/Cpl Maynard' – but his regimental number confirms he is the right man.

Official lists of POWs would be sent from the German Red Cross in Frankfurt, and the names would be checked against those known to the British Red Cross through enquiries from family and friends, and official War Office casualty lists. The main way of conducting this investigative work was through interviewing wounded men in hospitals, and a sophisticated mechanism for doing this was set in place. The Enquiry for the Wounded and Missing Department of the British Red Cross and Order of St John issued monthly *Enquiry Lists* with fortnightly supplements. Issues held at IWM, and believed to be the only known surviving issues are: [February 1915]; 18 May 1915; 26 June 1915; 17 July 1915, supplement B; 24 July 1915, supplement B; 31 July 1915, supplement B; 7 August 1915, supplement B; 14 August 1915, supplement B; 4 September 1915; 18 September 1915, supplement no. 2; 1 February 1916; 15 September 1916, supplement [photocopy]; 1 August 1917, no. 14 [1989 reprint by Sunset Militaria and Ray Westlake]; 1 October 1918, no. 17; 1 December 1918, no. 21. Names are arranged under regiment and battalion, and sometimes details of company and platoon (this is one of the few sources to give this latter information) and the date that a man went missing. The first of these is too late to cover Munyard's capture, but uncertainty about a man's fate could persist for months (five months was the usual maximum time a name would be listed in this publication).

Newspapers are another excellent source of information. Local newspapers contain details of casualties and prisoners from that community. *The Times* carries lists of men reported prisoner, and is available to search, by name, online (by subscription), though this can be a bit hit and miss. The *War Office Weekly Casualty List* was first published on Tuesday 7 August 1917 with information relating to casualties from 30 July 1917. Officers' entries contain surname, rank, initials and regiment. Warrant officers (WOs), NCOs and men are listed under regiment, surname, regimental number, initial and location of residence of next of kin. Main categories are 'killed', 'died of wounds', 'wounded' and 'missing', but these are sometimes followed up with 'previously reported missing, now reported died of wounds as a prisoner of war in German hands' or 'previously reported killed, now reported prisoner of war in German hands'. It includes Australian, Canadian, Indian, New Zealand and South African forces as well as repatriated POWs. The last list (no. 83) is dated Tuesday 4 March 1919. It is a difficult source to use and, although IWM does have a complete run of this it is not currently very accessible.

Regimental magazines should also list POWs, although some magazines ceased or had only partial publication during the war years. *The Suffolk Regimental Gazette* is a particularly good example. Issues between January and March 1916 contain a very useful 'List of NCOs and Men Prisoners of War in Germany', which has names in alphabetical order, with regimental and battalion number, and the camp where they were held. There are also details about men moved to Switzerland, and letters from POWs written to the Suffolk Prisoners of War Help Society.

There would usually be a significant time lag between a prisoner's capture and the report reaching the British press. Munyard's name does not seem to appear in *The Times*; with the volume of men listed it is not surprising that names slipped through the net. It is interesting to chart the progress of information filtering out to the British public with this first major land engagement in the last week of August 1914. *The Times* of 26 August reported significant casualties: 2,000 were mentioned. The public were obviously clamouring to learn more, with questions in Parliament about why further news was not forthcoming. All information came through the Press Bureau, which publicized the fact that it worked in consultation with the military and naval authorities, and could only release details if they did not compromise forces in the field. Families also had to be informed before the lists became public. By the last day of the month casualties were reported to have trebled to 5,000–6,000, and numbers of men arriving at hospitals in Britain were given. On 2 September the first casualty list was published, although only featuring officers' names. A few other ranks' names appeared on 4 September – but only those who were dead or wounded, not the more complicated state of missing. On 9 September a few officers were unofficially reported as POWs. The first list of officers officially recorded as POWs via Germany was only published in *The Times* on 9 October. Sometimes ad hoc lists appeared, such as a list of NCOs and men interned at Munsterlager published on 29 September 1914, and a list of Royal Naval Division (RND) men held at Döberitz on 26 November 1914.

In the meantime, an article on 5 September sent news via Denmark that a German newspaper had mentioned 680 prisoners arriving at Döberitz Camp on 1 September, and another 2,000 the next day. It reports that they 'occupy five enormous tents surrounded by a wire fence' and commented on the British soldiers' tattered uniforms. Munyard was presumably amongst these first prisoners.

Döberitz was Germany's Aldershot. Situated just outside Berlin, it was a large training area on sandy and dusty soil. Camps were organized within the twenty-one Army Districts of Germany. Each District had its

S Hillman's Representantes de las Nacional Aliadas [Delegates of the United Nations] *at Döberitz Camp. A propaganda image for the Spanish edition of* Hamburger Nachrichten, *this purports to show the varieties of different uniforms and nationalities found in a prison camp. This reinforces the point made about these camps being multi-national societies (© the artist/photo: IWM, PST 6957).*

own Army Corps Command, and the camps came under the control of the General and Staff of that District. Although barrack buildings or other large institutions would sometimes be taken over for prison camps, it was more common for camps to be very makeshift affairs to begin with. Often camps would be tented – though sometimes men were just expected to live in the open – until they built their own wooden huts. These chaotic conditions applied in Britain as well, but it should be remembered that Germany's haul of British POWs was dramatically outnumbered by Russian and French prisoners, exacerbating their problem of finding space and provisions for all these men. *The Times* of 14 September 1914 reported on the numbers of prisoners captured by Germany at that early stage: Russian (1,830 officers and 91,400 men), French (1,670 and 86,700), Belgian (440 and 30,200) and British (160 and 7,250).

Information in FO 383/159 at TNA contains a report of Döberitz, commenting on the conspicuous improvement at the camp from spring 1915. The report explained that the tents mentioned above were actually cavalry tents for sheltering horses, and that they were full of holes.

Although the autumn was miserable, early December saw a move to newly built – and overcrowded – wooden huts. Washing facilities were outside until the end of January 1915, when they were covered with a tin shelter, while the open latrines were situated in full view of the road until March. Hospital accommodation for 200 was also built. Food was reported as very poor and inadequate. The guards were reputed to be cruel, and punishments included flogging with horsewhips and being tied to a post. However, in the summer cricket, rounders and tennis were played, a marquee was used as a theatre and concerts were regularly held. By 1917 a rifle club was apparently in operation there with three air-guns. FO 383 contains an enormous amount of useful detail relating to prison camps and to individual POWs. There are frequent inspection reports, and also reports of visits to hospitals which often contain lists of the men who were hospitalized on that date.

Camp magazines were important, providing a morale boost for the men who created them, and interest and diversion for those who read them. They are also a mine of information about life in the camp, its in-jokes and often had interesting artwork. The Döberitz magazine placed a value on being read by those working on *Kommandos* (men were often sent away from the main camp to labour in working parties; the rate of pay varied between 15 and 30 pfennigs a day), as it enabled them to keep in touch with friends left behind, and keep up to date with happenings in camp. This publication is also quite unusual in that it completely recognizes the multi-national nature of life in this camp. There are three issues, each titled in one of the main languages of the camp – British, French and Russian – and these appear throughout each magazine. There is always a possibility that men involved in noteworthy pursuits, such as sports or amateur dramatics, were named in these publications. Munyard kept one issue – *Gazette de Döberitz*, no. 2, which contains a handwritten date of 9 May 1916 – no doubt because he is credited with writing the boxing column. This detailed the activities of that sport in the camp at the Gaff Club, and appreciatively mentioned the two punchbags sent out from Britain. The list of camps in Appendix 6 contains details of camp magazines held at IWM and some other institutions.

Photographs are also common; the men seemed to take great pleasure in signing these, and often putting personal details on the cards, and passing them on to friends. Photographers visited POW camps and the prisoners could purchase the resulting portraits, which would appear as postcard prints. No doubt it broke the men's monotony, and from the German viewpoint it contributed to their economy while allowing the British recipients to see how healthy their relatives looked in incarceration. Munyard had about 100 of these in his collection, and although the majority date from his later time in Switzerland, there are several from his German sojourn. Autograph books and sketchbooks fall into this category as well – it is always worth looking at any collections relating to a camp of interest because they often extend far beyond the named man of the collection. A really good example of this type of material, from Sennelager, can be seen on the internet through www.wfa-dorsetswilts .org.uk/articles/sennelager.htm.

The Surrey History Centre holds a remarkable album relating to the East Surrey Prisoner of War Care Committee (ESR/1/12/9). It was presented, together with a fountain pen, to Mrs Iva Longley, wife of the commanding officer, 'by her fellow workers whose names are here inscribed, as a small token of affection and as a memento of over four years work in the interest of our prisoners'. Many wives of senior officers ran organizations of this type, and Mrs Longley appreciated the importance of this volume for she wrote: 'This album is to be sent to the Depot East Surrey Regiment, Kingston, after my death for the regimental museum.' The album consists of 160 pages, full of cards from prisoners, often with minimal messages but sometimes with details of the camp or circumstances of capture, and virtually always with a signature and address (usually providing camp details), as well as letters from wives and mothers and prisoners, frequently thanking for parcels or airing concerns. Several postcards from Herbert Munyard are featured, including an undated one from Döberitz Camp with a design for Christmas 1915 addressed to Mrs Longley (with no message) and a card dated 2 September 1916 relating to a parcel that arrived on 12 July when Munyard was in hospital. Although imprisonment could forge strong, sharing relationships, hunger and deprivation brought out the worst in some people. Munyard was concerned for the welfare of the other men and wrote a letter on behalf of nineteen of them, informing the Care Committee that one of the sergeants in the battalion had been receiving the parcels intended for all and 'utilising them for his own use' while 'the undermentioned men here received nothing.'

The addresses given on the *Kriegsgefangenen postkarten* in the Care Committee album are helpful for placing a man, and some of these show that Munyard was one of the prisoners from Döberitz sent to the German-occupied Russian territory of the Courland (also known as Kurland, and now Latvia) as a reprisal. Information about this can be found in the Foreign Office correspondence from the Prisoners of War and Aliens Department at FO 383 at TNA. This is an absolute cornucopia of information about all aspects of imprisonment, including some reports on camps and queries relating to individuals, and it is well indexed. Arranged chronologically under the country principally referred to, it runs to 547 volumes (though many other countries apart from Germany and Austria-Hungary are included here). Individuals are often mentioned and you sometimes find lists of people. An instance of this is an earlier example of a reprisal. The Germans objected to the British segregating German submariners, who were held in prisons at Chatham (twenty-nine) and Devonport (ten), and responded by arresting thirty-nine British officers. Both sets of prisoners are named, together with the camps they were moved to (and even the weight gain of the Germans is recorded, proving they were not badly treated).

Files at TNA in FO 383/156–159 throw some light on the movement of 1,000 British prisoners from Döberitz to Libau and other locations in German-occupied Russian territory in May 1916. John Muir, a member of the RND said, 'I have no idea upon what basis these 1,000 men were selected. They had not made themselves conspicuous. It was suggested that they had more food from home than others and so would be better able to stand the fatigue of harder labour.' Another 1,000 prisoners were gathered from other camps in Germany, and most seem to have been kept in ignorance of their final location. Over 100 prisoners leaving Münster Camp III were told that their new address would be 'Friedrichsfeld, E.[nglander] K.[ommando] I, Libau'. This meant little to those not familiar with the concept of a parent camp for administration and post, from which working parties were sent out; the confusion is shown in the official correspondence, where it was seriously suggested that Friedrichsfeld may have changed its name. This movement of prisoners to the Courland was a reprisal for the British shipping some German prisoners from England back to France to work for them in Rouen and Le Havre, where it was thought that the British were breaking the accepted conventions by exposing the POWs to shellfire and making them conduct war work. Some images relating to this reprisal can be found online at: www.britisharmedforces.org/li_pages/regiments/dcli/duke_Friederichs feld.htm. Information about those who died can be found at: http://britishwargravesjelgava.blogspot.com/.

The documentation reveals public concern, and shows that the authorities were trying to establish exactly what the situation was. They were not helped by the Germans refusing to allow a United States representative to visit (this was allowed in mid-October 1916, albeit just to Libau). A detailed report was made by Hauptmann Draudt of the Prussian Ministry of War, although this was not believed by the British. The report does, however, provide some useful information about the Courland, as the area was collectively known. No. 4 Company (Munyard's unit), comprising 500 men and 24 NCOs was based at Libau in a former oil factory near the Baltic. Apparently their main complaints referred to the slowness of parcels, a lack of potatoes, mouldy bread arriving from Switzerland and that they had no football (the latter two issues were dealt with as a football arrived, and army biscuits were substituted for bread). No. 3 Company was at Wainoden, No. 1 Company at Angernsee and No. 2 Company at Mitau, primarily doing agricultural work, with 150 men based at Windau.

The conditions were undoubtedly difficult, and Munyard's health suffered, with resulting hospitalization. He sent a card from Libau on 1 July 1916 showing a large elegant-looking building described as 'My hospital in Russia'. A later postcard written on 26 August 1916 gave his new address as the Prisoner of War Hospital at Heilsberg, East Prussia. He referred to this as having 'shifted from Russia to another hospital'. His poor state of health would lead to him being exchanged to Switzerland, and his story continues later.

The other key documents at TNA are in WO 161. These consist of over 3,000 reports compiled by the Government Committee on the Treatment by the Enemy of British Prisoners of War, based on interviews with repatriated or escaped prisoners. However, this is really just a drop in the ocean considering there were estimated to be 192,000 British and Commonwealth POWs. There is a slim chance of finding the person you are looking for here, but the records are still of use because you can search under camp, name and unit. They also give a good cross-section of experiences that can help with understanding what many men went through. The records are available through Documents Online, and provide an excellent account of the many different experiences that POWs had. About forty transcripts can be found free of charge online at http://yourarchives.nationalarchives.gov.uk/index.php?title=Category:WW1_Prisoners_of_War_Interviews_transcripts.

There are occasional listings such as that found in AIR 1/892/204/5/696 – 'List of British Prisoners of War Interned in Germany: 13th March–4th April 1916'. This is very far from comprehensive but Friedrichsfeld is well covered, and details provided include name, rank, regiment and place of capture. Among other things, it provides a list of the seventy-five POWs moved from Muncheberg to Sagan in March 1916. What is remarkable about this list is the bizarre spellings of the home locations. The information came via the German authorities, and you can see how some of these iterations might have come about, such as 'Bradfort, Jorkstire', but others are more mysterious, eg 'Cumbrigde, Welli'. The regiments are also given in German fashion, eg '14 I R', and '12 Kav'. These difficulties would be amplified where people were unaware of the geography, and can cause problems for researchers today.

ADM 1/8420/124 is primarily concerned with the loss of HMS *Maori* and *Crusader* in May 1915, but has a list of men held at Giessen and officers at Heidelberg. Also included is a partial list for Münster Camp II.

Another potential source for men who were captured in the very early part of the war are the records of Princess Mary's Gift Box Fund. All men in service by Christmas 1914 were eligible to receive the embossed brass box, and this included those who had the misfortune to be taken prisoner before 25 December. The boxes were stockpiled at a store in Deptford, where they awaited the POWs' homecoming. In fact, the boxes had been sitting there so long that many of them had been pilfered, and the remaining cigarettes and tobacco had been rendered unfit for smoking and had to be replaced. The WWC at IWM (also available in some libraries as the Gale Thomson 'Women, War and Work' digital resource) contains the lists of the repatriated NCOs and men who were eligible for the box, as well as the details of those POWs who had died after December 1914. These can be found in the Benevolent Organizations section, and are arranged by regiment. Details vary, but will usually include a man's name and regimental number, plus name and address of next of kin. Often there will be additional details such as the date of capture, and occasionally the name of a camp. Most, but not all, regiments are represented, and the lists do not appear to be totally comprehensive, but they are certainly worth looking at for early captives. Unfortunately, there is no sign of Munyard in the East Surrey Regiment list at BO 2 1/71, possibly because he returned to Britain before the end of the war.

Regimental histories will also sometimes have lists of POWs, though this is far more likely for officers than other ranks. The internet can also yield information, often in the shape of online auctions or the sites of specialist dealers in postal items or money; postcards and POW currency are frequently offered for sale, with images attached. Some useful websites and forums are listed in the Quick Guide to Key Resources in Appendix 1, and also in the list of camps in Appendices 6, 7 and 8.

Finally, there is a very slim possibility that you may be able to hear a relative's voice, since sound recordings were made in POW camps in Germany. Wilhelm Doegen visited POW camps in order to record the voices and accents of British and Commonwealth POWs as part of a long-running project into the study of language and dialects. He was director of the Sound Department of Berlin State University and went on to found the Lautarchiv in 1920 at Humboldt University. All the men volunteered to be recorded, and had to complete a form that provided information about themselves. In 2008 the British Library acquired digital recordings of all the British and Commonwealth performances, and accompanying paperwork was also copied; although I have not been able to consult the originals of these (they are still being accessioned) the biographical infor-mation does appear on the website. Sixty-six recordings can be listened to on the British Library website at http://sounds.bl.uk/Browse Category.aspx?category=Accents-and-dialects. The men are principally reading the parable of the Prodigal Son, but there are also recordings of Indian soldiers singing traditional songs – these would need to be accessed at the British Library. Wilhelm Doegen was the editor of the interesting (and well-illustrated) book: *Kriegsgefangene Völker: Band I: Der Kriegsgefangenen Haltung und Schicksal in Deutschland* (Dietrich Reimer (Berlin: Ernst Vohsen), 1919).

An Officer's Experience

An officer's experience of captivity would be quite different from that of an ordinary soldier. There is a complete record of officers who were imprisoned: *List of British Officers Taken Prisoner in the Various Theatres of War Between August, 1914, and November, 1918* was compiled from records kept by Messrs Cox and Company's Enquiry Office, at Harrington House, Craig's Court, Charing Cross, London SW1. It was published in 1919 and republished in 1988 by the London Stamp Exchange. Cox was the bank of choice for most military personnel, and as the book says, 'a missing officer's cheque was often the first intimation of his being a prisoner of war.' The bulk of the book covers the Western Front, with the officers arranged by their regiment and battalion, and there is a helpful index. The information is not detailed, but usually provides the date that the man went missing, and the date of his repatriation (or date of death – sometimes with the location as well). Second Lieutenant R F Corlett is listed under the 1st and 2nd Battalions of the King's Own Yorkshire Light Infantry. His missing date is given as 18/11/16, and the date of his repatriation as 4/1/19.

Robert Frederick (known as Roy) Corlett's service record is at TNA

Second Lieutenant Corlett had a photograph taken at Ströhen ; this was a typical POW portrait, though probably more common for officers than other ranks. He had signed this, with details of his original battalion, not the one he was captured with. This image also appears on the cover in a stamp. It was used by the Isle of Man Postal Service for their stamp issue to mark the ninetieth anniversary of the end of the First World War, with each stamp featuring a man from the island (© IWM, Documents: Misc 886 and stamp on cover courtesy: Isle of Man Post Office).

(WO 374/15571), but this is not extensive. Many service records for returned officer prisoners of war will contain an exoneration from blame for being captured letter, but there is no trace of his here. Sometimes the Medal Index Card of an officer POW will contain the wording 'Exonerated Officers List', but this does not appear on Corlett's card. His service record tells us that his home address was 21 Burnside Terrace, Woodbourne Road, Douglas, Isle of Man, and that he was born on 7 July 1894. He attended the Collegiate School at Douglas, and passed through the Inns of Court Officer Training Corps before being commissioned into the 3/4th Battalion King's Own Yorkshire Light Infantry (KOYLI) on 8 June 1916. There is an Arrival Report relating to his return from captivity. This gives the information that his unit was the 4th Battalion KOYLI, 148th Brigade, 49th Division, but that he was attached at the time of his capture to 2nd Battalion KOYLI, 96th Brigade, 32nd Division (this neatly explains the discrepancy between the different battalion numbers he was

Watercolour painted by Second Lieutenant P Warburton at Ströhen Camp, showing the wooden huts and normal life going on. The deckchair and newspaper emphasized the difference from the men's camps, where they would be busy working. Boredom could be a real problem for officers, and was a major contributor to Barbed Wire Disease (© IWM, Documents: Papers of Second Lieutenant P Warburton, 06/73/1).

reputed to be serving with). He left Bad Colberg as a repatriated POW on 23 December 1918, sailed from Rotterdam on 30 December, and arrived at Hull on 31 December. On 1 January 1919 he appeared before the first of many medical boards. Corlett had been wounded when he was captured on 18 November 1916, and the board considered that 'his injury in the first instance was very severe,' and he was awarded a further two months' leave. Although he returned to Litherland Camp at Liverpool at the end of March, less than two weeks later he had been sent to the 1st Western General Hospital, and he does not appear to have gone back to army life before his demobilization in November 1919.

Documentation relating to the the Corlett family is available at Manx National Heritage. The anniversary stamp issued by the Isle of Man Post Office bearing Corlett's image features a phrase from one of Roy's letters home, explaining that the Germans had operated on him and extracted the bullet in his leg. He spent months lying on his back with a splint on his leg. After recovery he attempted to escape by trying to swim across a freezing river, but he was recaptured by the Germans, and this was probably how he ended up at Ströhen.

Second Lieutenant P Warburton of the 7th Battalion of the East Surrey

Bad Colberg looked superficially attractive. People had formerly paid to stay in this hotel complex, but the buildings were dilapidated, though appreciated after the primitive conditions of some of the other camps (© IWM, Documents: Misc 886).

45

Regiment was held at Ströhen and Bad Colberg, the same camps as Corlett. Obviously an artistic man, Warburton painted and also performed with the Phollies, Bad Colberg's Concert Party. His collection in IWM's Department of Documents (06/73/1) contains a delightful album of watercolours showing scenes from both camps (including landscapes painted on walks out). As well as an album of photographs (many of them signed), the souvenir number of *The Morning Walk* from 1918 is also held. This gives some idea of characters in the camp (the poet F W Harvey was held at Bad Colberg and featured heavily in a 'Poetry of the Great War' section of the magazine) and what life was like, including a humorous breakdown of 'A Day in the Lager'. You can also find some photographs from both camps, and pieces of ephemera, on the Gordon Jacob website at www.gordonjacob.org. Jacob was the conductor of the orchestra, as well as playing piano for the Phollies. Included are details of music that he wrote in the camp.

Ströhen was regarded as a bad camp, and closed at the start of winter 1917. Australian Captain John Mott made a successful escape in September 1917, and his debriefing interview can be found in FO 383/273; 'This is what is known as a "Strafe" Camp, and conditions are very bad indeed.' A *Strafelager* was a punishment camp, and, rather like Colditz in

A rather unusual image showing the Bad Colberg orderlies on the steps in a popular spot for photographs. There would always be some other ranks held in a camp for officers – the usual ratio was one orderly for between five and ten officers (© IWM, Documents: Misc 886).

Close up of one of the handsome villas of Bad Colberg, with officers enjoying the balcony and novelty of being photographed. Close up you can see the barbed wire, and also the more mundane wooden huts that supplemented the accommodation (© IWM, Documents: Misc 886).

the Second World War, habitual escapees were sent there. It is not surprising that many escapes were made from this camp – it is said to have held the record for the number of successful 'home runs'. About 400 men lived in its wooden huts, and the poor quality of the water is frequently commented upon, with the result that there were dysentery outbreaks. In 1917 the prisoners conducted a 'letter strike' where no one wrote home for six weeks, in the successful hope that the silence would initiate enquiries being made.

In contrast, Bad Colberg appeared to be a very attractive camp visually. It had been a sanatorium and was built over thermal springs, although the company running it had gone bankrupt before the outbreak of war, and the buildings were all rundown. The 245 officers and 70 orderlies there enjoyed luxurious bathrooms, good entertainment facilities and a full education programme. Commandant Kröner had a reputation as a cruel and violent man.

TNA has occasional listings of officers, and one interesting example occurs at CAB 45/129 in the *The 'Torgau History' of the Retreat from Mons in August 1914: Compiled from Accounts given by Officers who Were Made*

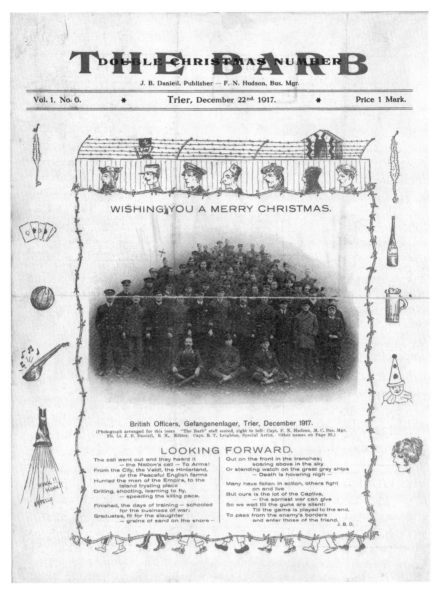

Camp magazines are often excellent sources of information. Officers' camps are more likely to have produced these as they had more leisure time, and IWM has a good range of publications. This special Christmas issue of The Barb *– from Trier – featured a photograph with names of all the officers who appeared on it (© IWM,* The Barb *– 22 December 1917).*

Prisoners-of-War during that Operation and Interned at Torgau-am-Elbe. This was secretly compiled within the camp, based on the personal experiences of officers who had been captured during that operation, and was smuggled out of Germany. A list of officers appears at the back arranged by unit, with the date that the officer was captured.

A list of sixteen naval officer POWs in December 1915 can be found in FO 383/109, providing ranks, names and camp where they were held. A partial list of officers at Heidelberg in May 1915 can be found at ADM 1/8420/124. IWM has a printed list of officer POWs at Crefeld dating from April 1917. It has been annotated and added to by pencil, and there are numbers that probably equate to the rooms where the men lived.

Regimental collections are also good places to look – for example, the Suffolk Regimental Collection at the Suffolk Record Office in Bury St Edmunds has a large alphabetical list of officers at the camp in Graudenz in a collection of papers related to Second Lieutenant J A Blanch (GB 554/Y1/28b). You can also find listings of POW officers in *The Suffolk Regimental Gazette* together with the camp they were in.

Camp magazines can be excellent sources, and those produced by officers tended to be more 'professional' and detailed than their other ranks equivalent since they had more time and facilities for creativity. These frequently mention people by name, and will sometimes contain complete lists of prisoners.

Indian Prisoners of War

The British Library holds some excellent material for Indian POWs in the shape of items from their Indian Soldiers' Fund records. This can be accessed in the Asian and African Studies Reading Room. 'List of Indian Prisoners of War Interned in Germany and Roumania' dated 15 October 1918 (F/120/272) is extremely useful. The POWs are listed under their regiment, in alphabetical order. Their regimental number, rank, name, German POW number and camp are given. The majority of the men were held at Halbmondlager, Wunsdorf, Zossen. Occasionally, there are more precise location details in the list, eg those for 2511 Rifleman Dambar Sing Gurung of the 2/2nd Gurkhas read: 'Matricule 3797, Kriegs-gefangenenlager, Baracke No. 28, Gottingen, Hanover', or Jemadar Pirzag Singh located at 'Offizier-Gefangenenlager, Room No. 68, Freiburg, Baden'. Attached to this is a twenty-page 'List of Indian Prisoners of War in Germany whose Deaths have been Reported to Us', dated 13 August 1918, containing date and place of death, and 'List of Indian Prisoners of War formerly in Germany and Roumania and now Repatriated to India', containing a rough date of repatriation, eg October 1918, or January 1919. Another, briefer, 'List of Indian Prisoners of War Interned in Germany' is dated 18 October 1918.

Halbmondlager was set up for Indian and French colonial troops to encourage them to change sides and fight with their Turkish 'brothers'. The name of the camp referred to the Ottoman half-moon symbol. The first religious mosque in Germany was built here, although it was not just Muslims who were held at Zossen, but Gurkhas, Sikhs, Hindus, etc. In 1917 most of these POWs were moved to the camp of Morile-Maculesti in Romania, where it was felt the climate would suit them better. Some information about the provision of aid to Indian POWs can be found in the 'Indian Soldiers' Fund Reports, 1914–1919' held in the library of IWM. These include some reports on the camp at Zossen, mentioning, for example, the four different kitchens in the camp enabling food to be prepared according to the men's different rites, and that fresh mutton (slaughtered in camp) was the only meat eaten.

Burial Records

Although a few graves of First World War British prisoners in Germany were left in their original sites – principally to respect Jewish and Indian burial rites – most were concentrated in cemeteries in four locations in Germany. Records would have been kept of where all the original burials were made, but the only records that survive at the CWGC today are for Niederzwehren. The Commission should have information relating to the original burial place of individuals buried there. Documentation with this information would also have been sent to the next of kin at the time, and it is possible this may still exist somewhere in the family.

The four locations are:

Berlin South-Western Cemetery – Located at Stahnsdorf about twenty-two kilometres from the centre of Berlin, this large cemetery was opened in 1908. No original British military burials occurred here, and it was the last of the burial sites to be chosen (in 1924) in order to relocate graves from eastern Germany. It houses 1,176 Commonwealth graves from 146 different locations. These include Döberitz, Altdamm, Stargard, Lamsdorf, Magdeburg, Stendal and Schneidermühl. It was located behind the Iron Curtain in Soviet territory before the fall of the Berlin Wall. The cemetery where Second World War casualties were buried, including large numbers of POWs, was located in the west of the city, in the heart of the British sector.

Cologne Southern Cemetery – More than 1,000 Allied prisoners were buried here during the First World War, and the cemetery was an obvious choice for concentration because the city was the headquarters of the British Army of the Rhine from 1918 to 1926. The large cemetery was opened in 1900; 2,482 servicemen are buried or commemorated here, from 183 burial grounds in Hanover, Hesse, the Rhineland and Westphalia.

Camps represented include Aachen, Dortmund, Dülmen, Friedrichsfeld and Trier.

Hamburg – Ohlsdorf Cemetery – Opened in 1882, this is the largest non-military cemetery in the world. During the First World War 300 Allied servicemen were buried here. Graves from over 120 burial grounds in Brunswick, Hanover, Schleswig-Holstein, Mecklenburg, Oldenburg, Saxony and Westphalia are located here (from camps such as Münster, Gustrow and Parchim).

Niederzwehren, at Kassel in Hessen – This cemetery was started in March 1915 for burials from the local camp, and nearly 3,000 Allied servicemen were buried here (including French and Russians). Over 1,500 bodies from 190 burial grounds in Baden, Bavaria, Hanover, Hesse and Saxony (including camps such as Hameln, Göttingen, Langensalza, Ohrdruf, Quedlinburg and Sennelager) were buried here.

There are 184 Indian POWs buried at Zehrensdorf Indian Cemetery, about thirty-eight kilometres south of Berlin. This was the burial place for the camp at Zossen, five kilometres away. Seventeen Indian civilians and five Indian merchant seamen are also interred here.

IWM has some paperwork belonging to Miss Constance Marx (86/75/1), who was involved with Red Cross work repatriating POWs and also locating graves in the Alsace-Lorraine area. Her documents contain some insight into the type of work this involved. There are also a few letters from men and families that she assisted, and lists of names and burial places.

There are graves of prisoners in cemeteries scattered all over Europe. A few men are buried in Austria. Poland has several POW graves in Posen Old Garrison Cemetery (now Poznan), with burials relocated from Czersk and Szczypiorno Prisoner of War Cemeteries. There are thirty-six prisoner of war graves in Jelgava in Latvia (formerly Mitau); these men died whilst they were working in the Courland after having been transported there in the same reprisal as Munyard.

Many prison camps erected memorials to men who died. These seem to have been funded locally, but I have been unable to uncover much information about them, other than photographs and brief mentions. Presumably their origins followed from the British Army tradition of everybody in a unit contributing a small amount of money – typically a day's pay – to finance a memorial to their comrades who had died in a particular campaign or posting. Cemeteries around the British Empire have obelisks or other structures marking the brief sojourn of units, while regimental chapels in this country have wall plaques. The memorials may have been designed by artistic POWs – the memorial at the predominantly Irish Limburg Camp was a Celtic cross, for example – and would have offered a productive activity for the designer/craftsman, and interest for the camp as well as the feeling that they were doing the right thing by their fallen comrades. The memorials may possibly have been executed by them as well, although this work is more likely to have been undertaken by German craftsmen. The CWGC has almost nothing about them, although they are outside its remit. There are, however, many general comments about how well maintained most of the POW graves in Germany were.

Record class RG 35/45-69 at TNA contains an incomplete collection of death certificates (General Register Office: Miscellaneous Foreign Death Returns). It may be worth a look in these, although I have never found these very helpful for POW research. These are mainly in French, and records for names beginning with C, F, P, Q and X are missing. These can be consulted online at the pay-per-view site www.bmdregisters.co.uk/#bmd.

Repatriation

The situation in Germany following the Armistice was extremely chaotic. Although up to that point the Red Cross parcels, which had kept the men alive, had arrived regularly, this was no longer the case. The Soldiers' and Workers' Councils had taken over from the military in most of the prison camps, and the revolutionary atmosphere in a country desperately short of food meant that the camps were now at risk of break-ins because of their food supply. Law and order was under threat and transport had virtually broken down. The Red Cross, reliant on their POW lists, no longer knew who was where – and consequently how many or where or if they should be sending their precious parcels – and the next few weeks would see an enormous effort made to establish the whereabouts of each man.

Although the official line was that POWs should remain where they were (notices were inserted in German newspapers to this effect), communications were not functioning properly. For many, the temptation to go home was too great, and they made their way through the British lines, and travelled back via the Channel ports (chiefly Calais). Some made their way to Holland. These journeys were often extremely difficult for weakened men with little or no food. The influenza epidemic and the large numbers of refugees and troops on the move also exacerbated the chaotic conditions. The north of Germany was most affected by revolutionary fervour, and this was particularly marked in some of the German ports, adding yet another complication to the evacuation issue. Some POWs were also set loose by their guards, and a few camps, such as Langensalza, were so overcrowded that they could not accommodate the 1,500 men returning from *Kommandos*, who were left to look after themselves as best they could. FO 211/469 reveals deep concern about this latter camp, which was extremely unsettled. A shooting incident on 27

November had resulted in sixteen POW deaths and twenty-four wounded men. The conditions there were very bad – men were sleeping on damp muddy floors because there were not enough bunk beds, while there were 1,000 POWs in the hospital with no medication or proper treatment.

The papers of Major General Sir Richard Ewart are held at IWM (73/88/1). He was posted to Berlin to help coordinate the repatriation of British POWs (and later, Russian POWs). His diary provides a clear account of the confused situation and bureaucratic muddles that occurred during this hectic period, complicated by unrest on the streets of Berlin.

TNA has documents that yield some information about the repatriation arrangements, eg 'Repatriation of British Prisoners of War under Armistice – Arrangements for Transport from Rotterdam to Hull – SS *Takada*' (MT 25/18) and 'Prisoners of War – British Military Repatriation Committee: Prisoners of War – Repatriation' (FO 211/469). This latter file is chiefly concerned with repatriation via Copenhagen. FO 383/474 and FO 383/475 are also useful, with the latter featuring daily minutes from the Transport Sub-Committee. *The Times* is also very informative: there seems to have been a desire to keep the public informed about what was happening, while at the same time emphasizing the complexity of the situation. Despite some problems, it appears to have been a very efficient operation, with 70 per cent of British POWs evacuated from Germany by Christmas Eve 1918. This was a much more advanced position than for other countries – France had 50 per cent evacuated, Belgium 40 per cent and Italy 30 per cent. There also had to be arrangements for hospital ships and hospital trains to evacuate those POWs not well enough to travel any other way. The Admiralty declined to offer ships for evacuation – the Royal Navy was busy with operations in the Baltic, and their vessels did not have the space to accommodate large numbers of POWs, who would have had uncomfortable journeys across the North Sea in heavy winter weather.

POWs arrived principally at Dover, Hull or Leith, having sailed mainly from Calais, Rotterdam (from mid-December, once the British had arrived in the Rhineland, POWs were evacuated to Holland on the Rhine by barge), Copenhagen, Danzig and other Baltic ports. Hamburg and Bremerhaven were initially not used because of fears of mines. The POWs were primarily sent to Prisoner of War Reception Camps at Waterfall Meadow Camp at Dover, or South Camp at Ripon for those arriving in the northern ports. They should have received a package either on embarkation (at Rotterdam) or when they arrived in Britain. It was distributed by the Navy and Army Canteen Board, and contained one briar pipe (and a bag for it), 2oz tobacco, twenty cigarettes (two packets of ten Gold Flake), ¼lb toffee, ¼lb chocolate and ¼lb sweet biscuits. The train journey from Leith to Hull took 'under four hours'. The men were given a hot meal on disembarkation, and also a packed meal to sustain them on the journey (consisting of a 9oz meat pie, ¼lb biscuits, two pieces of chocolate and 2oz of cheese). Pre-printed postcards were also sent informing family they had arrived safely in the country and were at or moving to the POW Reception Camp.

The India Office contains some interesting material in a document entitled 'Repatriation of British and Indian P/W, Consequent on the Signing of the Armistice' (IOR/L/MIL/7/18707). There are mentions of a few individuals, mainly but not exclusively Indian troops, but it also contains material about the war establishment of a Prisoners of War Reception Camp, and about how these camps functioned.

On arrival at the camps the men would be 'processed', though the aim was to keep them there no longer than forty-eight hours. It was very important that the men be accounted for, and the complex task of making sure the records were accurate was lengthy and time consuming. Ideally, they would be interviewed to see what details they could provide about missing men, but in practice this did not happen thoroughly with those

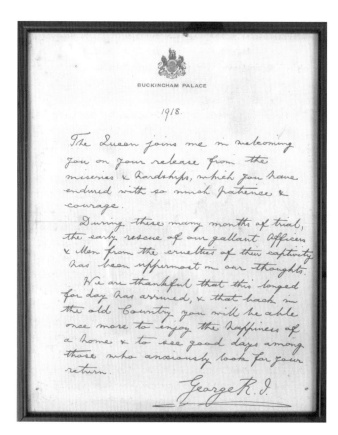

The royal letter given to returned POWs was often a prized possession. Many were framed, as this one was by Private W Keith of the Cheshire Regiment. The letters were produced by lithography and were an early example of the royal family embracing modern technology (© IWM, EPH 4582).

returning from Germany – it was far more successful with men returning from Turkey because there were longer gaps in their more complex travel arrangements when this work could be done. If the men were medically well enough they would be given their 'leave and duty' ration books, message from the King, and rail warrants to travel home for two months' leave.

On their arrival in Britain there was likely to be some coverage in the local press about returning POWs, and some communities threw a big homecoming event for their men. Local libraries and archives and regimental museums will be the best places to look for this information. The Queen's Royal Regiment gave bronze medals to be worn on a watch-chain to their repatriated POWs at an event in Guildford on 24 January 1919. Information about this can be found at the Surrey History Centre in QRWS/1/5/1 and QRWS/30/ELIAA.

Biggleswade was an excellent example of a community effort, and the WWC has a good collection of material about The *Biggleswade Chronicle* British Prisoners of War Fund. It hosted a Welcome Home Reception on 17 January 1919 for men of the town and the 150-plus captured men who came from within a nine-mile radius of the town. Programmes for their fund-raising concerts are also included in the WWC, and these feature photographs of some of the men who were POWs (Prisoners 5/1-/7 and 5/30). Another example is the Fenton Prisoner of War Help Society, where the programme for their Welcome Home event on 28 January 1919 includes the names of the POWs (Prisoners 7/6).

Finally, FO 383/475 contains information about 'the missing' and rumours of 'secret camps'. In early January 1919 more than 22,000 British POWs were unaccounted for; some of these would have materialized as the repatriations continued, but many of these men would have died – perhaps on working parties where they were buried with paperwork either lost or non-existent, or behind the Western Front, where they may have been killed by British fire. Cases of men reported missing were thoroughly investigated. The first POW lists from Germany in autumn 1914 were 'extremely imperfect' and later responses to individual enquiries 'quite useless'. Regimental lists of missing men were subsequently sent to Germany with forms for evidence to be entered about the fate of missing men. When the first POWs returned in 1915 they were systematically examined. The file records: 'Experience shows that if a man has been missing for six or seven months he is probably dead. This statement should not, however, be taken as applying to the March offensive as complete lists of prisoners have even now not been received from Germany.' The period of presumption of death had been decided in autumn 1915. This could be assumed after a minimum period of six months for officers and seven months for other ranks on the Western Front. It was extended to twelve months on the eastern fronts, although 'careful investigation and experience having shown that practically all living men were heard of earlier than this'. Around 80,000 cases were dealt with, and presumption of death was always deferred if the next of kin wished it.

Chapter 6

BRITISH CIVILIAN INTERNEES IN GERMANY

On the outbreak of war the Germans restricted the movements of all Britons, with wholesale internment of British men aged between 17 and 55 from November 1914. Before this date many men were imprisoned, but from November 1914 the procedure became regularized, with large numbers of Britons being sent to Ruhleben. A racetrack near Spandau to the north-west of Berlin, it was a primitive camp at the beginning, but soon acquired its own efficient internal organization run by the prisoners, and became home to some 5,500 men. All camp numbers fluctuated because new prisoners would arrive while others escaped, died or were moved, exchanged or repatriated. At the time of the Armistice 2,323 internees were held there.

Ruhleben was probably the best known of all the prison camps in the First World War, and was well documented in books. It was the main location for British civilian internees and, situated just outside the capital city, attracted a great deal of attention in the press. There was a full artistic

Nico Jungman's Panoramic View of Ruhleben Prison Camp, *showing the smoking chimneys of Spandau in the background. The grandstand is in the centre of the picture overlooking the racecourse on the right, with the stables behind on the left (© IWM, ART 522).*

life in the camp, and it produced two runs of English-language magazines: *In Ruhleben Camp* and *The Ruhleben Camp Magazine* – both held by IWM. There is correspondence in FO 383/523 that ensured that a full set was given to IWM; clearly these were gratefully accepted, and an interest in similar magazines from other prison camps was expressed. All Ruhleben magazine publications held by IWM (including French and Italian titles) can be found under the list of the camps. *The Ruhleben Camp Magazine* is full of cartoons and illustrations. There was also a thriving market in home-designed cards – 25,000 Christmas cards were sent from the camp in December 1914. The camp also had its own postal service. An exhibition about Ruhleben was held in London in early 1919 and attracted large numbers of visitors, despite the relatively high admission cost of half a crown. The forty-eight-page well-illustrated 'souvenir album' can

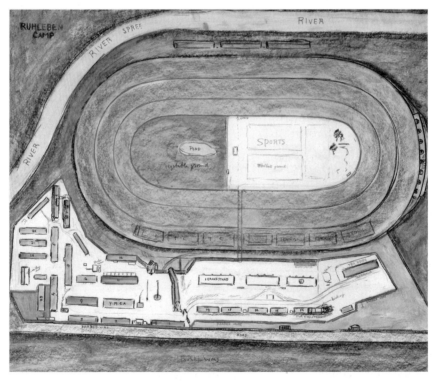

Nico Jungman's Plan of Ruhleben Camp: Key to Panoramic View *shows the previous scene from above. The River Spree forms a natural barrier. Although the camp covered quite a wide area the actual living accommodation was very cramped for over 5,000 men, which was its population when the camp was at its fullest, though numbers fluctuated (© IWM, ART 530).*

Men pulling carts laden with parcels to the Parcel Post Office at Ruhleben. The two carts were named HMS Lion *and HMS* Tiger *after ships that fought at the Battle of Jutland in 1916 (© IWM, K 45689-3 Ruhleben Sheldon Box).*

be seen at IWM. A well-supported Ruhleben Association met annually until 1964, and many of the inhabitants shared a close bond.

Although there is a U-Bahn station named Ruhleben, it is only in the general district of where the camp was. The site of the camp, unmarked and impossible to visit, now forms part of an industrial complex. The area was part of the British Sector of Berlin at the end of the Second World War, but no attempt was made to mark the spot where the camp had been. It seems a forgotten episode in the history of Berlin, with the only concrete remnant being a few graves in different cemeteries, though even these have nothing to mark the Ruhleben connection.

The camp was very much a melting pot of all classes and nationalities; a large constituency of the camp was merchant seamen. Ships and seamen had been interned on the outbreak of war if they were in German waters, and the crews of merchant vessels were traditionally very mixed – 200 black crew members were included among them. Men of the merchant marine were usually categorized as civilian rather than military prisoners, although there would continue to be debate about their status, and some men – especially the officers – did end up in military camps. As well as the usual businessmen, students and tourists, there was also a pro-German fraternity who felt themselves to be more German than British (some of whom were later offered the opportunity to leave the camp and serve in the German Army), which led to the usual factions and frictions that occurred in all camps of this type.

The merchant seamen are probably the best-documented contingent of the camp, although there are various useful pieces of documentation about other types of internee and individuals in FO 383 at TNA. FO 383/61 has a list of Hamburg bank clerks who were released from Ruhleben in April 1915, for example, and this includes their ages and the banks they worked for.

One of the best sources for Ruhleben is MT 9/1094, which contains three lists of 'Ruhleben Internees Compiled by the American Embassy at Berlin'. Again, as all prisoners are listed, the scope is far wider than the merchant seamen coverage you might expect from papers in the Ministry of Transport record class. The first list is undated, but appears to be from early 1915. Details included name, address, age, profession and barrack number, while merchant seamen usually have the name of their vessel added in pencil. It is also interesting to see the addresses that people gave as their home – large numbers are in Germany, but wider Europe was well represented too, with Britons being drawn from countries the Germans had occupied. Many of the British addresses belonged to merchant mariners. An unusual inclusion in this register is the descrip-

This decorated ox bone is a typical piece of POW art, created under wartime conditions, using material to hand. It was made in Ruhleben Camp by a group of British civilian internees with a Belgian connection, and their signatures form a record of their comradeship in captivity (© IWM, EPH 3802).

tion 'coloured' in brackets for non-white men. The second volume was dated September 1915, and has an additional section for remarks (eg if an individual was released or transferred). The third volume was dated September 1916, and is of special interest because it is marked 'Ruhleben Camp School Bookbinding Department'. This volume includes a neat little red stamp 'Volunteer, German Army' for those among the PG (pro-German) fraternity. There are also loose variously dated amendments giving details of releases, new inmates, men going elsewhere and movements within the camp as well as those going 'on leave'. For example, on 28 September 1916, a man delighting in the name of Admiral Wellington Nelson from Barrack 15 was recorded as 'gone on leave until further notice to Schweinfurt in Bavaria'. MT 9/1244 has Ruhleben Camp amendments for the year 1918.

Chris Paton's excellent 'The Ruhleben Story' can be found at http://ruhleben.tripod.com. This is an extensive site on the history of Ruhleben, which features a growing list of those in the camp, with biographical details where known, rough details of where they lived in the camp as well as pictures. It is interesting to see how the contributions from relatives and other researchers enrich the information available.

I was able to learn more about a painted ox bone in IWM Collections by using the American Embassy registers and Chris Paton's list. Bones would frequently be present in prison camp kitchens, and made an ideal canvas on which to paint or carve in a community short of paper and other commodities. This work provided the artist with a pastime to avoid the monotony and boredom of prison life, as well as a source of income, and a supply of souvenirs or gifts for the prison, local populace and relatives at home. This ox shoulder bone has been painted by M Morris, and has been signed by a cohort of people. Autographs are a gift for the family historian – it is always exciting to see a relative's name written in their own hand – but in this context it places the person within a group at a particular date. The bone is dated 1914–1915. The name of the artist, M Morris, can be found under the coat of arms and the British and Belgian flags. The registers reveal that 26-year-old Maurice Morris was a glass painter whose home address was 144 Rue Haekh, Brussels. He lived in Barrack 6, though he and presumably his 23-year-old salesman brother Benjamin had moved to Barrack 20 in the second list.

The Belgian connection of this ox bone – hinted at in the depiction of the flag – is continued with many of the other names (not all of which are legible), and a horse-racing connection is also indicated. Charles Luff, a 24-year-old commercial clerk, came from 43 Rue de Namur, Brussels, and was released back to that city in June 1916. A Thomas Luff who was four years younger was also resident at the same address, and in Barrack 15 (later 12). Trainer Samuel Archibald Heapy came from Warve in Belgium. Information from the list at 'The Ruhleben Story' tells us that he was formerly the leading jockey in Belgium, that he was training almost 100 horses there and gives details of thank-you cards written in response to parcels sent by the Jockey Club of Great Britain. Originally living in Barrack 12, he moved to number 2. Frederick or Frank Slade was a 31-year-old jockey with two addresses: Hoppegarten (a German horse-racing track at Brandenburg near Berlin) and 12 Avenue de Pesage in Brussels. He lived in Barrack 2, presumably near George Wedgwood, aged 32, another jockey from Neuenhagen, Hoppegarten. His British address was Sandringham Road, West Hartlepool, and he was released to England in June 1916. J Shatwell was also a jockey at Hoppegarten. From Ashton-under-Lyne, he was a member of the Ruhleben Lancastrian Society. The 47-year-old William Davison was a stableman from Rue Linée 64, Brussels, Nord St Josse Belgium. He lived in Barrack 7, but moved to number 8.

However, there was another William Davison in the camp, and he died there. It can be a problem when you find people with exactly the same name, which is why any supplementary details can be helpful. The second William Davison was a merchant seaman and we can find him on the list of First World War merchant naval POWs at Marcus Bateman's site at http://wanborough.ukuhost.co.uk/POW/POW.htm. This is an index taken from MT 9/1238, *List of Merchant Seamen and Fishermen Detained as Prisoners of War in Germany, Austria-Hungary and Turkey, Board of Trade Printed List, 31st May 1918*. The website allows you to search for the name of an individual or the name of a ship. Putting in the surname 'Davison', the following details come up: Camp [presumed to be Ruhleben unless otherwise noted], Surname [Davison], first name [W], occupation [Master], address [36 Jackson Street], town [Sunderland], county [Dur], birth/age [blank], ship [Cogent ON 87351], comments [deceased].

This list also appears in MT 9/1991 at TNA, where it has been annotated with date of birth, and dates of release. There are also lists for 12 October 1916, 31 March 1917, 31 July 1917, 30 September 1917 and 31 December 1917 – many of these have also been annotated. A similar list dated 21 September 1915 appears in FO 383/65.

There is a variety of material in the very thick file MT 9/1597, including lists of repatriations from Ruhleben, exchanges, lists from other camps (eg merchant seamen interned at Crefeld in 1917). It also contains enquiries from individual seamen, and correspondence relating to all aspect of merchant marine imprisonment, including the vexed question of their actual status.

MT 9/1240 has lists with details of general camp amendments, and also German forms filled in by men of the SS *Jumna* and *Turritella* on capture, providing such details as name, place and date of birth, name and address of next of kin and details of the vessel that captured them and when and where this took place.

Burial Records

The CWGC does not have details of civilians who died in the First World War. The CWGC records merchant seamen who perished as a direct result of war activity, but not those who died in prison camps. Thus there is no comprehensive list of non-military fatalities, and because bodies of civilians could be repatriated back to Britain after the end of the war they may not have remained in Germany. The graves of those who died inside the camp at Ruhleben can be found in Section 39 of 'In der Kisseln' Cemetery, Pionierstrasse 82-156, 13589 Berlin-Spandau. There is nothing to mark it as a First World War burial place except the dates 1914–1918 at the bottom of each headstone. The low-set grave markers are extremely plain, bearing just an initial or first name, surname and the date of the man's birth and death. The men were buried according to the physical location where they died – many of these men died in the camp hospital, but there were other medical establishments that men might be sent to,

General view showing First World War plot where Ruhleben graves are located in Spandau 'In der Kisseln' Cemetery (© the author).

and they would be buried in cemeteries close to these places. If a relative died in another camp in Germany you can check with the local authority for war burials in cemeteries in the area. It is worth making the point that the death rate at Ruhleben was not as high as at other prison camps; it has been estimated that fifty to sixty men died at Ruhleben. Some of the internees were older men, and, though an agreement to repatriate those aged 45 and over was made in 1916, this only began to happen in any large numbers from the beginning of 1918, when many were transferred to the Netherlands.

Medical facilities were good on the whole. If a man couldn't be treated in the camp, he could be sent out to other institutions such as the Berlin POW hospital in Alexandrinenstrasse or Dr Weiler's Sanatorium. There was no real shortage of food once Red Cross parcels started coming through, though it was certainly true that those with more money fared better than those without.

Eleven of the graves in Spandau belong to merchant seamen (two of whom were 'forty-fivers' – many of the older senior merchant mariners seem to have lived in Barrack 8): Robert Bowditch, William Davison, Thomas French, William Hazell, Charles Jennings, Fred Norton, Edward Russell, William Stewart, David Thomas, George Tyndall and Robert Wilks.

Documentation relating to merchant seamen is good, and there are also death registration records to look at. There is considerable correspondence about this in FO 383.

FO 383/65 provides information about how deaths were recorded according to German death registration regulations. The information included the first and family name, profession/trade and domicile of the notifier, place, date and hour of death, first and family name, age, profession/trade, domicile and birthplace of the deceased and, if married, the first and family name of his wife, or single status, and the first and family name, profession/trade and domicile of the parents of the deceased. The cause of death, place of burial, position of grave and effects of deceased were not required by law and not entered in the register, but the Germans professed willingness to reply to enquiries made, and the British Government received 'special and exact lists of all personal effects of English prisoners of war'.

FO 383/428 contains considerable information about William Davison's death. He was arrested on 1 August 1914 in Hamburg (some merchant seamen were rounded up before the outbreak of war), and arrived at Ruhleben on 6 November 1914. He died at the camp of *Gehirn-schlag* or a stroke. The time of death is usually given, and he died at 4.45pm on 19 January 1918. He was buried on 24 January 1918 at 2.45pm at Friedhof 'In der Kisseln'. The location of his burial is given as *Feld* (field) 40, *Reihe* (row) 20, *Grab* (grave) 2. Eight internees attended the funeral. His wife's details were given as Isabella Margaret Davison, née Harrison of Sunderland. He had a long list of effects, which are all itemized, including one *Seesack* (seabag) (which among other things contained twenty-three pairs of socks), and one leather bag.

FO 383/474 contains an issue of *The Guild Gazette: A Journal of the Imperial Merchant Service Guild*, dated September 1918, which has a roll of honour, and also a separate section on 'The Interned Seafarers'. One column reads:

Died in Internment
We are very sorry to report the deaths in internment of the following highly esteemed and respected members of the profession, whose names are being duly recorded on the Roll of Honour:–
Captain E RUSSELL, SS 'Bury'
Captain W DAVISON, SS 'Cogent'
Mr W E S Wood, Chief Officer SS 'Borderland'

It also contains a section on Ruhleben prisoners' release, and the pressure being applied to expedite the release of all merchant seamen. A letter encouraging this was published from Th. Wiese on behalf of the

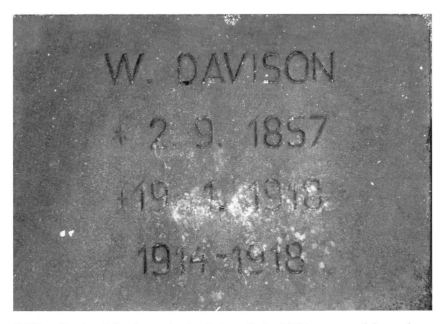

William Davison's headstone is simply inscribed with his name and dates of birth and death. The dates '1914–1918' are the only indication that this is a war grave (© the author).

men of the German merchant marine, sent from Douglas on the Isle of Man. The magazine also contained a photograph of twenty-three named merchant marine officers at Salzerbad in Austria-Hungary.

Women were not usually interned. When war broke out, British women were generally repatriated back to Britain, but there were later examples where imprisonment did happen, usually for short periods. Holzminden was the usual camp women were sent to. A group of high-profile women held there from 27 June 1916 were the five stewardesses serving on the SS *Brussels* when it was captured by the Germans. The captain, Charles Algernon Fryatt, had been sought by the Germans because of an incident the previous year when he had attempted to ram a German U-boat, and he would later be court-martialled and executed. All his crew were interned, although the stewardesses, Clara Elwood, Mrs Alice Elwood, Kate Bobby, Edith Smith and Mrs Katherine Stalker, were only imprisoned for a limited time. They had a grim experience though, and were horrified at 'the extreme prevalence of vermin throughout the camp' and the poor food, as well as the low moral standards of many of the imprisoned women. Detailed accounts of their experiences can be found in FO 383/209. Their captivity was relatively short: they were released in November 1916.

The situation in Austria-Hungary was different. Some British subjects were formally interned in camps, of which Katzenau, near Vienna, was the main one. The majority of Britons were merely confined – allowed to stay in their own homes, but with close contact with the police. In fact, when the food situation worsened as the war progressed, some of those who were still living at home preferred to be interned in order to receive Red Cross parcels, although their numbers did not exceed 350. Fewer than fifty of these were merchant seamen.

Online Sources

http://pds.lib.harvard.edu/pds/view/12382737 – Maurice Ettinghausen Collection of Ruhleben Civilian Internment Camp Papers held at Harvard Law School Library consists of twelve boxes of ephemera. You can see the full text of magazines and newspapers such as *Ruhleben Daily News* and *Evening Star*, as well as the Italian *Messaggero* and *L'Eco* and French *La Vie Française*.

http://pds.lib.harvard.edu/pds/view/13136016?n=152 – John C Masterman Collection at Harvard Law School Library.

http://www.lysator.liu.se/~padrone/ruhleben/index.html – James McCarthy's sketchbook from Ruhleben.

http://yourarchives.nationalarchives.gov.uk/index.php?title=Ruhleben – Your Archives pages at TNA.

http://ruhleben.tripod.com/ – 'The Ruhleben Story'.

www.ruhleben.com/index.php – Stefan Hartmann is very interested in the internment camp as well as the general district of Ruhleben, and his forum, 'Ruhleben ein Stadtteil zwischen Charlottenburg und Spandau in Berlin', offers a great opportunity for an English–German dialogue.

http://ssa.nls.uk/ – Search under Ruhleben on the Scottish Screen Archive site and you can watch 'Return of the Interned', showing some civilians returning to Leith from Ruhleben in 1918.

Chapter 7

BRITISH PRISONERS OF WAR IN TURKISH HANDS

The experience of prisoners held by the Turks in some ways seems to be a precursor of what was to happen in the Far East in the next world war. Most prisoners found themselves in a totally alien situation, where escape was hardly considered a possibility owing to the hostile outside environment where white Europeans would be highly conspicuous and had little knowledge of local language and geography. A punishing climate, swelteringly hot by day and bitterly cold by night, coupled with difficult terrain and a shortage of water and the danger of disease provided challenges similar to those that would occur in the Far East a quarter of a century later. The men were inadequately supplied with food that bore little resemblance to any diet they were used to. They were also put to hard labour building railways.

There was a shockingly high death rate, much worse than in Germany. It has been estimated that 70 per cent of British POWs died in, or on the way to, Turkish camps. Over 3,000 POWs died on the gruelling marches from Kut el Amara in 1916, and those that arrived exhausted at the Baghdad railway camps were immediately set to work by the Turks, with little concern for the astronomical casualty rate. Official information filtered back to Britain from the Ottoman Empire very slowly, with the result that the Government and families at home were very much in the dark about what was happening. The Reverend Harold Spooner's experiences below explain why so many men have unknown graves and why keeping records proved difficult. The Turks were initially reluctant to allow neutral inspections of the camps, but, as was usually the case, there seemed to be some improvements in the latter part of the war. Red Cross parcels getting through ameliorated the situation, for example. It also needs to be said that the rations and living conditions of the POWs were similar to those of the Turkish Army, as required by international law. The poor treatment received was not necessarily deliberately inflicted cruelty – although, as always, the commanding officers set the tone for the camps, and there were good and bad. The parallel with the Japanese in the Second World War continues here, as exactly the same situation

68

applied: Japanese living conditions and rations were similar to those the POWs were given, and the POW treatment would not have seemed abnormal within the culture of their captors.

The information relating to Turkish captivity is also more difficult to find. Comparatively fewer men were imprisoned, and although there are a respectable number of officers' accounts, the voice of the ordinary soldier, sailor and airman is much rarer. Writing diaries was forbidden, letters were more erratic and were much less frequent between Britain and Turkey than between Britain and Germany. Officers were able to correspond with their relatives, though this was a frustrating experience, with questions asked in one letter not being answered until many replies later, if at all. IWM has only a small amount of this type of material for the lower ranks, although there is enough to glean some insight into the experience. Exhausted from their hard work, the men would not have had

Frederick Nelson received his first letter from England in January 1916. His first letter arrived home in May 1916. Many letters and parcels never reached their destination or were severely delayed. This much-stamped and annotated envelope was sent from Manchester on 17 October 1915, but though it arrived at Galata/Constantinople on 14 November of that year, it apparently never reached its recipient and was returned to his home address on 27 May 1920 (© IWM, Documents: Papers of F Nelson, 07/59/1).

the energy to write, even if they had had the wherewithal to do so. Frequent moves — where one often had to carry all one's own luggage – and pilfering by either Turkish guards or Arab looters when travelling across the vast empty distances of the desert meant that the men left captivity with very few belongings. Frederick Nelson's story below is held at IWM (07/59/1), but this is in the form of written-up talks that he gave about his experiences. Although his collection has excellent paperwork and a couple of photographs, the acquisition of these date from after the end of Turkey's war.

An Other Rank's Experience

The first prisoners of the Turks were taken at Gallipoli. Initially conceived as a naval operation, this ill-fated campaign (April 1915–January 1916) was an attempt to open up a new front, assist Russia and gain control of Constantinople and the Dardanelles Straits. The number of prisoners involved was not large (31 British officers and 374 other ranks), and most were captured as individuals or in small groups. It is likely that most experiences would have been similar to that of Private Frederick William Nelson, whose captivity began on 7 August 1915. He had volunteered for the army on 3 September the previous year, apparently falsifying his age. His service record still exists, but nowhere on the surviving documents is there an age or a date of birth. His family believed he gave this as 31 July 1895, but he was in fact born on 31 July 1897. At just 18 years and one week old, following several dramatic months on active service, he found himself a prisoner. Nelson had joined the Lancashire Fusiliers in Salford, and less than a week later had sailed from Southampton to Egypt. He appeared to have no previous service, and no military training before he left the UK. On 2 May 1915 Nelson embarked from Alexandria for the Dardanelles, where his unit, the 1/8th Territorial Battalion of the Lancashire Fusiliers formed part of the 125th Infantry Brigade of the 42nd Division. Nelson had already been slightly wounded, and was suffering from the almost-universal Gallipoli complaint of dysentery, but he could not be sent to hospital because of the shortage of manpower. He was tasked, with three others, to guard the water supply as a 'soft option', but when four men from another battalion arrived to take over this role he was forced to return to his unit, where he went over the top and was taken prisoner.

On the first night of his capture Nelson described being walked around behind the lines to ensure that the men lost their bearings. Another major event was having his boots 'liberated' – the Turkish soldiers would systematically go to the back of the column and remove boots or other property from the prisoners. The food was also commented on. The first morning he had 'half a chippattee (one name for a kind of elongated pancake made of brown flour) and a drink of water'. The following day there was a meal of boiled maize which was 'immediately nicknamed "bullets", for the yellow peas were as hard almost as their namesakes.' This was served in a 'carawanna' dish, 'a shallow circular metal dish about 15 inches in diameter'. Catering for ten men, it would be put on the floor, where they had to squat and eat with a spoon: the man 'with the fastest spoon stroke gets the most dinner.' He later described the excitement of seeing a carawanna dish piled high with luscious fruit looking like plums or damsons – only to experience severe disappointment on tasting olives. He later described how 'you might put your spoon in the carawanna and bring it out with a sheep's eye, or a jawbone with all the teeth in.' Another POW remembered tripe with fur attached.

The men sailed from Gallipoli to Constantinople (and were concerned about the submarine threat, again echoing the Far East situation in the next war), where they had to submit to a humiliating triumphal march through the city, and were later temporarily housed in Stamboul Gaol. Nelson also mentions being filmed with about 100 other men, walking

Group photograph taken in August 1915 at Stamboul Gaol for propaganda purposes. Nelson is standing to the right of the left lamp post, wearing a fez at an angle. He discovered the photograph in a shop in Constantinople after the Armistice! (© IWM, Documents: Papers of F Nelson, 07/59/1).

71

around the prison yard for a propaganda film. A group photograph was taken on this occasion.

An excellent and little-known source for POWs in this campaign has recently been published in Turkey: *Prisoners of War at the Çanakkale Battles: Testimonies and Letters: Volumes I and II* edited by Dr Ög Alb Ahmet Tetik and published by the General Staff of the Turkish Armed Forces (Ankara: Genelkurmay Basimevi, 2009). When taken captive the men were obviously formally interviewed: they wrote their own name, number and unit, and the information they provided was written down in Ottoman Turkish. The details their captors were looking for included when the men arrived at Gallipoli and where they were captured, and they all seem to contain a statement to say they had not been ill treated. These have been reproduced in facsimile form (and you can actually see the prisoner's signature), together with an English/Turkish translation. Frederick Nelson's entry reads:

> I landed on the shores of Çanakkale on May 5. I could not change my clothes since then until the day I was taken prisoner in a trench across the Asçibaba on August 7. I was in the trench for all that time. I got infested with lice. The 5th, 6th, 7th, and the 8th battalions were fighting against the Turks in Asçibaba. I am 18 years old. I was working as a clerk at the Karabez(?) [sic] Chocolate firm in Manchester. I joined the army on the fourth of last September at my own will. In terms of water, I have never experienced shortage of water while I was in Asçibaba. I have nothing to complain about the Turks.

The reference to 'Karabez' is interesting. Presumably it is a phonetic rendering of Cadbury's, which was possibly a better-known chocolate firm to the Turks than the one for which Nelson worked. His army record contains the details that he was employed as a book-keeping typist for Messrs J S Fry and Son, 27 Hanging Ditch, Manchester (Fry's was a Bristol-based firm that was taken over by Cadbury's in 1919). Ironically, his company launched one of its most famous products – Fry's Turkish Delight – in 1914.

The second volume of this publication contains other interesting material, including details of the men who were taken POW with Nelson, or at least on the same day. Private H Rosevere from his own unit, and six men from the 7th Battalion are listed, together with two men from the Worcestershire Regiment, one from the Hampshire Regiment and one Frenchman. The report from the interrogations is also given. It was written by S Command of the Department of Intelligence – the actual value of it is questionable – but I think it worth including here for what it adds to the general picture of the capture process:

Below is the summary of the interrogation of the prisoners, from the 7th and 8th Lancashire Regiments affiliated to the 42nd Division 4th Infantry Brigade, caught at the 10th Division Front.

The division mentioned is a territorial division. It first went to Egypt and landed on Gelibolu on the eve of attack. Only a small portion of the division is composed of new units. The Corps Command they are affiliated to is in England. Having had their training in England they were sent here.

The 8th Lancashire Infantry Regiment Commander was Colonel Tallaux, who died two weeks ago. Commander of the Infantry Brigade is General Trith(?). They landed on the shore of the Ilyas Cape. As it is understood from their testimonies they are living in their dugouts and trenches. Landings are conducted early in the morning, before dawn, and in the evenings after the sunset. The 7th Lancashire Regiment Commander Colonel Macour(?) was wounded by a howitzer shell.

General Douglas came to the trenches a couple of times. He thinks he is not in to region [sic]. The last attack, he says, was carried out by two regiments. (Most probably they are affiliated to his division.)

Their division went to Limnos four days ago to rest; and it had been to Bozcaada for once earlier.

[They say] they are all tired and weary of the war. Their ration is not good. [They say] they are especially thankful for being fallen prisoners. One of them says that he joined the army just for the glittering of the uniform. He say if he were given a second change [sic] or even 1.000 lira he would not repeat the same mistake. He says he is praying for not repeating the same mistake, but that he is afraid of not complying with the orders.

The final materials of relevance in this publication are facsimiles of letters which were sent from and to some of the POWs. Presumably these have been intercepted and/or taken from POWs, and they have been underlined to show what the Turks regarded as important for intelligence purposes. There are also a few letters that appear to have been dictated by POWs from hospital beds after their capture. There are not great numbers of these, but this is a fascinating publication, with an idiosyncratic index that highlights the problems of transliteration and foreign language materials, and shows that these problems are exactly the same as they were almost a century ago.

Another related item held at IWM is *British and Dominion Servicemen Captured at Gallipoli who Died in Captivity*, by Patrick Gariépy (Eugene, OR: P Gariépy, 1999). This records that Private Henry Rosevere, captured with Nelson, was one of these unfortunate men. He died in Anatolia on 11

March 1917, and is commemorated on the Angora Memorial in Baghdad War Cemetery. The detail contained in this publication varies, but it does sometimes provide personal recollections, cause of death, personal effects and who they were returned to, and references to obituaries.

Nelson travelled by train to Angora (now Ankara), where he stayed until the end of November. There were two meals a day; the first, at 10am, was a small amount of wheat boiled in a large amount of water, and the second, at 5pm, would typically be one small potato and a small piece of meat. The men were then forced to march to Kiangherai, a journey of four days. Many men died here, and Nelson comments, 'It seemed to be all the biggest men who died, whereas the thin, weak, bags of bones like myself managed to peg along somehow.'

TNA has a useful list of British POWs in Turkey dated February 1916. This can be found in AIR 1/892/204/5/697. Frederick Nelson appears in this, along with details of his unit (down to company level, he was with B Company of the 8th Battalion of the Lancashire Fusiliers). His regimental number is given as 2398, and his camp appears as Kiangri [sic]. A note at the top of the list reads: 'The United States Ambassador states that 318 of the undermentioned prisoners of war who were interned at Kiangeri [sic], together with some of those at Afion Kara Hissar, have been transferred to Bazanti, the present terminus of the Anatolian Railway near the Taurus Mountains.' The list also includes details of men known to have died, and as well as name, rank, number and unit, provides details of where the man was captured, where and when he died (which might include the hospital where he was being treated), the cause of death and his home address. The location in the AIR record class is an interesting demonstration of the melting pot principle referred to earlier, where you can find information in unexpected places, simply because men from all the land, sea and air forces were held together, and this particular list seems to have been retained in only one place.

Bazanti, referred to above, was a terminus. Different camps worked out of there, and we know from Nelson's papers that he went to Bilemedik in March 1916, where 'the Turkish Government washed their hands of us as far as food etc was concerned and we had to earn our living or starve. The guards of course remained.' The men had a choice of working on the surface (for 8 piastres/1 shilling and 4 pence per day) or in the tunnels for 12 piastres. The men worked for a fortnight from 6am to 6pm, and then for a fortnight from 6pm to 6am, but by September were all weakened by malaria and dysentery. Nelson was sent on a two-day train journey to Afieu Kara Hissal [sic], where he stayed for some time. He was selected to be exchanged to England, but missed the November 1917 exchange because he was ill in hospital with malaria.

Nelson's service record has details of 'Weak eyesight, aggravated by sun in Egypt, and during internment in Turkey by medical treatment

Nelson was among the crowd of released POWs and crew of HMS Superb. *The photograph was taken at Constantinople on 15 November 1918 (© IWM, Documents: Papers of F Nelson, 07/59/1).*

there eg numerous doses of quinine. Also Malaria Fever (Turkey) and Dysentery contracted July 1915 on Gallipoli', and he is listed as having been treated in hospitals at Haidar Pasha, Malteppe, Afion Kara Hissar and Bilemedik. An examination at 2nd Western General Hospital on 25 February 1919 claimed he had no disability. His date of arrival in the UK was given as 8 December 1918, and he was demobilized on 19 March 1919.

There are various lists that can be found in the Foreign Office files. For example, FO 383/335 contains three useful partial lists of prisoners. One lists 136 British POWs at Ada-Bazar, under their name, unit and regimental number. There is also a list of 41 WOs and sergeants at Angora in November 1917. The same period is covered in a list of POW naval ratings. The details include camp, name, number, rate and name of vessel. FO 383/336 contains a list of British POWs who died at Tarsus (some of these appear to be civilians). FO 383/227 reveals brief details (name and vessel or unit) of the Roman Catholic British and French POWs at Afion Kara Hissar who received a Christmas gift (32 piastres and 9½ paras) from Monsignor Dolci, the Apostolic Delegate at Constantinople; 47 officers and men are listed here. FO 383/459 contains a list of men of the 1/5th Hants Battery RFA, and the camps they were held in, together with lists of those known to be alive but not located, and those whose fate is unknown. FO 383/456 contains several lists of POWs, for example, at Afion Kara Hissar dated September 1918. There is a list from Magnesia, which includes the ages of the men listed, a list of officers at Kedos and nominal rolls of Indians at Konia. There are also two short lists of names of POWs working for the Baghdad Railway Construction Company.

Another very interesting document in FO 383/227 is 'British Prisoners of War in Turkey: Report of an Enquiry made by the War Prisoners' Fund of the Oxfordshire and Buckinghamshire Light Infantry', dated May–June 1916. Although this does not have a list of names it does attempt to make sense of and provide information about the various camps, and gives numbers of men from different regiments who were held in different camps. Interesting little snippets from this include the fact that goats could be purchased at Bozanti for 2s, and the example of a letter written home by a soldier complaining that he had not heard from his mother. The Turkish censor apparently added to this, 'Dear Mrs Lee – Do not write more than four lines at a time, and I am sure they will be received by your son.'

Regimental collections are also useful for lists. The Norfolk Regiment's Casualty and Sickness Ledger provides details of POWs of the Germans, Bulgarians and Turks. The regimental museum also has a useful Kut Nominal Roll, and it is instructive to compare the two. The first contains an entry for Private H Airey of the 2nd Battalion who was wounded on 2 January 1916. He is 'Presumed Prisoner of War. Enquiries made in Turkey, no indication that soldier still living. Date of death between 29.4.16 and 24.5.17.' The Kut Nominal Roll, obviously compiled later, and probably drawing on the Reverend Spooner's information described below, provides the information that he died at Yarbaschi on 28 July 1916.

An Officer's Experience

The campaign in oil-rich Mesopotamia (present-day Iraq) led by the Indian Army resulted in the capture of around 21,000 British and Indian troops and followers. Of these, over 10,000 were taken at Kut el Amara. The men, who had been besieged in the small town since December 1915 following earlier attempts to take Baghdad, were not in good shape when they surrendered to the Turks on 29 April of the following year. They were also completely unprepared for the ordeal that awaited them. The officers had a difficult time, but as always their situation was much better than that of the rank and file; they travelled by river to Baghdad and were then marched to their camps. Most of the men were forced to walk hundreds of miles on a nightmare journey to the working camps in Asia Minor.

The son of a clergyman, Harold Spooner was born on 17 February 1880 and began his service with the Indian Ecclesiastical Establishment in 1911. The documents appointing him to the Bengal Ecclesiastical Establishment on probation on 28 January 1911 are held at the British Library in the India Office Records (IOR/L/PJ/6/1058 file 265). This file contains his application form dated 5 September 1910, recording three and a half years in the 1st Wiltshire Volunteer Rifle Corps and stating, 'Am used to organizing and looking after outdoor games, Cricket, Football, Hockey, Tennis, etc. Have been tried for Wiltshire at Cricket and have my County Colours for Hockey'. Referees describe him as 'assiduous, accessible and attractive' and 'athletic and manly and likely to have a good influence both with officers and civil servants'. He sailed for Calcutta on the Peninsular and Oriental SS *Sardinia* on 4 March 1911. Before serving with the Indian Expeditionary Force in Mesopotamia he was attached to the Middlesex Regiment.

Spooner's entry in *List of British Officers Taken Prisoner in the Various Theatres of War between August, 1914 and November, 1918* can be found at the back of the volume where the various non-Western Front campaigns are listed. His name appears under a section called 'Kut Garrison', as Captain H Spooner, Army Chaplains Department. The only information attached to this is the date of his repatriation, which is given as 1/1/19.

Rev H Spooner is also listed under the Indian Ecclesiastical Establishment in *The Times* on 7 June 1916 (over five weeks after the event). Under a heading 'The Defenders of Kut' there is an incomplete list

The Reverend Harold Spooner with his Sikh orderly during the siege of Kut el Amara (© IWM, Q 107194).

of 200 officers believed to have been taken at Kut el Amara. Only officers are listed here, and the newspaper is anxious to make it clear that no news has yet been heard from the Turkish Government.

The Reverend Harold Spooner's documents at IWM (76/115/1) are remarkable for the level of detail they reveal about the besieged defenders of Kut and also about what happened afterwards. He was immensely aware of his responsibilities, visited the sick when he could, and sought to record as many details as possible relating to the men who did not return. He was always anxious to give solace to families at home and provide information that he knew would be wanted. In his movements around Turkish territory he was concerned about the care of the cemeteries that would be left behind and made it his business to do whatever he could for the prisoners, to record details of ill treatment and discover the fate of as many as possible.

Spooner's concerns began even before the British and Indians left Kut. Anxious about the fate of the cemetery 'with all its neatly kept graves, 300 of them, at the head of each being either an iron or a wooden cross with the soldiers name and regiment on it', he spoke to the Turkish commandant, who

> promised that he would have it respected, and sent his orderly to show him the exact spot, and gave him orders to see that it was not molested in any way. I went with the said orderly, explaining to him our anxiety to have the graves honoured and preserved. The next day, however, I took a funeral there, and found that all the wooden crosses had been stolen, and on the following day all the iron ones had also gone, and one noticed little Arab children running about the streets waving these crosses as if they had been flags. The wire fencing had been taken away and foot-paths made right across the graves, the wall of the cemetery was broken down, and the place resembled an ordinary thoroughfare.

The Reverend Spooner was aware that the Turks were not responsible for this since the damage had been done by the local Arabs, but he was deeply disappointed that the Turks had not prevented this and had not kept their promise. This was to be a pattern that repeated itself.

An appalling march from Baghdad to Castamuni was experienced, in which men who were too exhausted or ill to continue fell out and were left to die where they lay if they were not spotted and rescued by their weakened comrades. An incident described by Harold Armstrong in *Turkey in Travail* typified the cultural rift between the men who found themselves in this situation. A British soldier critically ill with dysentery lay near the road, and one of the Arab guards had put sand in his mouth to kill him. The British soldiers who noticed this were outraged at this flagrant murder, yet when challenged the Arab believed he was being kind and saving the man from being savaged by jackals while still alive. The other surprise on this journey was the kindness of the Germans that they met. Allied with the Turks, the Germans were usually horrified to see fellow Europeans being treated as the POWs were. They shared food, and the Reverend Spooner wrote at a stop at Demi Kupu how 'One of these Germans used to attend our funerals and afterwards he would make a cross to put at the head of the grave, writing on it some words of sympathy.'

They arrived at the officers' camp at Castamuni on 29 July 1916, and the initial impression was favourable:

Our billets were Armenian houses and Greek school buildings; they were furnished with beds and a certain amount of other things, and meals were provided in a restaurant close by. Some 80 officers had been there for about six weeks, and they all looked fairly clean and fairly cheerful. Walks were arranged for twice a week, and they had started what was known as football – the ball consisting of a leather football case stuffed with straw. Officers were also allowed to attend the Turkish baths, and to purchase what they needed in the local bazaars.

A coloured drawing of the church at Castamuni, from the Collection of the Reverend Harold Spooner (Courtesy Lt Col A P Spooner MBE; IWM, Documents: Papers of the Reverend H Spooner, 76/115/1).

The Reverend Spooner was very critical of the fact that the Turks did not – initially at least – recognize his status as a religious man. He frequently writes of his difficulties in getting a space for a chapel, and he was also irritated by the preferential treatment the Turks gave those of their own religion: Indian troops were not treated equally, with Muslims receiving superior treatment. He was presented with candlesticks and a cross by a local Greek priest on 19 August, in gratitude for the kindness shown by the officers to the local Greek poor (charitable collections had been made, and these were especially appreciated because of the plight in which the POWs found themselves). The cross now appears to be held at the National Army Museum. When the officers left Castamuni, Father Anastasias offered to pray for the souls and tend the graves of those who remained in the cemetery.

Spooner was also irritated by the communication problems; these go some way to explain why knowledge of what was happening in Turkey was so poor. On 17 November 1916 he wrote:

> Have received long lists from the War Office with the names of those who have not been heard of since the fall of Kut-el-Amara. I have given about 150 names from my diary, and have returned it to the Commandant, who has promised to send it to GHQ Constantinople, for transmission to England. I wish to state here that on three occasions I did this sort of work for the War Office, and have heard that these names never reached home. Whether Tufik Bey, our Commandant, was at fault, or whether those in Constantinople, I am unable to say.

Some information did get through via irregular means. FO 383/459 contains a lengthy letter from Major General Sir Charles Mellis to Lloyd George, sent from Broussa on 1 February 1918, which was illicitly sent via a Russian officer who was exchanged. In it he writes of the sufferings of the Kut garrison, drawing on his own experiences but also quoting the Reverend Spooner. This letter contains reports and statistics, but Spooner makes the point that 'Some commandants seem to have been quite *human* and at some hospitals troops have been treated well.' As well as the online catalogue, the Foreign Office card catalogue in the Research Enquiries Room can be checked (the file numbers on the cards need to be converted to contemporary references, but this is quite easy following the instructions). Not all of these documents have survived, but there are some references to the Reverend Spooner in this for 1918 and 1919. In FO 383/461, correspondence was raised in April 1918 to find out more about the soldiers buried in Kut Town Cemetery, and it is suggested that one of the three garrison clergymen might be able to help (the Reverend Spooner at Kastamouni, the Reverend Father Mullen at Psamatia, but most recently reported in Haida Pashar Hospital and the Reverend A Y Wright at Afion Kara Hissar). Father Mullen replies with a lengthy letter explaining the sources that would need to be consulted, first of which is 'a. The Rev H Spooner, C of E Chaplain to 6th Division who is official Registrar'. Mullen gave a rundown of the locations where graves were likely to be, and provided listings of the Roman Catholic officers and men who were buried in Kut Old Town Cemetery. There were queries as to whether anything had been heard from Wright or Spooner, but nothing appeared to be there – no doubt one or other of the letters got lost *en route*.

On 11 October the party Spooner was travelling with arrived at the camp at Changri (although he later wrote that Kiangheri might be a better spelling) after a four-day journey. On this expedition he recorded that some of the old guards from Castamuni invited the POWs to sit with them and warm themselves around their bonfires. He comments, 'The old Turkish soldier is often found to be a very kind hearted man.' Changri, however, is summed up in one word: 'damnable'. Although earlier arrivals had spent weeks cleaning:

> The whole place swarms with vermin and mosquitos. It is so bad in the summer that even Turkish troops cannot inhabit these barracks. The rooms are just bare barracks with no glass in the windows, great holes all over the floors, and the wind appears to come from every quarter. Officers have to sleep on the floor because there are no beds, in fact there is no furniture of any sort – no tables, no chairs, no washhandstands – and the insanitary state of everything is indescribable. The water in the barrack square is undrinkable and our orderlies have to fetch it in water bottles from two miles away. No officers are allowed to go for walks but are only allowed in a field outside the barracks from 10am to 4.30pm . . . Though the nights were bitterly cold many officers preferred living out in the open to living inside those terrible rooms.

The camp was very unhealthy, and a move to Yozgad followed. The Reverend Spooner requested that he be sent to a camp with no chaplain so he could minister to the men, and although this was granted he did not feel up to making another arduous trip immediately. He was allowed to wait for a month as he wished, and had an interesting journey where he was able to speak to some of the men *en route* (despite Turkish orders not to let this happen):

> [At] No. 3 Camp, 7th Regiment, Little Yozgad, I was fortunate enough to arrive just as the men were leaving off work and sitting down to a meal. They seemed very excited at seeing their officers again, and proceeded to give one food and make one feel very much

at home among them, and they sat around and told me of their experiences. No words can express what these poor fellows had been through with regard to exposure, starvation and sickness. They had endured terrible sufferings for nearly two years, but the conditions now were very much improved. Parcels were coming along fairly frequently, and the new conditions seemed to be due to a change of commandant, their present one being Sherif Bey – previously commandant of the guard at the officers' camp at Castamuni. He seemed to be doing all he could to help our men.

On 17 June 1918 he arrived at Bor, where he found a camp with 100 British other ranks, 100 Indian other ranks, 50 Russians and 40

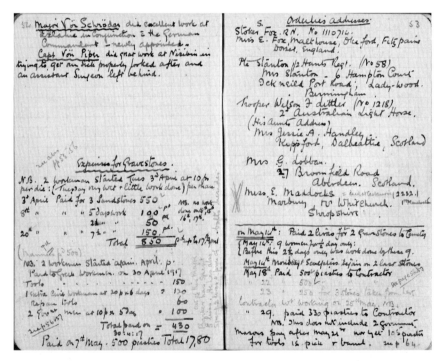

Sample page from one of the Reverend Harold Spooner's notebooks and diaries. In often tiny handwriting he would record all sorts of details he considered of relevance, including lists of men. This spread has information about the costs of gravestones at Castamuni, notes on German officers who were helpful and the home addresses of some of the orderlies. He would have written to Miss Maddocks when her brother(?) died – his original grave can be seen on page 83 (Courtesy Lt Col A P Spooner MBE; IWM, Documents: Papers of the Reverend H Spooner, 76/115/1).

Romanians, together with the medical officer, Captain Murphy. He found the camp to be a reasonable one, with the main problem being the nearby hospital at Nigdé, to which men had to march. On 18 November 1918, when the men were preparing to leave the camp, the commandant made a gracious speech, and was cheered by them: '. . . on the whole he had been good to them and never wished to see them ill-treated.'

The journey to Constantinople, where they arrived on 29 November, was something of a nightmare as well. On 23 November, they arrived at Konia, and the Reverend Spooner made a point of meeting Father Antoine, a Catholic Armenian who had buried twenty-three British soldiers. This entry sums up the difficulties that would surface when the authorities were trying to account for what had happened to those who were missing:

> I copied the names of those soldiers out of his burial register, but as they are spelt phonetically it is difficult to make them out. He also told me that seven out of these had arrived actually dead; there were

A drawing of Castamuni Cemetery dated 30 September 1917. The four graves at the top, from left to right, belong to Stoker Thirkell, Lieutenant Reynolds, Lieutenant Locke and Commander Crabtree. The grave at the lower level belongs to Gunner O'Mahoney and Lance Corporal Maddocks (Courtesy Lt Col A P Spooner MBE; IWM, Documents: Papers of the Reverend H Spooner, 76/115/1).

no names given of them, and they were buried in three large graves. This perhaps is a good instance of the behaviour to our dead by the Turks, and why so many names have not reached our Government because they did not take the trouble to find them out.

Officers who were Turkish POWs are generally very well documented. The book *From Kastamuni to Kedos: Being a Record of Experiences of Prisoners of War in Turkey, 1916–1918,* written by many hands and edited by C L Woolley, Capt RFA (Oxford: Blackwell, 1921) contains a nominal roll of officers in the three camps covered in the book. Details include the place and date of capture, and the name of the camp(s) the individual was in, and the date they arrived. It also includes details of the other rank orderlies. Reverend H A Spooner MC is listed as serving as CF (Chaplain to the Forces), and having been captured at Kut on 29 April 1916. It provides the information that he arrived at Castamuni on 28 July 1916, but was also held prisoner at Changri and Bor.

Magazines were produced in Britain by families who were pooling information, and these provide an interesting counterpoint to the camp magazines. An excellent example of this is the *Yozgad, Broussa and Constantinople Magazine,* copies of which can be seen in the Major General Sir Ernest Walker papers at IWM (76/128/1). Snippets of letters received by families were published in this, and there was an attempt to spread details to friends and relations who may not have heard from their loved ones for some time. *The 'Kronical': Kastamuni Kronical* was based on the same idea, although produced in a less sophisticated way, and there are other titles that sound similar, although these are not held by IWM and I have not had sight of them. I am not aware of anything similar for those held in Germany, but perhaps the smaller numbers and the comparatively fewer camps, together with the fact that many of the POWs belonged to the Indian Army, and their families probably knew each other was a bond that led to this phenomenon. A committee was formed specifically in relation to the Prisoners of War Captured at Kut (which seems to have broadened out to officers in what were regarded as some of the unhealthier camps), with the aim of pressuring for their exchange or repatriation. A petition to this effect can be found at TNA in FO 383/459, including some signatures of friends and relatives in the UK, and lists of the 'representatives' and the POWs they are representing. A caustic comment written on the top reads: 'These people, like everyone else, seem to think that you have only to express a wish and that Turks will then carry it out.'

All three of the padres – the Reverends Mullen (Roman Catholic), Wright (Wesleyan) and Spooner (Anglican) – were created Members of the Military Division of the Most Excellent Order of the British Empire 'for valuable services rendered in connection with the defence of Kut-al-

Amarah', dated 3 June 1919. This was published in the *London Gazette* supplement of 23 October 1919, and can be found online at www.london-gazette.co.uk. This was also announced in *The Times* of 24 October 1919 under the heading 'The Defence of Kut: Further Honours and Awards'.

There is also a brief file dated 5 October 1917 relating to the three clergymen and whether the Ottoman Government was issuing pay to them. This is located in FO 383/335.

Spooner's post-war experiences were mixed. He returned to India after helping the authorities piece together the facts relating to the fate of the Kut garrison. His experiences, no doubt coupled with the sense of responsibility that he bore, led to a nervous breakdown. The documents invaliding him from the Indian Eccelesiastical Establishment on 1 November 1928 'on account of melancholia' can be found at the British Library in IOR/L/PJ/6/1965. What is certain is that without the information that he so assiduously compiled, our knowledge of what happened in this bleak episode would be much poorer. Many had cause to regard him as, in the words of one of the wounded whom he visited at Kut, 'our incomparable padre'. His eldest son, Pat Spooner, was to follow in his footsteps by serving with the Indian Army and earning an MBE for escaping from an Italian POW camp (this is described in the Second World War companion volume).

Indian Records

The British Library has good listings of Indian POWs in its Indian Soldiers' Fund Committee material.

'List of Indian Prisoners of War in Turkey in Asia' (IOR Mss Eur F120/274) is a 296-page compilation of periodical lists numbers 1–7 that are also held, and it appears to be comprehensive. It is divided up by regiment, and then contains regimental number, rank, name, camp number and place of internment. For example, 599, Sepoy, Manga Khan, 310, Airan, Secteur Taurus Sud is listed under the 26th Mule Corps. It also has details of Indians attached to British units, eg 323 Sweeper Juman Isar attached to 2nd Norfolk Regt., Daridja Cement Factory. In a few cases the camp is not known and so no address is given.

'List of Indian Prisoners of War in Turkey in Asia whose Deaths have been Reported' (IOR Mss Eur F120/275) is arranged under regiment. It contains regimental number, rank, name, date of death, and last address. For example, 3887 Sowar Mohammad Ishaq of the 7th Lancers died at Entilli on 30 March 1917.

Burial Records

Haidar Pasha Cemetery in what was Constantinople, and is now Istanbul was given to the British Government in 1855 and contains about 600 burials from the Crimean War. There are 366 war graves, with a large number of these being British POWs from the First World War, although there are also burials from the post-war occupation. Seventy-seven British and Indian graves here were relocated from Feriköi Protestant Cemetery in Constantinople.

Baghdad War Cemetery contains nearly 6,000 First World War graves, and this is the burial site of many of the POWs from the Mesopotamian campaign. Again, graves were concentrated here in the late 1920s; for example, 91 graves were moved from Adana Protestant and Prisoner of War Cemeteries, 198 graves from Afium Kara Hissar Armenian Cemetery, 369 from Bagtche Prisoner of War Cemetery, 33 from Kurbali Prisoner of War Cemetery, 94 from Nigde Greek and Prisoner of War Cemetery, 145 from Yarbashi Prisoner of War Cemetery and 134 from Tarsus Armenian Cemetery.

A large percentage of graves in the Mesopotamian theatre were lost or unmarked, and these names are commemorated on the Basra Memorial. The current situation in Iraq means that at present the Baghdad Cemetery and Basra Memorial are not accessible.

Civilian Internees

The number of civilian internees held in Turkish hands was given by the Central Prisoners of War Committee as 120 at the end of December 1916. These were mainly merchant seamen, and their principal camp was at Magnesia, near Smyrna. A list of civilian Turkish internees who arrived at Alexandria for repatriation on 9 November 1918 is given in FO 383/459 (a list of five stowaways is also included).

Repatriation

The repatriation of POWs from Turkey was very much overshadowed in the British press by the far larger numbers of prisoners returning from Germany. The dangers of travelling across a mined sea, and also shortage of shipping, meant that the preferred route for the men to travel home was by land. They would leave Turkey via Smyrna. Accomodation was arranged in a small village called Paradise just outside the port, where they were able to use the modern and comfortable facilities of the American Mission School. The passage to Alexandria (or Port Said) took about two and a half days. After a break in the city, the men would have another three- or four-day voyage to Taranto. From here it would be an

Released POWs in Constantinople wearing distinctive 'blanket cloth' suits mixing happily with incoming soldiers from the 3rd Middlesex Regiment of the 28th Division who formed part of the Army of Occupation (© IWM, Q 13949).

arduous six- to eight-day train journey to Calais. After the Channel crossing back to Blighty, the men would find themselves in Dover (Waterfall Meadow Camp), where they would be processed as quickly as possible and allowed to go home.

Some of the information about repatriation sources in the Germany chapter is also relevant here. FO 383/462 at TNA has a list of British officer POWs repatriated from Turkey reported at Alexandria on 6 November 1918. There is also a list dated 18 November 1918.

FO 383/456 contains a 'List of Civilians Released from Turkey' – this is in the form of a telegram from Alexandria dated 7 December 1918. Details are sparse: just a surname and initial, and the names are mainly non-European sounding. There is also a document dated 27 December 1918. A separate sheet is attached with names of some officers and the date they disembarked at Alexandria.

Chapter 8

BRITONS EXCHANGED
AND INTERNED IN
NEUTRAL COUNTRIES

Holland

Not all men confined during the First World War were held on enemy territory. Some of the first captives taken in 1914 were from the Royal Naval Division, which had been hastily despatched to assist the Belgian defence of Antwerp. Inadequately trained and ill equipped, the RND arrived on 5 October 1914, the day that the Belgians began their evacuation. The situation was chaotic and confused, and 1,500 men of the 1st Royal Naval Brigade crossed over the Dutch border rather than fall into the hands of the Germans. They were to be interned in the neutral Netherlands for the duration of the war. Hundreds of RND men also became POWs in Germany as a result of this episode.

The interned men of the 1st Royal Naval Brigade found themselves in the city of Groningen on 11 October 1914, and this was to be their home for the next four years. The Dutch Government, in accordance with the Geneva Convention, sent all brigade medical personnel back to Britain. Initially lodged in overcrowded military barracks, with some men sleeping at Fongers Cycle Works, they moved into the camp they called HMS *Timbertown* on 18 January 1915. The name came from the wooden huts that made up the camp whilst the 'His Majesty's Ship' prefix was a nod to the nautical nomenclature that was a distinctive part of naval life and tradition. The original men would be joined in January 1916 by crews from the submarines *E 17* and *H 6*, which were both wrecked on the Dutch coast. Although all members of the brigade were initially held together, officers were segregated soon after several commissioned personnel escaped. The remaining officers (with the exception of Commodore Wilfred Henderson) were transferred to the moated Fort Wierickerschans, Bodegraven.

The Times newspaper of 26 October 1914 contains a list of men who were interned in Holland. There is also supposed to be a list held at TNA in ADM 116/1317, but this is currently missing.

'1st R.N. Brigade Operational Orders: 1st R.N. Brigade: Organisation, Recreation, Occupation, etc.', held at TNA in ADM 116/1318 is a very detailed account of the camp. Much of this information is duplicated in 'Report on Internment Camp at Groningen by Commodore Wilfred Henderson, 1st R.N. Brigade' (ADM 1/8422/142), but this volume also includes rather fragile fold-out architectural plans for the bath and wash house, the administration hut, the cook house, the latrine block, a battalion hut (A, B and C huts were given to the Collingwood, Hawke and Benbow Battalions respectively, and each accommodated about 500 men), the recreation hall, guard house and gymnasium and bowling alley.

The Camp Magazine: Groningen, Holland: Being the Periodical of the 1st Royal Naval Brigade, Interned in Holland provides an excellent overview of life there. The first issue was produced in April 1915, and was continued monthly until November 1918. Over 2,000 copies of each issue were produced, and men were encouraged to send copies home. The profit that this publication produced financed the free issue of the daily *Camp News*; IWM has an incomplete run of this single-page typescript paper for 1917 and 1918; it contains news items, lost and found announcements, details of concerts, lectures, classes being held that day, warnings against a proliferation of vegetable stealing, exam results, etc. The April 1918 editorial of *The Camp Magazine* complained of the struggle to produce an interesting publication:

> As the months have rolled by it is quite safe to say that the compila-
> tion of the Magazine has grown more and more difficult, for it is
> essentially a Camp production, and to fill it each month with topical,
> readable matter has been both tedious and trying. The Camp as a
> whole is not a large or brilliant community, and our daily existence
> is devoid of any striking incidents.

The men were obviously very well aware of their situation and that they were extremely fortunate not to have been taken prisoner by the Germans. They actively raised funds for their comrades in Germany. For example, the June 1915 issue of *The Camp Magazine* reported that 104 10lb parcels of clothing were despatched to Döberitz, as was £8 18s 4d, raised at a performance given by The Follies at the Timbertown Empire.

Signalman Fred Penley led the The Follies theatre company, which had its first performance outside the camp on 16 March 1915. It performed around the Netherlands for civilian audiences besides entertaining the internees. As well as raising funds for POWs, typical causes supported included Belgian refugees in Holland and the poor in Groningen.

A report in *The Times* on 3 November 1914 recounts how the internees

Programme for The Follies featuring humorous advertisements devised by the men (Courtesy Mr G D Clarke; IWM, Documents: Papers of H E Clarke, 05/3/1).

would participate in a ten-mile route march every morning between nine and noon (except Sunday, and this would be reduced to one and a half hours in 1916). It also reported on the popularity of football (the camp teams would play against local Dutch teams, and IWM has a document relating to this (99/43/1) compiled by G Helsma); sports are one of the areas that are reported very well in *The Camp Magazine*. As usual there was a wide range of clubs and organizations, including a wool-workers' club, chess club, tennis club and the Interned Old Boy Scouts Association. This latter body consisted of about thirty men who met on Wednesday evenings between 6 and 7pm for 'the training of scoutmasters, the study of boys for their general improvement, and for social intercourse'. A sad incident occurred on 6 November 1915, when 'Shrapnel Jack', a smooth-haired terrier who had attached himself to the brigade in Antwerp and had been a popular member ever since, was at the head of a scoutmasters' training march and mortally wounded by a speeding car. A bulldog named Nigger was presented by the Westminster Tobacco Company to the camp in July 1915.

The main difference between the prisoners in Germany and the internees in Holland was the freedom the latter enjoyed. They were still guarded in the camps but they had more liberty and a friendlier environment in which to live. The Dutch were generally welcoming, and many friendships, including marriages (and some children without the formality of marriage), were to be the result. Weddings tended not to be reported in the magazine, as there seemed to have been some reluctance to have this information published in this way.

One of the advantages of being interned in Holland was the possibility of having leave. The practice of giving parole – undertaking not to escape while given some liberty or preferential conditions – was an issue that caused much debate during the war. Only officers were eligible for parole, but the decision was made that it should not be permitted, and officers had a duty to try to escape. Parole was allowed in Holland (because the officers were interned in a neutral country), and this practice was extended to allow those who had a very sick near relative to return to visit them in Britain. This was extended to all the naval internees, and expanded to become a four-week period of leave at home once a year as a reward for good behaviour. An undertaking had to be signed to

Pass from 1918 authorizing Harold Clarke to be absent from the internment camp at the stated times. Effectively he was free to wander around Groningen every day between 1.30pm and 12.30am (Courtesy Mr G D Clarke; IWM, Documents: Papers of H E Clarke, 05/3/1).

promise to come back and not conduct any work for the war effort. This was only abused on a very few occasions (with the culprits being arrested and brought back to the camp). Incidentally, this privilege was not allowed to POWs who had been exchanged to Holland – it was only open to the original naval internees.

Harold Ernest Clarke, a member of Benbow Battalion, who recorded his war reminiscences for IWM in a sound interview (4817), recalls having two leaves, and that 'we all went back without any trouble at all.' One of his trips apparently lasted three months because of difficulties with shipping. Leave was usually recorded on their service record, which can be downloaded from TNA's Documents Online. His card has the date of his first leave blank, merely saying 'On leave from Holland expiring 6.10.16', while his second period reads, '[illegible day].12.17. On leave from Holland expiring 10.1.18.'

The camp suffered great hunger in the spring of 1918; food was in very short supply in the country, and the men were unable to receive food parcels from home. There was a hunger demonstration in May, and the June issue of *The Camp Magazine* was actually censored because of Dutch sensitivity about the food situation. The levels of rations are given, with the comments that if the food was not available it could not be issued, and that the British, unlike the Dutch civilians, were unable to supplement their diet. The prizes for a swimming competition revealed that standard food had become a sought-after commodity. A white loaf was offered to the individual who won the 100 metres handicap, and 9kg of potatoes for the mess with the highest aggregate points. Clarke remembered: 'We really were in a bad way with food . . . we went for three or four months without any meat of any kind whatsoever, living principally on cabbage and potatoes.' Three slices of brown bread would be issued daily, for breakfast, tea and supper, and he recalls filling up on cold water. In August 1918, tins of corned beef, salmon and biscuits arrived, and Clarke recollected that he 'never appreciated bully beef so much in my life as I did then'.

The Dutch personnel in charge of the camp were primarily naval or marine officers (though the camp was under overall military, not naval, authority), and all spoke good English. Clarke recalled they 'couldn't care less about the war', and were simply conscripts on 10 cents a day. He remembered one occasion when four men were allowed out under the charge of a sentry; they found this rather a nuisance, until it transpired that the sentry had lived in Manchester for fourteen years, and they got him 'gloriously drunk and carried him and his rifle back'.

The men also needed to keep their minds busy, and there was a thriving library and a growing educational programme. Initially there was just one classroom, but this grew to three rooms, and classes were also held wherever they could be squeezed in. In July 1918 thirty-eight candidates sat Board of Trade exams which would benefit a mercantile marine career, while sixty internees were registered for Royal Society of Arts examinations, which included Advanced and Intermediate Dutch. The University of Groningen also opened its doors to allow the internees to attend lectures if they wished. Creative types who enjoyed making things became active with the Arts and Crafts Department, which was initiated by Able Seamen Hapgood and Peters, who carved coloured designs onto pipes, and later expanded into making wooden boxes. This became a thriving organization – the first exhibition was launched on 15 May 1915, and their products were sold in British shops such as Selfridges.

Those who died were buried in Groningen Southern Cemetery, and there are usually detailed obituaries and accounts of the funerals. The first to die was Seaman John McLeay, who was one of 106 men from the Isle of Lewis serving with the Royal Naval Reserve (RNR) imprisoned in the camp. A list of the 106 Lewis men in the camp can be found at www.wereldoorlog1418.nl/englishcamp/lewis/list.html. McLeay's obituary reported that he was not fluent in English – Gaelic being his native language – and that he had been instrumental in campaigning for a Gaelic minister for the many men in the camp who spoke this language. The Reverend D MacDougall officiated at his first service on 13 June 1915, and the following week John McLeay found himself in hospital. Prior to this he had conducted the services himself. He died of pneumonia on 26 August 1915 (his parents had recently lost another son to the same disease). There was also a detailed description of the Dutch crowds that lined the two-mile route to the cemetery, the procession led by Dutch mounted police and the brigade band, and of the funeral, attended by all the 'Gaelic Scotchmen' and other friends and representatives. He was buried with full military honours with Dutch soldiers firing three military salutes. Even the wreaths are described, including one in the shape of an anchor made from roses grown in the camp by Seaman Lunnes of the Gardeners' Staff.

The Commonwealth War Graves Commission provides a variant spelling for his name: John MacLeay was aged 38, and the son of John and Annie MacLeay. It also has the information that he was born at Shadar Barvas, Lewis. IWM has *Loyal Lewis: Roll of Honour [1914 and After]* (Stornoway: Stornoway Gazette, 1920), where he is mentioned under the Lower Shader section of the Airidhantium School District. Three sons of John MacLeay Senior served in the RNR: Donald, who survived; Angus, who drowned on the *Iolaire*, leaving a widow and four children; and John. His entry reads: '*JOHN, Collingwood Battalion, R.N.D.; interned in Holland after fall of Antwerp, and died at Groningen 26th August, 1915; aged 31.' The roll of honour has been transcribed and is available online at www.adb422006.com/ROH/index.html. Another relevant site is Faces from the Lewis War Memorial at http://facesmemorial.blogspot.com.

Other useful sources for the camp at Groningen are:

Donald Macleod died the following year, and his nephew remembers him in a blog: http://5dalmore.blogspot.com/2008/02/my-uncle -donald-dies-in-groningenmarch.html.

There is a series of articles on the Groningen at the Dutch site De Eerste Wereldoorlog, 1914–1918: www.wereldoorlog1418.nl/ englishcamp/index.html#ek.

A search using the term 'Groningen' on the Royal Naval Museum's *Sea Your History* site brings up good photographs and other material: www.seayourhistory.org.uk.

The Groningen Camp website contains scans of some of the camp magazines: www.groningencamp.co.uk/index.html.

There is an article on the camp at Groningen at www.firstworldwar .com/features/englishcamp.htm.

Many men joined ex-service or ex-prisoner associations, and these might provide some clues about their experiences as these events often produced signed menus, programmes or photographs. This is evidently only the second reunion of the 1st Royal Naval Brigade from Groningen, in 1938, but there was a good turnout, and Clarke obviously enjoyed the evening enough to purchase a photograph (Courtesy Mr G D Clarke; IWM, Documents: Papers of H E Clarke, 05/3/1).

Towards the end of 1917, officers, NCOs, civilians and invalided servicemen began to arrive in Holland on exchange from Germany. They were concentrated in The Hague and Scheveningen area, where they lived in houses and hostels. It had been hoped that some men would be able to get employment there, but jobs were very scarce, and POWs could only obtain a job if no Dutch employee was available. This meant that classes and workshops had to be arranged to keep the men busy and usefully occupied. When the war ended in November 1918 the organization established in Holland was helpful when the country was deluged with POWs waiting to be repatriated.

The British Empire Fortnightly: A Magazine for Interned Britons was published fortnightly from 18 March 1918. IWM has all seventeen issues, with the final edition being published on 8 November 1918. It contains general articles of interest, marriage and death coverage, wonderful advertisements and provides a general picture of life in The Hague.

As well as the graves in Groningen, already mentioned, some military internees are buried in The Hague.

Switzerland

Those POWs chosen to be exchanged to neutral Switzerland had passed a medical board (there was a long list of serious ailments which rendered a POW eligible). The POWs then travelled to Constance, where they

Cartoon drawn in the The Optimist, *the camp magazine for Friedrichsfeld. It shows Ginger Cox, with his crutch in the cart, being conveyed to Switzerland (© IWM, The Optimist – 16 April 1916).*

would again be examined by German and Swiss doctors. It was not a foregone conclusion that having gone through the lengthy and often difficult journey they would pass across the Swiss border. Some men were sent back, and some were kept back for the next inspection. Those who did arrive in Switzerland were overwhelmed by the welcome they received – large crowds greeted the trains, packages from the British colony were handed out at Zurich station, and welcoming parties and refreshments appeared at Berne. The principal camps for the interned British POWs were Mürren and Chateau d'Oex. Other locations used were Rougemont, Rossinières, Gunten (Lake Thun), Manor Farm (a chalet opened by the former *pension* owner Miss Simpkin as a convalescent home for twenty officers and men, and located on Lake Thun), Signal de Bougy, Vevey, Lausanne, Seeburg and Meiringen (known as 'centres for industrial instruction').

The men had all been selected because of their ill health or disabilities, and hospital provision and treatment centres were important. Leysin was the main hospital centre, but some cases were sent to Lucerne. The air was good, but one padre commented on how difficult it must have been for incapacitated men to come to a winter sports paradise, when many were unable to participate.

The first British exchanged prisoners arrived in Switzerland on 29 May 1916 and reached Chateau d'Oex the next day. The thirty-two officers are listed at TNA in FO 383/216. There were also 272 men who travelled out on this journey. A list of all these men can be found in FO 383/218, and this also includes some information about where they were to be interned in Switzerland. The other information is name, rank, regiment, where they had come from and their ailment. However, this is all given in German and is often rather unintelligible. The lists were regarded as useless and had to be sent back. As the improved lists did not arrive until 12 June, the men arrived without documentation, and there was considerable administrative confusion. A copy of the anglicized improved list can be found in AIR 1/892/204/5/698, although it still contains some rather dubious regiments! This also includes a list of thirty-seven named officers who arrived on 12 August 1916.

FO 383 is, as usual, an excellent source, and contains some lists of men arriving and also leaving to return to Britain, but these are not comprehensive. The same procedures applied to the German POWs who were exchanged from the UK. Some lists of names of German POWs can also be found here.

One of the best sources for names in Switzerland are the nominal rolls for imprisonment. Lists for most months, usually broken down by area into Chateau d'Oex, Mürren and Leysin can be found in FO 383, and give a very interesting insight into the misbehaviour of the troops, and the punishments. As might be expected, drunkenness is the most frequent offence, but insolence, being out of bounds and overstaying leave also feature quite regularly. A relatively frequent punishment was being sent to the 'Inebriates' camp at Bougy'. Consistent bad behaviour could result in being sent back to Germany, as happened in April 1917 to Private J Ralph of the King's Own Scottish Borderers. He was apparently a 'stubborn, insubordinate, insolent and ungrateful man' and consistent drunkenness had meant he 'has not proved himself worthy of the benefits of internment in Switzerland.'

Herbert 'Bert' Munyard was exchanged to Switzerland at the end of 1916, and billeted at the Alpenruhe Hotel in Mürren. Many of the 100 or so postcards in his collection feature Swiss scenes, including cards of the British Interned Gymnastic Team and the British Interned Variety Company.

Munyard's papers contain three issues of the magazine *BIM: British Interned: Murren* (vol. 1, no. 3, July 1917; vol. 2, no. 2 and 4, February and May 1918). The first issue was produced in June 1917 under the auspices of Major Charley. The July 1917 issue is very detailed and has a breakdown of the happenings in the different hotels. Thus, under the Alpenruh Hotel [sic]: 'We all highly appreciate the generosity of "Bert" in presenting an engraved silver medal, to be won by the best all-round sportsman of the hotel. Luckily for the remainder of us, he is barring himself.' He has marked it with a X and the simple annotation: 'me'. The August 1917 issue reports that 'Private Munyard' has left the Alpenruhe because his 'duties on the police necessitate his residing at the Palace'; he still retained his place on the Alpenruhe sports teams, though. The Palace Hotel was mainly used for officers, and had particularly good sports facilities, including an ice rink, though this closed as a hotel towards the end of 1917. Details of mothers and wives who were visiting are listed under the different hotels. However, later issues are not so detailed, and are less 'personal', and from January 1918 the coverage is much wider, extending to all of the British interned in Switzerland. IWM has a run of this: vol. 1, no. 2–10, July 1917–[December 1917], and vol. 2, no. 1–10, January 1918–31 October 1918, with the issues being very slight towards the end.

The interned prisoners were not allowed to return to Britain on leave, but they were able to have wives and mothers out to stay with them. This came about because, as soon as it was announced that these exchanges were to take place, officers' wives went out to visit or live with their husbands, and there was an outcry that the ordinary soldier could not afford the same luxury. The French Government had arranged for three-week marital visits, and they did this by subsidizing railway fares to Switzerland and accommodation. *The Times* on 30 August 1916 took up the call to have a similar system in place for the wives of ordinary British servicemen – it was estimated that it would cost £12 for a visit, and that if the British Government wouldn't fund it, then an organization such as the

A charming image showing the group of five brides (appropriately dressed and clutching their wedding bouquets) who got married on 23 May 1917. Emma and Bert are marked by a cross – Emma is the central bride with Bert standing directly behind her. Presumably the vicar to the right of Bert is the Reverend Bulstrode (courtesy Mrs Molly Ford).

Red Cross should. By 2 September over 200 applications to visit had been received, and money was flowing in, with more than £2,000 being received. Lord Derby gave a cheque for £200 for this purpose.

The first visit took place at the end of September 1916, and over 600 women eventually took advantage of this service. There was provision for fifty wives at both Mürren and Chateau d'Oex. A party of about sixteen women would go to each destination each week, accompanied by two lady guides. In October 1917 the visits stopped being run on a regular basis, owing to transport difficulties, but special cases were still accommodated. The Red Cross had been involved in arranging visits for relatives to dangerously ill servicemen on the Western Front, so this was an obvious extension of that facility, though more complicated. Wives and mothers were the preferred relations (later there was a greater emphasis on wives, but sisters were definitely discouraged, presumably because they would be too much of a temptation for hundreds of men starved of female company). IWM has film footage of 'British Soldiers Interned in Switzerland' (IWM 453). Dating from the summer of 1918, it is thirteen minutes long. There is also some very brief footage in 'Topical Budget 264-1' (NTB 264-1) relating to visits by wives in autumn 1916.

In August 1916 soldiers were given permisson to get married in

Switzerland. The Red Cross also took fiancées out specifically for this purpose in their parties of relatives. Bert Munyard had been writing to Emma (or Emmie) Carpenter since he became a POW – originally addressing cards formally to Miss E Carpenter at the Trafalgar Cinema in East Greenwich where she worked. On 20 March 1917 she received a letter from the Red Cross saying they had had an application from L/Cpl H Munyard asking that she might be allowed to visit him, and they were now asking 'whether you will be willing to go to Switzerland to marry him if we can arrange it'. This followed a letter from Bert on 5 February asking her to go out and visit him (at which she wrote in her diary, 'What next?'). Although a press report dated 8 June 1917 in the *Kentish Mercury* described the engagement as 'one of some standing' that had 'stood the strain of long separation', this was not the case. Local newspapers are excellent sources, and this press report is quite detailed and includes a wedding photograph. Regimental magazines can perform the same function, though the East Surreys did not publish one for the First World War. The Munyards' marriage was to be a long and happy one, although Emma must have been very anxious about the journey into the unknown, across a submarine-infested Channel and war-torn Europe. The civil wedding ceremony took place at Berne with five other couples on 22 May, with a church blessing at Mürren the next day. The wedding certification is in the collection. Incidentally, the marriage blessing service was

Conveyance to the church in Mürren looks a lot of fun! Emma is a blur of veiled white on the patriotic British and Swiss cart, and the soldiers seem to be enjoying the spectacle (courtesy Mrs Molly Ford).

conducted by the Reverend R Bulstrode whose papers are at IWM (87/10/1); he mentioned that he once conducted five weddings in one day, so it must have been exceptional to officiate at so many simultaneously.

Emma kept a diary of her journey to Switzerland:

8 May 1917	– Started for Switzerland. Stayed at YMCA at Bloomsbury on 9th, 10th and 11th.
11 May	– Went to Southampton. Arrived 4pm. Sailed for France on SS *Hantonia*.
12 May	– Arrived 6am. Stayed in Paris for the day. Left 8.30pm.
13 May	– Arrived Swiss border 7am. Left at 11am for Berne. Met Bert at 3pm.
14 May	– Bert sworn in at the British Consulate.
15 May	– I was sworn in at the British Consulate.
16 May	– Went to Murren – had a good time.
17-20 May	– In Murren.
21 May	– In Berne.
22 May	– Married in Berne.
23 May	– Service in Church of England, Murren, Switzerland.
24 May–20 June	– In Murren.
21 June	– Started journey home. Stayed in Paris.
22 June	– Left Le Havre. Sailed on SS *Vera* at 10pm.
23 June	– Arrived safely at about 5am. I do miss Bert.
24 June	– Arrived home.

A year later Munyard returned home. The *War Office Weekly Casualty List* dated Tuesday 2 July 1918 reported in the daily list of 24 June that 'The following soldiers, who were prisoners of war in Switzerland, have now arrived in England'. 'Munyard 8429 A.' [sic] is listed under the East Surrey Regiment.

The exchanged British POWs were all blighted by ill health, which had prompted their exchange in the first place. Consequently, there were several deaths and eighty-four military graves are located at Vevey (St Martin's Cemetery). These men were originally buried at Arosa, Berne, Chateau d'Oex, Chur, Clarens, Constance, Couvet, Fribourg, Interlaken, Laufenburg, Lausanne, Lauterbrunnen, Leysin and Sierre.

The internment of British POWs in Switzerland officially ended on 21 December 1918. Colonel Picot, the British officer in charge of the interned, wrote *The British Interned in Switzerland* (London: Edward Arnold, 1919), which is available at IWM and online at www.archive.org/details/british-internedi00pico.

Chapter 9

GERMAN PRISONERS OF WAR IN THE UNITED KINGDOM

Numbers of German prisoners of war in the UK built up slowly, with the majority of the early captives being naval. Initially, civilian internees greatly outnumbered military prisoners and it was only in 1916 that the balance was reversed. By the end of the war, 319,138 Germans and 10,429 Austrians had been captured on the Western Front, while German naval prisoners numbered 6,410 and 9 from Austria.

As in Germany, the provision of prison camps was secondary to the effort of mobilizing the country for war and extending provision for the rapidly increasing British Army. It is also worth making the point that names of the camps sometimes bore only a loose connection to where they actually were. This also happened with military camps, which were frequently named after the nearest railway station.

The first permanent prison camp was sited at Dorchester, and by early 1915 the number of camps had grown to thirteen. The Directorate of Prisoners of War under Lieutenant General Sir Herbert Belfield was established in February 1915 and this streamlined the organization for looking after German POWs. Figures rocketed to 48,572 (and 1,316 naval prisoners) at the end of 1916, and a year later there were 118,864 (1,635) in 142 camps in England, 14 in Scotland and 1 at Oldcastle in Ireland. A dramatic escalation in numbers in 1918 led to over 250,000 men being held in over 500 camps. There is a list of camps in Appendix 8, and Nic Nichol's *Not Necessarily Behind Barbed Wire: Places of Internment in the United Kingdom of Great Britain and Ireland During the First World War [1919–1920]* is a great resource. The POWs remained in Britain until after the various peace treaties were signed, as there was a fear that conflict might reignite. The prisoners were also a useful source of labour for the British Government. A photographic book published in 1916, *German Prisoners in Great Britain*, showing images of POW life in some of the original camps is now available online at www.archive.org/details/germanprisonersi00bolt and can be seen, in different editions, at IWM.

There had been much critical comment in Britain about their citizens being forced to live in horseboxes at Ruhleben. In fact, racecourses were large self-contained sites with some ready-made buildings that often lent themselves to accommodating groups of people. German POWs and internees were housed at Newbury racecourse, and here you can see the men outside the stables (© IWM, Q 53359).

Records for these German prisoners are quite sparse and erratic. Only two lists of German POWs survive at TNA – WO 900/45, dating from 1915, and WO 900/46, from August 1916. These large-format lists are divided into various categories documenting both military and civilian prisoners interned in the UK, in France, and outside both countries, those hospitalized and those who had died. An example of information gleaned comes from the section on naval combatants interned in the UK: 1st Leutnant A von Schönemarck, 26068, who served on SMS *Blücher*. His home address was Klopstockstrasse 49, Berlin. He died of wounds at the Edinburgh Castle Military Hospital on 29 January 1915. Other lists are referenced, but as these have not survived it is not possible to see the details they contained, or how they might have added to the information. The later list also gives a man's age, and sometimes date of birth as well.

Leutnant von Schönemarck was probably among the twenty-three wounded sailors who landed at Leith on 24 January 1915. The British had sunk his ship in the North Sea the previous day, resulting in many fatalities. The survivors were taken to Edinburgh Castle, where the wounded were treated in the Military Hospital. Captain Erdmann, who commanded the vessel, was another casualty, dying of pneumonia on 16 February. Those who became POWs were taken to Stobs Camp, where the central space was named 'Blücher Square', and their captain was remembered by 'Erdmannstrasse', leading off it.

German First World War naval records should be held at the Deutsche Dienststelle (www.dd-wast.de/), but army records are more difficult. All First World War service records relating to Prussia are believed to have been destroyed. First World War German army casualty lists between 1914–1917 are now available through Ancestry (http://search.ancestry.com/). The Bavarian State Archives (www.gda.bayern.de) has service records for those serving in Bavarian units, and these *Kriegsstammrollen, 1914–1918* have recently been digitized and made available via Ancestry (http://search.ancestry.com/). Records for Baden and Württemberg may be available through the Landesarchiv in Stuttgart (www.landesarchiv-bw.de).

WO 162/341, 'Report on the Prisoners of War Information Bureau' at TNA is full of details about the administration of this office, and the work undertaken to ensure full documentation was made of POWs and civilian internees. It contains a useful collection of the various types of forms that were required for different circumstances. Although most of these are blank, some have been used, for example a rather tattered example of Army Form W 3034, which contains details of German POWs in No. 4 POW Convalescent Depot (NCOs) at Trouville in France. It lists regimental number, rank, name, corps and particulars of the wound or sickness from which the POW was recovering.

The National Army Museum has a splendid collection relating to 191 P/W Coy in France (9611-92-67 to 131). It contains a mass of good official documentation, including 'Correspondence, Records and Returns of Prisoners of War Companies: November, 1916' (SS 522). It also includes '191 Prisoners of War Coy: List of Tokens Collected from the Undermentioned Prisoners of War, on Being Sent Away from the Above Named Company for Repatriation'. This features lists of names with amounts in francs and centimes, although very few of the columns for money are filled in. The collection also includes a sample of a label that would have been attached to a POW *en route* to the UK.

FO 383 at TNA is almost as good a source of information for German POWs as it is for British, and contains all sorts of useful material. There are camp inspection reports, as well as papers relating to individuals and issues concerning them. German POWs exchanged to Switzerland are often listed, and these lists usually provide the name of their previous camp. 'Report on Visits to Internment Camps' (CAB 45/207) is also worth a look; it states that civilians generally gave more trouble than military prisoners!

Another useful source for reports of visits to camps is the Society of Friends Library. The Friends Emergency Committee for the Assistance of Germans, Austrians and Hungarians in Distress conducted their own inspection visits (FECVRC/CAMPS/2/1-7), and these have a different tone from the official Red Cross or Protecting Power visits documented at TNA. There was very much a sense of the visitors recognizing individuals – an example was the genuine pleasure that a reporter found in unexpectedly re-meeting Zwade, a Prussian guard cadet at Brocton Camp in 1917. He was an excellent football player who had successfully organized teams to play in previous years at Frongoch, and it was hoped he would do the same at his new camp. Another instance was a visit to Stobs in October 1916, where the dreadful monotony of the diet and its effect on those with weak digestion is commented on. Apparently the visitor shared a meal of bread and margarine with the men, but was so ill during the night that he was unable to resume his inspection the next day.

The camp at Brocton is particularly well covered at IWM, with several collections relating to it. Lieutenant Colonel Sir Arthur Grant was the commanding officer, and his collection (78/31/1) contains reports on the camp, and some details of letters written by the POWs, a document relating to complaints made by the POWs, an account of a day in the life of a POW, copies of some (beautifully designed) theatre programmes and issues of the camp newspaper *Deutsche Zeitung*, news cuttings, a report made on the shooting and subsequent slight wounding of a POW in 1918, photographs of a wooden box made for him by POWs and a plan of the camp and the theatre.

Letters and documents in the H M Thompson collection (P433) are also informative. He was a member of the 162nd Company of the Royal Defence Corps and was involved in administering the camp. Included in his collection are seventy-one lists (some duplicated) of German POWs from various camps who were brought to Brocton for medical boards. The lists were undated, but were divided by camp, and usually include serial number (merely the running order of the men from the camp on the list, and often not filled in), regimental number, rank, surname, first names, age, home address, disease and category. The final columns, 'decision' and 'remarks or decision of review board on final examination', were left blank. There is also an English translation of an account by E Wolff of his military experiences, and his time as a prisoner at Brocton (82/35/1).

As in Germany, a few men escaped, although most were quickly re-captured. FO 383 at TNA has material about some of these, and there is a fascinating document in HO 45/10883/345466. This contains a list of POW camps in this country, including details about when some were closed. It described the new system for notification of escapes and recaptures introduced in January 1918. Between then and the date of the document (September 1918) there had been 244 escapes, although most men had been picked up quickly. The new system alerted the chief constable in the area of the escape, who would then notify the chief constables of other areas, including port areas and counties on the coast. There had previously been much duplication of effort and recaptures were often not reported, resulting in resources being wasted hunting for men who were no longer free. It contains a splendid map of the area around Sutton Bonington, near Nottingham (now part of the University of Nottingham), showing when and where twenty-two escaped German officers were caught after their tunnel breakout in September 1917.

The British were anxious to utilize the pool of labour that the German other rank prisoners provided. Although women were increasingly taking over men's work, there was still a shortfall. Trade unions were initially opposed to the use of POW labour, but this was resolved by ensuring POWs were not paid more than the local rate for the job. From February 1916 POWs could be used for labour outside their camps. The employers paid the authorities, who gave the POWs a set allowance, and kept the rest for maintenance costs. Rates of pay varied between ½d and 2d per hour, although agricultural work could be better paid. Money could be an incentive, but prisoners were also often keen simply to get out of the camps and have something to do. The Ministry of National Service file NATS 1/1330 at TNA has some reports of POW camps from 1918 (although only a tiny sample of the total, they are useful if you are able to find the camp you are looking for, and they provide some idea of the variety of work that was undertaken). One example was the Old Boot Depot on Fairhill Road in Irlam, where seventy-five prisoners travelled from Leigh POW camp every day to grade cast-off army boots (though the grading work was an activity that women could have done, the work was heavy since each pair of boots would weigh about 4lbs, and the volume that these came in – arriving in sacks of between ten and fifty pairs – meant the prisoners were better placed to deal with it. There was always a marked reluctance to allow women to mix with POWs). Another camp, at Easton-on-the-Hill near Stamford, was opened in April 1918. It had grown to 600 prisoners by the time the report was conducted in early September. The POWs built two aerodromes – one at Wittering and one at Easton (working under the command of the American military). Both now form the RAF Wittering site that has been in almost constant use since 1916, though the early role played by POW labour has been forgotten.

POWs often favoured agricultural work since, although hard, it compared favourably with most industrial labour and there was often the opportunity to enjoy better food (either provided by farmers or through 'appropriation'). Many POWs were from rural backgrounds and familiar with the work. The authorities were initially concerned about the public reaction to seeing Germans working in the open countryside and the perceived security threat. Civilian internees set the precedent for doing agricultural work in the spring of 1915, but usually in very small numbers, in non-restricted areas and only those aliens deemed to be from

Private Charles Kirby is reputed to have guarded German POWs at Somerleyton Hall in Suffolk. This photograph was taken in Lowestoft, which adds more credibility to this family lore. He appears to be wearing a Suffolk Regiment cap badge – he transferred to the Royal Defence Corps in 1916 – so this dates from the first half of the war. His previous military experience is depicted in the medal ribbon for the Queen's South Africa Medal and the Long Service and Good Conduct stripes on his lower left arm, representing twelve years' service (© the author).

'friendlier' nations. Document HO 45/10881/340400 at TNA reveals that in January 1917 seventeen Hungarian subjects of Romanian origin were sent to the Forest of Dean – a prohibited area – to break up rough common ground for cultivation. All seventeen names were included (which is unusual in a file where lists of names have usually been weeded out). By autumn 1917 some 70,000 German POWs were working nationwide. Their role was particularly important on the land, helping to grow crops to feed the country.

Charles Kirby, my great-grandfather, had been a regular soldier. He joined the Suffolk Regiment in 1888 and saw service in Egypt, India and Burma before being demobilized in 1896. He was recalled for the Boer War, where he had the misfortune to be taken prisoner at Rensburg in 1900. When he found himself guarding German POWs he would have had first-hand experience of what they were going through. Too old for active service in 1914, he nevertheless rejoined the Suffolk Regiment. He served at home for the duration of the war, and luckily his service record has survived. However, this does not tell us where he was located, only the units he was with: initially the 4th Battalion, and then, from the end of April 1916, No. 53 Protection Company of the newly formed Royal Defence Corps. He was an ideal candidate to guard the growing number of German POWs – he knew how to handle a gun, had plenty of military experience to draw on and was too old to be deployed in the front line. A file relating to the 'Organization of the Royal Defence Corps' can be found at TNA in WO 32/18622. It shows that by far the largest role undertaken by the formation was working in POW camps. It also reveals that the establishment of a Protection Company was six officers (one major/captain, one captain, four subalterns), one company sergeant major, one company quartermaster sergeant, twelve sergeants, sixteen corporals and 264 rank and file. This was fine when the troops were guarding men in one central camp location, but as more POWs were working on the land in small groups it proved impossible to provide the requisite number of NCOs – for example, on isolated detachments one NCO should accompany four men. Eastern Command was the worst affected since it had the greatest number of small units of POWs in the country. Another vital but little-known role played by the Royal Defence Corps in relation to POWs was that, having a barracks near to Thurloe Place, the home of the CPWC, they provided the manpower that brought goods in to be packed for the prisoners' parcels and carried them out to the transport – a very heavy and demanding task.

My family has a postcard of Somerleyton Hall in Suffolk, with a message written on the back to say that grandfather guarded German POWs there. Charles wrote a diary of his wartime activities, but sadly this has now vanished. There was no camp in the Somerleyton area, so he was presumably guarding POWs in a migratory gang. Horace Thompson, the administrator at Brocton Camp and no fan of military organization, described how the system worked in a letter to his mother on 16 August 1918:

> The scheme is a splendid one – of course a civil and not a military one. It has been designed by a national committee working through local committees, formed in counties. Our part of it is to organize camps, and depots. It is this way. There are a number of prisoner camps, roughly one in each county, sometimes 2 or 3. Under these there are depots, having control of a number of groups. There may be 30 to 100 men in a group, and perhaps 6 groups in a depot. Then attached to depots and camps are migratory gangs of 10 prisoners, who move from farm to farm according to program [sic] arranged by the local committee, doing harvesting and other work. We shall have close on 1000 men in these gangs. Gangs are guarded by 2 men, who can also work if they wish (and be paid by the farmer) and the men are given quarters in some building at night. Their food comes every other day from the nearest camp or depot, delivered by motors arranged from the local committee. And no doubt they'll get a good bit from the farmers. This is about as complete a scheme as I have ever seen, it reflects great credit on the inventors of it.

Generally, the Germans were conscientious workers and the systems worked well. The list of camps in Appendix 8 shows this hierarchy. The Suffolk area came under the control of Pattishall in Northamptonshire, which had responsibility for as many as 133 agricultural groups.

It was quite common for large country houses to have parted with many of their horses for the war effort, and so there was often the facility for POWs to sleep in the stables. Somerleyton was a large estate and while German POWs laboured in the grounds or in the vicinity, the family's heir, Sir Francis Saville Crossley, of the 9th Lancers, was a prisoner in Germany. He was captured in 1914, and spent at least some of his period of captivity at Crefeld prison camp.

The papers of the County War Agricultural Committees in the various county record offices may contain records of POW labour, and are worth checking.

Women had also been working in the countryside to offset the shortage of labour. The WWC at IWM reveals a concern to keep members of the Women's Land Army (WLA) and German POWs away from each other, but this was not always possible. A letter from the Women's Branch of the Food Production Department of 26 August 1918 addressed the 'Employment of Land Army Women and German Prisoners'. It stated:

German POWs resting and having a meal under the watchful eye of a British soldier in September 1917 (© IWM, Q 54032).

While in the opinion of the Department it is always inadvisable to have Prisoners of War and women working together, it is considered necessary in the interests of the harvest, and in order to meet the practical difficulties of arranging labour at this time, to allow both prisoners and women to be employed under certain well defined restrictions . . .

The farmers themselves can do more than anyone else to keep everything in order. It should be impressed upon them that any trouble or wrong behaviour is likely to endanger the supply to them of both or either form of labour. It is in their own interest, therefore, as well as in that of the country generally that every care should be taken. It is specially important to guard against the women and the prisoners having intercourse at mealtimes, or before or after working hours.

WLA members were issued with *Rules of Conduct for Members*. These stated: 'Every recruit in the Women's Land Army must promise: I) To behave quietly II) To respect her uniform and make it respected III)

This scene in Suffolk in 1918 shows everybody working together to bring in the all-important harvest. Small boys and girls and old men are alongside German POWs and Women's Land Army members, and all look comfortable together (© IWM, Q 31044).

To secure at least eight hours rest each night IV) To avoid communication of any sort with German prisoners.'

Burial Records

The German equivalent of the CWGC is the Volksbund Deutsche Kriegsgräberfürsorge. The website at www.volksbund.de can be searched to find the graves of those who died in the two world wars, although registration is necessary. It differs from the CWGC in that it is not a government-funded body; when it was established in December 1919 it was a privately funded organization consisting of members who had the aim of maintaining German war graves and cemeteries abroad. There is a large cemetery in the middle of England at Cannock Chase in Staffordshire where most of the graves of German First and Second World War servicemen can be found.

The cemetery is the resting place of 4,940 German war dead, containing 2,143 First World War graves, and 2,797 from the Second World War. They were moved from 706 burial places, with the long process beginning in 1960 when an eighteen-man team came from Germany to survey the situation. The exhumation work began the following year, and there are immensely detailed files about this at TNA. The driving force behind the move was maintenance of the graves; various types of graves in differing states of repair were scattered around the country. If they were all brought to one place they could be cared for centrally, and the German Government could say that any other than these approved burial sites were outside its jurisdiction. An agreement was made on 16 October 1959 between the Federal Republic of Germany and the UK to establish the cemetery. The cemetery opened in June 1967.

Both military and civilian personnel were included, though Austrians were not (Austrian military personnel for the Second World War were reburied here, but not civilians). Eighteen bodies were repatriated to Germany at the wish of their families, but only one of these was a casualty of the First World War.

The 'War Graves in the Channel Islands and Isle of Man' file (HO 284/84) at TNA contains details about the exhumation of the German war dead. Those from the Channel Islands were taken to the Mont d'Huisnes Cemetery in France, though forty Germans remained at Fort George in Guernsey because it was a military burial ground. 'Removal of Various Bodies: German Servicemen' (HO 282/21) has lists of the bodies exhumed from different cemeteries around the country, and acts as a roll of honour for German POWs who died in this country. It is organized by county and cemetery, and as well as name and date of death, it often also gives the precise location of the original grave.

Less than five minutes' walk from the Cannock Chase German War

A typical headstone at Cannock Chase German Military Cemetery – two people are named on the front, and two on the back. Although civilian and military graves are generally kept apart, this gravestone has an internee and a soldier named on it, both of whom died after the Armistice (© the author).

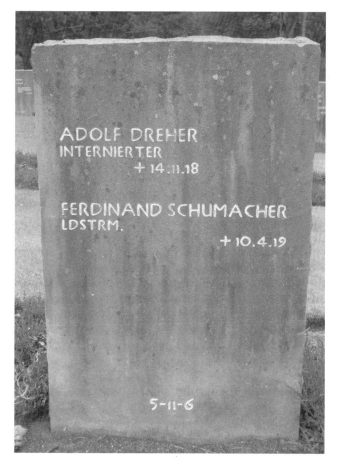

Cemetery is the CWGC Cannock Chase Military Burial Ground. This adhered to the ruling that any Germans who were interred in a military burial ground remained in their original graves. The CWGC can provide the names of the Germans and Austrians who are buried in their cemeteries. The headstones look very similar to the standard British stones, but contain a 'German-style' cross, the name of the soldier and the date of his death. These headstones were only erected in 1962. The 220 Germans and a single Austrian outnumber the 24 British and 73 New Zealand First World War graves. Many will have died at the 1,000-bed prisoner of war hospital located at Brocton Camp, and large numbers were victims of the 1918 flu epidemic. Horace Thompson in a letter to his mother of 1 November 1918 writes of the bad outbreak of flu in the camp. The severity meant 'that all movement of men is stopped. Thus we are having a respite, and an opportunity to catch up back work, which is very welcome.' Later in the same letter he says there are about 300 cases, some of whom have died: 'These Huns die very easily.'

The commanding officer of the camp or hospital where a POW died was responsible for marking his grave, if this had not already been done by fellow POWs. Army Council Instruction No. 1319 of 1917 provided guidelines for this, with a specified design, ('a simple wooden cross bearing full regimental particulars and date of death of deceased painted or stencilled on it') and the ruling that it must not cost more than 5s. The wooden cross was to be painted white ('three coats white lead in oil and neatly lettered').

Chapter 10

GERMAN CIVILIAN INTERNEES IN THE UNITED KINGDOM

O ver 53,000 Germans were recorded as living in England and Wales in the 1911 Census, with the majority of these in London, although there were sizable German communities scattered all over Britain. Many Germans worked as waiters, bakers, butchers, tailors and hairdressers, though all classes and occupations were represented, including women governesses.

In the period leading up to 1914 there had been a growth in anti-German feeling, and this was exacerbated when war actually broke out. Legislation to update the Naturalization Act of 1870 (which allowed an alien to become a naturalized citizen after just five years In Britain) was overtaken by the outbreak of war, and was strengthened during 1918.

The Aliens Restriction Act, introduced on 5 August 1914, placed limitations on those who were now considered enemies. It was necessary to register, usually at the local police station, and a permit would be required if an 'alien enemy' wished to travel further than five miles from his home address. Tourists and merchant seamen were also caught up in the war fervour.

In the autumn of 1914 there had been reciprocal exchanges of women and children, men over military age or unfit for service, doctors and ministers of religion. File HO 45/11522/287235 at TNA contains useful counts of different categories of aliens and how many of each there were in the country at various times in the war. In May 1915 there were about 14,400 'German female adults' in the country; 5,000 of these were single German women, 4,400 were German-born wives and 5,000 were English women married to Germans.

During this period there was a great antipathy towards those with foreign names. In response to this climate of poular feeling, the royal family changed its name, from the Germanic 'Saxe-Coburg-Gotha' to the familiar 'Windsor'. Few others were able to take this step. In October 1914 the Aliens Restriction (Change of Name) Order had been introduced, and

George Kenner's Alien Enemy Registration Certificate, which includes his photograph and signature. For those unable to write, there was space on the reverse for thumb prints. This had to be carried at all times, which accounts for the rather dilapidated state of the form (Reproduced with the permission of Christa Kenner Bedford/photo: IWM, ARCH 27).

this ruled that name changes required the home secretary's permission. Eighteen months later only twelve permits had been issued, and eleven of these were to British-born wives or widows.

Internment of enemy aliens who were perceived as threatening British national security began in the first days of the war. Merchant seamen were also among the first to be held, following the seizure of their ships in British ports. Anti-German sentiment and rioting in October 1914 resulted in a policy of general internment for males of military age (between 17 and 55 for Germans and between 17 and 51 for Austrians), though this was not rigorously applied until the following year, owing to a shortage of accommodation. The sinking of the *Lusitania* by a German submarine on 7 May 1915 caused riots to break out in the ship's home port of Liverpool. These later spread to other parts of the country, with German shops and property being attacked, and a resulting public call for internment. Turks and Bulgarians tended not to be interned unless they were suspicious characters or had no obvious means of support.

Early accommodation for those interned was often temporary, for example, Olympia Exhibition Halls were quickly brought into use for internees living in the London and South-East England area, and also for merchant seamen. The halls ceased to perform this function in December 1914. Another temporary, though expensive, solution until spring 1915 was the requisitioning of ships to hold both military and civilian prisoners. The *Canada*, *Tunisian* and *Andania* lay off Ryde, the *Scotian*, *Ascania* and *Lake Manitoba* lay off Gosport, while the *Ivernia*, *Saxonia* and *Royal Edward* were moored off Southend. There is quite a lot of information about these vessels and their POW use in an unpublished item held at IWM. Barry Chinchen has done a fantastic job in compiling a folder of facsimile ephemeral material relating to First World War internment in the United Kingdom: 'Aliens, Internees and Prisoners of War in the UK, 1914–1920'. Some of the material from TNA is reproduced here but he has drawn on other sources as well, and it is well worth a look.

More permanent camps were established at locations such as Alexandra Palace, opened in May 1915 (before that date it had housed Belgian refugees), and Douglas and Knockaloe on the Isle of Man. Alexandra Palace was very often used as a transit camp for those travelling elsewhere, or being repatriated. Men who lived in the London or South-East area were often accommodated there to allow their wives and children to visit them – about 3,000 of the men fell into this category.

An Internee's Experience

George Kenner was originally a Bavarian, who had been born Georg Kennerknecht on 1 November 1888. His diary, various papers and some delightful drawings of the three camps he was interned in are held at IWM (ART 17053-19096). Artworks are also held in museums close to where the camps were: the Surrey Heath Museum (www.surreyheath .gov.uk/leisure/tourism/shm/default.htm) for Frith Hill, the Manx Museum (www.gov.im/mnh/heritage/museums/manxmuseum.xml) for the Knockaloe pieces and Bruce Castle Museum (www.haringey .gov.uk/brucecastlemuseum) for missionary portraits from Alexandra Palace. Kenner came to England in 1910, where he worked as a process artist and established his own company with a colleague – Waddington and Kennerknecht. His partner is believed to have been the person who supplied him with art materials during his incarceration. In August 1914 he had to register: 'we Germans had to be quiet, and were not allowed to go beyond 5 miles from our residences.' After the sinking of the *Lusitania* he was gathered, with many friends, at Waterloo Station. About 350 men travelled to Frimley at 5pm on 12 May 1915 to their tented camp:

> Frith Hill was a Soldiers Camp, accommodating 2000 German Prisoners of War, but 300 Civilian Prisoners were already interned there, who greeted us with wild acclamations: 'Have you Newspapers?', 'Fill your straw-mattresses well!' and other suggestions. Each man received a knife, fork, spoon, dish, towel and kitchen soap, 3 blankets, and one straw-mattress with pillow-case, (which we filled at once). Thus fitted out we moved behind the barbed wire, 10 men in each tent, which were rigged up for us by the German soldiers.

Tea, bread and margarine were shared out. New men arrived constantly, and 200 tents rapidly filled up with 2,000 prisoners. As usually happened in the internment camps, order was established quite quickly by the inmates, and a captain was selected for every ten tents. Sandstorms regularly caused discomfort, as did leaking tents (which were repaired with wax candles). Those who could afford it could pay to move into a

This peaceful idyllic scene shows the commanding officer's tent with his two children and was one of the first paintings that George Kenner made at Frith Hill Internment Camp in the summer of 1915. Kenner described how the 'nice pleasure grounds with flowers and evergreen trees . . . refreshed the eye' (© Christa Kenner Bedford/photo: IWM, ART 17060).

better section; 120 men did so and enjoyed more privacy – only four to a tent – as well as cement paths, flowers and plants and the services of a paid cook. The men made their own entertainment: there was a band of zither players, a string band and a singing club; sports were perennially popular too: 'footballs and boxing, German Faustball [similar to volley-ball] and croquet sports'. As well as entertainment, there was the possibility of working, with some men working in the fields, 'led there by military escort'.

Kenner, however, had found his own occupation: he wished to continue practising his artwork, and managed to gain permission not only to paint in the camp, but also to create portraits of the commanding officer's wife and two daughters. The lack of female company was one of the things that men most missed when incarcerated, so this must have been pleasurable for him, as was the opportunity to be, temporarily at least, on the other side of the wire. He was aware that he was 'free of care'

P.o.W. Camp, A Sunday Morning, July 1915

This picture, entitled P.O.W. Camp: A Sunday Morning, July 1915, *shows the scene that Kenner would have been most familiar with. The equipment necessary for everyday life is located in and around the canvas tents, and washing is hung up between them. The barbed wire fence can just be seen beyond the sea of canvas (© Christa Kenner Bedford/photo: IWM, ART 17065).*

as a bachelor, and observed many of the married men amongst his fellow internees ageing rapidly and finding life very difficult as they both missed and were extremely worried about their families. Visitors were allowed every Tuesday and Friday – for a mere twenty minutes.

The men themselves had become a tourist attraction; people were interested to see what 'the enemy' looked like and would cluster around the barbed wire to observe life going on in the camps. Vera Brittain wrote about her trip to Frith Hill Camp for a spot of sightseeing in September 1914 in her book *Chronicle of Youth*, and noted the sign forbidding this activity being ignored by everyone in the crowd.

On 29 September 1915 Kenner was moved to Alexandra Palace. 'We were led to the upper storey of the West-wing of the building, where for everyone was prepared a plank bed, consisting of two stands and three wooden boards.' The beds by the walls had clothes hooks, but the rest had

Early Morning, Post Office, Barbers, Seamen Modelling *by Kenner shows the incongruities of camp life. The exotic plants are a legacy of Alexandra Palace's days as a entertainment venue, with wooden partitions dividing the vast space into places for different functions. Men sit having their hair cut while others write letters and do handiwork in what is effectively a thoroughfare* (© *Christa Kenner Bedford/photo: IWM, ART 17080*).

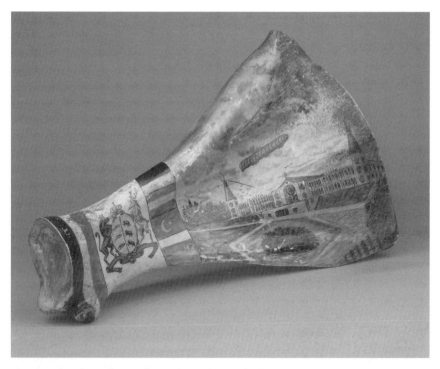

A painted ox bone from Alexandra Palace, which provides a counterpoint to the Ruhleben ox bone. Still brightly coloured, a zeppelin flies triumphantly over the palace, while the coat of arms of Würtemberg and German, Austrian, Turkish and Bulgarian national colours add to the patriotic feel of the piece. On the reverse has been painted 'Erinnerung an Alexandra Palace Camp 1915–16' (© IWM, EPH 766).

to lay their things over their baggage. About 2,800 prisoners were housed in A, B and C Sections. In C Section Kenner shared his room with 450 men. Other rooms in the section were the ground-floor skating rink which housed 400, and two smaller rooms with seventy-five men in each. The lack of privacy and difficulty in getting away from people was one of the reasons why many preferred to be in places such as the Isle of Man – at least living in the more primitive huts there meant men were not concentrated with so many others, and there tended to be more of a 'family atmosphere' in these.

Some 'peace and repose' was offered in the reading room, while the covered terrace allowed exercise even in bad weather. The palm garden now served as a hospital, and the windows were painted green as a camouflage from the perennial danger of attack from zeppelins and air raids. No alcohol was allowed, and smoking was only permitted in certain doorways or in the open. Kenner described merchant seamen occupying their time by making lovingly recalled ship models, which could be either sold or given as gifts. It is interesting to see the ox bone art noted at Ruhleben also being practised here. It also featured at Leigh POW camp, and the *Leigh Chronicle* of 26 February 1915 reported two examples of exactly the same type of bone decorated there. The first contained a poem on one side and decoration of a flag and coat of arms, the back containing the names and regimental details of the artist's friends who had died in the war. The second bone featured a large eagle and German flag, with the words 'Zur Erinnerung an meine', 'Mitt Gott Fur Koenig und Vaterland' and 'Gefangenschaft Jn. Templemore, 1914–15'.

The crowded conditions and shortage of personal possessions meant vigilance had to be applied to belongings to ensure they were not pilfered. Kenner described how you had to watch your washing dry; if left unattended, it might not be there when you returned. This distressing

A drawing showing a POW giving a lecture on history at Alexandra Palace. This is taking place in the theatre, hence the prominent 'Fire Proof Curtain' message. It is well attended – all camps encouraged POWs to lecture on things they knew about in order to entertain and inform their comrades (© Christa Kenner Bedford/photo: IWM, ART 17089).

consequence of prison camp life was to resurface when he was at Knockaloe, when his warm leather sketching gloves were stolen. This and the loss of some artwork in the post temporarily discouraged him from painting.

In June 1916, Kenner was moved again, this time to the hutted camp of Knockaloe on the Isle of Man. Although originally intended to take 5,000 occupants, the camp was extended as the need to intern more men grew. Three more camps were formed at that location, and these were divided into twenty-three compounds – each of about 1,000 men. The circumference of the camp was about three miles – 695 miles of barbed wire had been used to construct the fences. Kenner described his new surroundings:

> The sleeping places were like the berths of a ship, 2 and 3 over each other, and the luggage was put under the lowest berth. Every 1000 men had 10 hut captains and one Superior. An English Blue Guard, whom we called 'Blue Bottles' attended to Post and Cantine [sic]. The last mentioned had not so many luxuries as the one at Alexandra Palace.

Sunday appears to have been a special day – the prisoners were counted every day except for Sunday, and a treat was baked on that day: 'There was also a back-room to prepare dough, where a German baker every Sunday sold butter-crumble-cake, generally called "Panzerplatten" [armour plates].' Food would become more of a problem as the war progressed, and in April 1917 the rations were reduced. Kenner speaks of the hunger that the men felt – some were reduced to eating grass even though it made them ill. Flour from Spain was sent by the Red Cross and made into rolls, but generally the Germans had difficulty with their parcels from home, simply because the blockade meant that food was so scarce in Germany there was literally none that could be spared to send to POWs. When the charmingly named 'love-gift' parcels did come from Germany they were very much appreciated, but their arrival was all too rare.

Meanwhile, the British were pursuing a policy of sending back 'useless mouths' to Germany – at least those who were too old to play an active part in the war effort. Great distress was caused by this as many men had made their homes in Britain and did not want to leave. Many had British-born wives, and HO 45/10833/327753 at TNA contains an appeal from the head captains of Camp 4, Knockaloe, addressed to the Under-Secretary of State, Foreign Office, POW Department. Dated 18 May 1918, it enquired about the fate of those who had English connections and wished to remain in the UK. It stated that of the 4,400 internees in Camp 4, 459 had families in the UK. The average number of years spent in England had been twenty, while the average number of years of marriage was thirteen,

Waiting for Dinner in the Huts *shows an interior from Knockaloe, Kenner's third camp. The cluttered wooden hut has bunk beds around the walls, and tables running down the central aisle. Clothing and other items are scattered around inside, and enamel plates and mugs are on the table (© Christa Kenner Bedford/photo: IWM, ART 17056).*

with an average number of two children. Married men were usually sent to Alexandra Palace if their families were in the south-east of the country so that they could have visits. Although some of internees would have had families living nearer to the Isle of Man, proportionally there were a greater number of single men living there. Family visits were a major concern both to the men and to their families on the outside.

Even though Kenner had no wife he did not want to return to Germany – he had started a business in Britain and wanted to remain here, but that did not prove possible. He left the camp in February 1919, and only managed to retain his artwork, which today forms such wonderful testimony to his internment experiences, because the guard was interrupted when it was his turn to be searched. He bluffed that he had already been examined when the guard came back to him, and was thus able to retain all his belongings. His arrival back in Germany in March 1919 was a bleak experience. The defeated country was hungry and desolate and people were wrapped up in the struggle for survival. Though he married and started a family, two small children died in infancy, largely owing to the privations in Germany. In 1927 the Kenners emigrated to the United

States of America. Margarete, his wife, spoke little English, and German was the language always used at home, but they never returned to the country of their birth. What happens after the end of a war is always just a footnote in the larger story, but for many Germans who had built lives in the UK, after suffering years of misery in the camps, their homes and businesses were destroyed, their families faced great difficulties and they had to return to a now alien country and begin their life all over again. In February 1919, there were 19,831 internees in the UK (16,442 of whom were Germans), by May this had reduced to 5,000, most of whom wanted to remain in the UK. Only 16 per cent of the 24,450 men interned at Knockaloe were allowed to remain in the UK.

British-born wives of Germans were included as enemy aliens, although regarded as less dangerous than native foreigners. Their plight was particularly difficult because, when their husbands were interned, they had usually lost the earner in the family, and many found themselves destitute, especially since family and friends frequently abandoned them. Grants were not given to British-born wives until November 1914, and application for these had to be made to the local Poor Law Union. The more generous London rates allowed up to 10s per week for wives and 1s and 6d per child under the age of 14. Less was allowed in the country. The rates were raised in May 1915 to 11s 6d and 1s 9d respectively, and in February 1917 to 12s 6d and 3s.

FO 383 at TNA contains personal correspondence from people in distress in both Britain and Germany (and also people of both nationalities in other places such as India and Africa). The human suffering of war is plainly seen as those left stranded or poverty stricken write for assistance, often to be met by the unmovable barriers of officialdom.

There were other organizations that could help. The Society of Friends established an Emergency Committee for the Assistance of Germans, Austrians and Hungarians in Distress at the end of August 1914. This originated in response to difficulties resulting from the outbreak of war – 500 people were reported to be seeking assistance from the German Benevolent Society, with the largest group being dismissed waiters.

The Society of Friends has an excellent library that can help with this. The periodical *The Friend: A Religious, Literary and Miscellaneous Journal* is a good source for the war years. Items are indexed under 'Peace service', and 'Emergency Committee for helping aliens' and 'Detention camps' are likely headings. This gives some examples to show how assistance has been provided, but these are usually supplied just with initials instead of full names. The text of *St. Stephen's House: Friends' Emergency Work in England, 1914 to 1920* also provides a good history of the work done. It is available online at: www.isle-of-man.com/manxnotebook/fulltext/sh1920/index.htm.

Some lists are held in the Friends Emergency and War Victims Relief files. For example, there are Mendicity Reports dating from 1915. These include the number of the case, name, address, nationality, circumstances of wife and child, and information about money. An example reads: '2608 – Harry Hermes, 81 Grosvenor Terrace, SE. German, wife English. No children. Have been having a grant from us for some time.' Many of these appear to be cases where there are doubts about the authenticity of the claim.

Another example is a seven-page listing of names and addresses, all dating from 1914–1915. These sometimes give details of where someone has been interned. For example, 'Case 1012, Julius BLOOM, 9 Queen's Road, Aldershot at Stratford Camp, Sept 17 1914'. There are also some pages relating to the Austro-Hungarian Emergency Committee. These are dated 9 November 1914, and were obviously completed in a hurry, since in no cases are addresses given, and they have not been signed by the recipient of the relief, but initialled by someone else. These include an individual whose documents are held at IWM (06/83/1): 'Name [Cseh, Benj.] Address [all left blank] Occupation [tailor] Nationality [Hung. – either A or Hung] General remarks [left blank] Cash – s- d [10/-] Meals granted: breakfast – Dinner – Tea [left blank], Lodging [blank] Signature of applicant [EH]'.

FEWVRC/EME/07-09 is a promising collection, but not currently available, because of its fragility. There are three boxes relating to emergency cases selected for preservation. These appear to provide details of individuals and the help given, but cannot be properly examined before they have been conserved. These will probably prove to be only a small percentage of the number of cases that there were.

The WWC has informative material relating to the Friends Emergency Committee in the Relief section, although this is unlikely to mention names.

The Society of Friends also has good collections relating to the camps themselves. There are a number of magazines (which are detailed in Appendix 8). There are also some reports of visits to camps. One especially good example is FEWVRC/CAMPS/1/7, 'P.O.W. Camp Central Committee Administration Camp IV: Report: Knockaloe Civilian Prisoners of War Camp I.O.M.' This contains a committee list, detailing names and position; the names run into three figures. As well as E. Cecil Kny, the camp secretary, and the usual more senior positions, executive committee clerical staff were named. It is an extremely detailed report which contains several photos: for example, a picture of the Gazette office and of some of the graves in the cemetery.

TNA contains camp reports in FO 383, but there is an extremely thick file in the shape of HO 45/10947/266042, 'Knockaloe: Civilian Prisoners of War Internment Camp, I.o.M.: Final Report and Statistical Record on the Internal Administration of the Prisoners of War Camp No. IV, 1915–1919', dated 15 March 1919. This features autographs of people in chief positions, and a plan of the camp. Although there is usually an emphasis on the Germans and Austrians, there is a very interesting 'Report on a Visit of Inspection to the Places of Internment of Turkish and Bulgarian Civilian Prisoners of War at Knockaloe and Douglas in the Isle of Man from November 5th to November 12th 1917'. This provides the statistics that there were 19,278 men in the four compounds at Knockaloe. The breakdown was 65 Turks, 22 Bulgarians, 2,433 Austrians, 16,622 Germans and 136 others. Virtually all the Turks and Bulgarians were destitute to the extent they couldn't even afford to buy cigarettes in the canteen, and most were unable to speak English. Generally they received no parcels or money from home or the UK. A very occasional gift was received from the Swedish Legation and the Bulgarian POWs each received £1 every Christmas from the Bulgarian Red Cross. The report contains a letter from Mustafa Mehmed 5533, in Camp 4, Compound 6, Hut 6B:

> Amongst the many grievances and hardships which the Turkish subjects interned here have to suffer, the most painful and deplorable one is that regarding our religion. Ever since the beginning of our internment no opportunity whatsoever has been accorded to us to profess even the minor points of our Creed. We are not even permitted to render the last services to our dying men in hospital. We have repeatedly applied to the Authorities for a small place in one of the huts, where we could pray and perform our religious rites, however such applications have been refused. The same applies to our application for work. What we are continually asking for is work which would enable us to earn a few pence, in order to enable us to supplement our meagre rations.

Another interesting document is a translation of a German report, circulated by the Admiralty in CAB 37/123/37. 'German Report of Concentration Camps, November 21 1914' contains messages that had got back to Germany through illicit means. For example, at Frith Hill there were complaints of nothing to eat but mutton broth for seven weeks, while one secret message read, 'Eat much moss'. Information revealed under a stamp on a postcard from Douglas read, in what must have been minuscule writing: 'We have suffered much: at Olympia we were beaten, many have broken stones, even I. Here sanitary arrangements wretched, damp, wet; many no boots and a clay soil. Food horrible and little, revolution soon.'

There is also an excellent collection on the Cornwallis Road Workhouse, usually called Islington Camp, in MEPO 2/1613, which includes a large-scale plan. It is full of fascinating little facts that contribute to an understanding of life in there – for example, there were six bath tubs, and each inhabitant could have one twenty-minute hot bath a week. It contains a list of nine men who were sent away to the Isle of Man (obviously regarded as a punishment posting) because their letters to Germany had contained comments implying they were starving. The camp was run by the police authorities and the population of about 650 were guarded by just one sergeant and four policemen. Ex-internees who had been repatriated often complained of their treatment once they had returned, but this file contains an article written by 55-year-old Carl Hans Stielow in a war-time issue of *Die Woche*. He described it as 'a palace among the Prison Camps of England' and looked back on the experience 'with not unfriendly feelings'.

Unfortunately, lists of internees do not appear to exist unless you are looking for someone of more mature years. The initiative to exchange men of 45 and over resulted in the compilation of lists of men eligible for this, and these appear in HO 45/11522/287235, 'Interned Male Civilian Prisoners of War of the Age of 45 and Upwards', an outsize document. These were compiled around October 1916, and there was an attempt to distinguish those men who wanted to return to Germany from those who did not. The lists from Douglas are more informative than most, and include details such as 'Son serving in R.A.M.C.'

The Manx National Heritage Library holds a 'Register of Prisoners of War Interned at Douglas Aliens Detention Camp'. It also has an excellent collection of documents and books, and has produced a very useful bibliography at: www.gov.im/mnh/heritage/library/bibliographies/internment.xml.

The Times dated 17 January 1919 had a list of exemptions from internment or repatriation issued by the Aliens Advisory Committee. It gives 259 names, with their place of residence and the grounds for exemption.

TNA has produced useful guides to its holdings for *Internees: First and Second World Wars, Immigration* and *Naturalisation and Citizenship: Grants of British Nationality.*

A very few Alien Registration Cards are available on Documents Online. There are only about 600 and most of these will have more relevance to the Second World War than the First. These are only a drop in the ocean, though – they come from MEPO 35, and so only cover the London area, but there would originally have been tens of thousands of these.

The Anglo-German Family History Society also comes highly recommended: www.agfhs.org.uk/index.html. It is a very friendly self-help society that has useful name indexes, and should be able to help you in your research. The society has also erected plaques at Alexandra Palace and the Isle of Man to commemorate the internment experience.

Burial Records

Most graves of German civilian internees have now been relocated to the German War Cemetery at Cannock Chase. You can read more about this in Chapter 9.

Other alien nationalities have remained where they were buried; for example, eleven Turkish internees who died at Knockaloe are buried at Patrick Cemetery (as are two German Jewish graves that have remained in their original location, and thirty British guards who died there). The internment experience is very much remembered on the Isle of Man, and a visit to the island will be helpful to try and place the internment experience. A useful website for this is: www.iomguide.com/internment -camps/knockaloe.php.

Internees who died at Alexandra Palace were originally buried in the Great Northern Cemetery at Southgate. There is a memorial that records the names of those who died in the cemetery near the entrance. The Anglo-German Family History Society has also erected a memorial at Alexandra Palace.

Appendix 1

QUICK GUIDE TO KEY RESOURCES FOR TRACING PRISONERS OF WAR AND CIVILIAN INTERNEES IN THE FIRST WORLD WAR

Main Sources

International Committee of the Red Cross (ICRC)

Archives Division and Research Service, International Committee of the Red Cross, 19 Avenue de la Paix, CH-1202 Geneva, Switzerland
www.icrc.org/eng

The ICRC holds surviving First World War POW and civilian internee records for all nationalities. However, these records are currently unavailable until 2014, when the records will go online.

The National Archives (TNA)

The National Archives, Kew, Richmond, Surrey TW9 4DU
www.nationalarchives.gov.uk
Tel: 020 8876 3444

TNA has useful information sheets and guides for tracing both POWs and civilian internees, as well as Army, Royal Navy, Royal Air Force and merchant navy personnel. These are available on the website. Also ask to see the very helpful file compiled by Alan Bowgen relating to First World War POWs, which is held behind the Enquiries Desk.

TNA holds surviving First World War service records (although if an individual served after 1920 their records are likely to still be held by the Ministry of Defence):

Army
Officers' records – WO 339 and WO 374
Other ranks' records – available online at www.ancestry.co.uk
Medal Index Cards – available at www.ancestry.co.uk and TNA
Documents Online at www.nationalarchives.gov.uk/documentsonline.

Royal Navy
Most service records available via Documents Online (as above),
including those for Royal Naval Division and Royal Marines.

Royal Air Force
Officers' records available via Documents Online (as above), and Royal
Flying Corps and Royal Naval Air Service records available through
Army and Royal Navy sources above.
Airmen's service records for numbers in the range 1–329,000 are available
at TNA in AIR 79.

Merchant navy
Records are scattered in many places, and many relating to the First
World War have not survived. Little is available online except 'Campaign
Medals Issued to First World War Merchant Seamen', available via
Documents Online (as above).
   Wide variety of records available at TNA, but most useful probably in
MT 9.
   Marcus Bateman's site at http://wanborough.ukuhost.co.uk/
POW/POW.htm features an index from MT 9/1238.

Most useful record series at TNA generally are:
   WO 161 (now available on Documents Online – as above), which
consists of around 3,000 interviews with escaped or repatriated POWs.
   FO 383 – Prisoners of War and Aliens Department correspondence files
of the Foreign Office – very well indexed on the online catalogue.

For internees in this country, Home Office files HO 45 and HO 144 are
likely sources, though little material has survived.

For internees in Ruhleben the lists in MT 9/1094 are invaluable.
   Chris Paton's excellent 'The Ruhleben Story' can be found at
http://ruhleben.tripod.com/ while Stefan Hartman's www.ruhleben.com
/index.php has great potential for German–English dialogue.

Post-First World War service records are generally available to proven
next of kin for a £30 fee, though this can take several months. A generic

online application form can be found at: www.veterans-uk.info/ service_records/service_records.html. The relevant addresses are:

Army Personnel Centre, Disclosures 4, MP 555, Kentigern House, 65 Brown Street, Glasgow G2 8EX. Initial contact may be made by telephone (0845 600 9663) or by email (disc4@apc.army.mod.uk).

Director of Naval Personnel, Naval Disclosure Cell, Mailpoint G-2, Room 48, West Battery, Whale Island, Portsmouth, Hampshire PO2 8DX.

RAF Disclosures, Room 5, Trenchard Hall, RAF Cranwell, Sleaford, Lincolnshire NG34 8HB.

Commonwealth War Graves Commission (CWGC)

Commonwealth War Graves Commission, 2 Marlow Road, Maidenhead, Berkshire SL6 7DX

www.cwgc.org

Tel: 01628 507200

Best starting point for tracing those who died as POWs.

Imperial War Museums (IWM)

Imperial War Museums, Collections Enquiry Service, Lambeth Road, London SE1 6HZ

Email: collections@iwm.org.uk

www.iwm.org.uk

Tel: 020 7416 5342

IWM has a great collection of art, books, documents, exhibits, films, magazines, photographs and sound interviews. It also produces information sheets offering guidance for tracing POWs, as well as Army, Royal Navy, Royal Air Force and merchant navy service personnel.

IWM offers an enquiry service and you can make appointments to conduct research at the address given above.

Useful British Sources

British Library, 96 Euston Road, London NW1 2DB

www.bl.uk

Holds India Office Records, Sound Archive and also Newspaper Library (at Colindale).

Fleet Air Arm Museum, RNAS Yeovilton, near Ilchester, Somerset BA22 8HT

www.fleetairarm.com

Tel: 01935 840565

Liddell Hart Centre for Military Archives, Michael Howard Archives Reading Room, King's College London, Room 302, Strand Building, Strand, London WC2R 2LS
www.kcl.ac.uk/library/archivespec/collections/LHCMA.aspx
Tel: 020 7848 2015

Liddle Collection, Special Collections, Leeds University Library, Woodhouse Lane, Leeds, West Yorkshire LS2 9JT
http://library.leeds.ac.uk/liddle.collection
Tel: 01133 435518
Good collection for First World War, and particularly strong on Ruhleben.

Manx National Heritage Library, Douglas, Isle of Man IM1 3LY
www.gov.im/mnh
Tel: 01624 648000
Very good information sheet available at www.gov.im/mnh/heritage/library/bibliographies/internment.xml

National Army Museum (NAM), Royal Hospital Road, Chelsea, London SW3 4HT
www.nam.ac.uk
Tel: 020 7730 0717
The new online catalogue is really helpful: www.nam.ac.uk/inventory/books/index.php.

National Maritime Museum, Romney Road, Greenwich, London SE10 9NF
www.rmg.co.uk
Tel: 020 8312 6516

Royal Air Force Museum, Department of Research and Information Services, Grahame Park Way, London NW9 5LL
www.rafmuseum.org.uk
Tel: 020 8205 2266

Royal Marines Museum, Eastney Esplanade, Southsea, Hampshire PO4 9PX
www.royalmarinesmuseum.co.uk
Tel: 02392 819385

Royal Naval Museum, HM Naval Base (PP66), Portsmouth, Hampshire PO1 3NH
www.royalnavalmuseum.org
Tel: 02392 727562

Also hosts very useful *Sea Your History* site: www.seayourhistory
.org.uk.

Royal Navy Submarine Museum, Haslar Jetty Road, Gosport,
Hampshire PO12 2AS
Email contact preferred: archives@rnsubmus.co.uk
www.rnsubmus.co.uk
Tel: 02392 510354

Society of Friends
The Library of the Religious Society of Friends in Britain, Friends House,
173–177 Euston Road, London NW1 2BJ
www.quaker.org.uk/library-and-quaker-centre
Tel: 020 7663 1135

Other archives, libraries and museums can be located through these
websites. There are too many regimental museums to list here but the
Army Museums Ogilby Trust website is invaluable for locating these:
www.armymuseums.org.uk.

Regimental museums can also be located in the publication *The AMOT
Guide to Military Museums in the UK* (London: Third Millenium, 2010).

ARCHON – archive contact details generally: www.nationalarchives.
gov.uk/archon

National Register of Archives
www.nationalarchives.gov.uk/nra

Sources for the Commonwealth

Australia

Australian Army First World War service records are at the National
Archives of Australia:www.naa.gov.au/collection/explore/defence
/service-records/army-wwi.aspx

Australian War Memorial, Treloar Crescent, Campbell ACT 2612,
Australia
www.awm.gov.au

Mapping our Anzacs
http://mappingouranzacs.naa.gov.au

Canada

Canadian Army First World War service records are at: www.collection-scanada.gc.ca/databases/cef/index-e.html

Canadian Virtual War Memorial
www.veterans.gc.ca/eng/collections/virtualmem

Canadian War Museum, 1 Vimy Place, Ottawa, Ontario K1A 0M8
www.warmuseum.ca/cwm/home

New Zealand

Auckland War Memorial Museum
www.aucklandmuseum.com/

Auckland War Memorial Museum Cenotaph Database
http://muse.aucklandmuseum.com/databases/Cenotaph/locations.aspx

New Zealand History Online
www.nzhistory.net.nz/war/researching-first-world-war-soldiers

Paperspast – a project by the National Library of New Zealand to digitize New Zealand papers.
http://paperspast.natlib.govt.nz/cgi-bin/paperspast

South Africa

Ditsong National Museum of Military History, PO Box 52090, Saxonwold, 2132, South Africa
www.ditsong.org.za/militaryhistory.htm

Sources for the Central Powers

Austria-Hungary

Austria has excellent military records, and the Kriegsarchiv website has pages in English and a helpful pdf information sheet entitled 'Genealogy in the Vienna War Archives'.
Kriegsarchiv, Nottendorfergasse 2-4, A-1030 Vienna, Austria
http://oesta.gv.at/site/6154/default.aspx

Military conscription registers are held at the National Achives of Hungary.

Magyar Oszágos Levéltár, Bécsi Kapu tér 4, H-1250 Budapest, PO Box 3, Hungary

www.mol.gov.hu/angol/bal_menusor/about_us.html

Germany

All First World War army service records relating to Prussia are believed to have been destroyed.

The Bavarian State Archives, Generaldirektion der Staatlichen Archive Bayerns, Schönfeldstrasse 5, 80539 München, Germany

www.gda.bayern.de

The state archives have service records for those serving in Bavarian units, and these 'Kriegsstammrollen, 1914–1918' have recently been made avaiable via Ancestry (http://search.ancestry.com/).

Records for Baden and Württemberg may be available through the Landesarchiv in Stuttgart.

Landesarchiv Baden-Württemberg, Eugenstrasse 7, D-70182 Stuttgart, Germany

www.landesarchiv-bw.de

Deutsche Dienstsstelle has records of German First World War Naval personnel.

Deutsche Dienstsstelle (WASt), Eichborndamm 179, D-13403 Berlin, Germany

www.dd-wast.de/

German War Graves

Volksbund Deutsche Kriegsgräberfürsorge e V, Werner-Hilpert-Strasse 2, 34112 Kassel, Germany

www.volksbund.de/

Turkey

Ottoman Archives, Başbakanlik Osmanti Arşivi, Daire Başkanligi, Sirecki, Istanbul, Turkey

Websites

Anglo-German Family History Society
www.agfhs.org.uk

Australian War Memorial information sheet: www.awm.gov.au/research/infosheets/pow/ww1/

Australian War Memorial *Stolen Years* online exhibition: www.awm.gov.au/exhibitions/stolenyears/

Black Sheep Index – commercial site that offers index for mentions in newspapers (that can be purchased). For First World War POWs, name, rank, unit, location and date are given: www.blacksheepindex .co.uk/SOUL.htm

British Magazines During the Great War – site reproducing articles from illustrated magazines, with some good POW material: www.greatwardifferent.com/Great_War/NewsMedia/Media.htm

Dublin Fusiliers – nominal roll of Royal Dublin Fusiliers POWs: www.dublin-fusiliers.com/Pows/list-prisoners.html

Europeana Erster Weltkrieg – First World War in pictures, letters and memories: www.europeana1914-1918.eu/en

Feldpost – website relating to German war letters and collections where they are held. Primarily concerned with Second World War material, but the First World War is also covered: www.feldpost-archiv.de/english /index.html

Firstworldwar.com – a multimedia history of the First World War: www.firstworldwar.com/photos/prisoners.htm

The Great War Archive at the First World War Poetry Digital Archive: www.oucs.ox.ac.uk/ww1lit/gwa

King's Own Royal Lancaster Regiment Prisoner of War Care Committee: www.kingsownmuseum.plus.com/pwcc.htm

Long Long Trail – probably the best website on the British Army in the First World War: www.1914-1918.net

The Manchesters – nominal roll of Manchester Regiment POWs: www.themanchesters.org/pow.htm

National Ex-Prisoner of War Association – primarily concerned with the Second World War, but there is an interest, and some newsletter items relating to 1914–1918: www.prisonerofwar.org.uk

Peace and War in the 20th Century – McMaster University Library: http://pw20c.mcmaster.ca/life-prison

Prisonniers de Guerre – French site with photographs and lists of POW camps: http://prisonniers-de-guerre-1914-1918.chez-alice.fr/photoset-cartespostales.htm

POW camps in Sussex: http://sussexthegreatwar.wordpress.com/

Western Front Association – broader interest in the First World War than the name would suggest: www.westernfrontassociation.com

Worcestershire Regiment – website with POW accounts and nominal rolls: www.worcestershireregiment.com/pow_stories.php

Discussion Forums

Useful places to discuss First World War POW research:

AGW14–18 Forum: German First World War discussion forum – members only: http://de.groups.yahoo.com/group/agw14-18

Forum Eerste Wereldoorlog – Dutch forum which has a 'POWs of the First World War' section under the heading of *Algemeen* as well as international pages: www.forumeerstewereldoorlog.nl

Great War Forum – many knowledgeable members happy to share information: http://1914-1918.invisionzone.com/forums/index.php?act=idx

Milex – German discussion forum relating to the First World War: www.milex.de/forum/

Pages 14-18 Forum – international pages on French forum, which at time of press has a few posts on POW matters, and could be potentially very useful: http://pages14-18.mesdiscussions.net/

Vermisstenforum – German forum with an English section relating to the missing, primarily after the Second World War, but there is some coverage of the First World War as well: www.vksvg.de/index.php

Appendix 2

BRITISH PRISONERS OF WAR HELD BY THE BULGARIANS

The Salonika Campaign (sometimes called the Macedonian Campaign) began in autumn 1915, when British troops became involved in this Balkan region to support the Serbs against a Bulgarian, German and Austro-Hungarian attack.

All officers and most men were held at Philippolis, although the men were widely employed on working parties. The first POWs were taken in autumn 1915, and a year later the numbers held were 15 officers and 510 other ranks. An exchange of thirty POWs was made in August 1917. A second exchange took place in September 1918, when seventy-two other

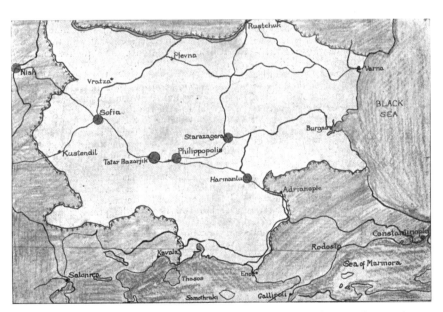

Map showing main POW camps in Bulgaria. Taken from the March 1918 issue of The British Prisoner of War *(with kind permission of the British Red Cross Museum and Archives).*

ranks and five officers gained freedom. The CPWC gives the total numbers of POWs held by Bulgaria as 49 officers and 1,237 other ranks.

FO 383/127, 'Relief to British P. of W. in Bulgaria' contains lists of the 423 British POWs in Bulgaria in 1916 (though there is debate about the numbers and potential discrepancies), alphabetically by name, rank and regiment. There are also separate lists of men at Philippolis, Drenovetz, Gorno Panitchervo, Radomir and Sofia, and various working parties, Tirnovo, Vratza, and men in hospitals.

FO 383/252 contains a list of twenty-nine incapacitated POWs, giving name, regiment, town and county of birth. Also a list of eleven Bulgarian POWs to be repatriated, with details of their injuries (they were mainly amputees). Correspondence throughout spring and summer 1917 relating to the exchange mentioned above, though names and numbers do not necessarily correlate. This volume also contains interviews with some repatriated POWs conducted by the Government Committee on the Treatment by the Enemy of British Prisoners of War (similar to those found in WO 161).

The WWC at IWM contains sixty-two cards or letters in Prisoners 3/1-/62. These were mainly sent by POWs in Bulgaria thanking Lady Dodds for parcels received from the Red Cross.

WO 95/4945 contains a box of war diaries from the Salonika line of communications relating to British-run POW camps for Bulgarians and Turks: Nos 1, 2, 3, 4, 5, 6, 7, 8, 9, 10, 11, 12, 13, 14, 15, 16, 17, 18, 19 and 21 POW camps, also Karaissi and Guvezne and Ajvasil and Gloucester Gully. As with all war diaries, these vary in the amount of information they contain, but they are usually very interesting documents. They are generally very good for details of British personnel in camps and the transport of POWs. They also cover what is happening in the camp, reporting problems with health, reluctance to work because of reduced food rations and escapes, and occasionally some POWs are named.

Prison Camps in Bulgaria

Apriloff (Hospital) – 6th Division Hospital, Alexandravoska, Gladstone Hospital, Minkoffschool Hospital, Knights of Malta Hospital, Hotel Europe
Bellovo
Costenetze Bania
Drenovetz
Drama – Hospital
Elli Dere, Ost Rumelien
Gornipanitcherevo (also Gorno Panitchervo)
Gümürdjina

Levonovo
Nisch – Hospital
Ochonié
Pechtera
Philippolis
Radomir, Ost Rumelien – 2nd Hospital, Radomir City
Sevlievo
Sliven
Sofia
Starazagora
Strumnitza
Tatar Pazardjik
Tirnova (also Tirnovo)
Uskub (Scopia) – Hospital
Vratza

Appendix 3

BRITISH PRISONERS OF WAR AND INTERNEES IN EAST AFRICA

The Central Prisoners of War Committee gives the total number of POWs held in East Africa as 30 officers and 164 other ranks. A number of civilians, mainly missionaries, were also interned.

FO 383/176 has a list of 'British Civilians in East Africa' – though this is rather confused since the initial list relates to the Cameroons. However, there is a subsequent list of 'British Subjects Interned in German E. Africa', dated January 1916. There is correspondence from the Universities' Mission to Central Africa with names. This is followed by a 'List of British Prisoners of War and Other British Subjects Interned in German East Africa'. This features 138 people by name, rank or profession, and regiment or vessel (or place and date of death).

Prison Camps in East Africa and Magazines

Kiboriani: *Kiboriani Daily Mail* – photocopied handwritten issue for 25 December 1915.
Kilimatinde
Moragoro
Tabora: *Prison Times* – not held by IWM.

Appendix 4

ABBREVIATIONS AND GLOSSARY

Abbreviations

ADM	Admiralty
AIR	Air Ministry
BRCS&OSJ	British Red Cross Society and Order of St John
CO	Colonial Office
CPWC	Central Prisoners of War Committee
CWGC	Commonwealth War Graves Commission
FO	Foreign Office
HO	Home Office
IA	Indian Army
ICRC	International Committee of the Red Cross
IPOWA	International Prisoner of War Agency
IWM	Imperial War Museums
KOYLI	King's Own Yorkshire Light Infantry
MT	Ministry of Transport
NAM	National Army Museum
NCO	non-commissioned officer
POW	prisoner of war
TNA	The National Archives
RND	Royal Naval Division
RNR	Royal Naval Reserve
WLA	Women's Land Army
WO	War Office
WO	warrant officer
WWC	Women's Work Collection (held at IWM)

Glossary

Filialager	working camp
Kommando	working party
Lazaret	hospital
Sammellager	collection or transit camp; the main camp for working parties, eg Friedrichsfeld or Güstrow
Stammlager	parent camp
Strafelager	punishment camp

Appendix 5

SELECT BIBLIOGRAPHY

General Sources

Parliament produced many Command Papers relating to POWs throughout the war. These very informative sources have all been bound together at the IWM Library under the title 'Command Papers Releating to Prisoners of War'.

Das Archiv des Ausschusses fur deutsche Kriegsgefangene der Frankfurter Vereins vom Roten Kreuz (Leipzig: Verband Deutscher Kriegssamlungen, 1921) [excellent bibliography of English and German sources].

Bury, Right Reverend Herbert, *Here and There in the War Area* (London: Mowbray, 1917).

Die Eiche: Vierteljahrsschrift für Freundschaftsarbeit der Kirchen ein Organ für Soziale und Internationale Ethik, vol. 3, no. 3 and 4, July 1915 [press reports, official correspondence and letters relating to British POWs in Germany and German POWs in UK. All German text].

Jackson, Robert, *The Prisoners, 1914–18* (London: Routledge, 1989).

Jones, Heather, *Violence against Prisoners of War in the First World War: Britain, France and Germany, 1914–1920* (Cambridge: Cambridge University Press, 2011) [Studies in the Social and Cultural History of Modern Warfare].

Moynihan, Michael (ed), *Black Bread and Barbed Wire: Prisoners in the First World War* (London: Leo Cooper, 1978).

Moynihan, Michael (ed), *God on our Side* (London: Leo Cooper, 1983).

Picot, Lt Col H P, *The British Interned in Switzerland* (London: Edward Arnold, 1919).

Reports by the Joint War Committee and the Joint War Finance Committee of the British Red Cross Society and the Order of St. John of Jerusalem in England on Voluntary Aid Rendered to the Sick and Wounded at Home and Abroad and to British Prisoners of War (London: HMSO, 1914).

Roxburgh, Ronald F, *The Prisoners of War Information Bureau in London: A*

Study, introduction by L Oppenheim (London: Longmans, Green, 1915).

Speed, Richard B, III, *Prisoners, Diplomats, and the Great War: A Study in the Diplomacy of Captivity* (New York: Greenwood, 1990).

Thomas, Lily, *Memories Grave and Gay: Of Burton Prisoners of War and the Local Work with Allusions to War-time Legislation* (Derby: Bemrose, 1919?).

Vance, Jonathan F (ed), *Encyclopedia of Prisoners of War and Internment* (Santa Barbara, CA: ABC-CLIO, 2000).

The Work of the Central Prisoners of War Committee, 1916–1919 (London: Charles Cull, 1919?).

Yarnell, John, *Barbed Wire Disease: British and German Prisoners of War, 1914–18* (Stroud: History Press, 2011).

East Africa

Briggs, J H, *In the East Africa War Zone* (London: Church Missionary Society, 1918).

British Civilian Prisoners in German East Africa: A Report by the Government Committee on the Treatment by the Enemy of British Prisoners of War (London, 1918).

Holtom, Ernest C, *Two Years' Captivity in German East Africa: Being the Personal Experiences of Surgeon E C H, Royal Navy* (London: Hutchinson, [1919]).

Spanton, Ernest F, *In German Gaols: A Narrative of Two Years' Captivity in German East Africa* (London: Society for Promoting Christian Knowledge, 1917).

Germany

Bilder aus den Gefangenenlagern des Garde-Corps (Potsdam: Stiftungsverlag in Potsdam, 1918) [Photographs of Döberitz, Dyrotz, Weinberglager, Halbmondlager and Müncheberg].

Bond, Lt Col R C, DSO, *Prisoners Grave and Gay* (Edinburgh: William Blackwood, 1934).

[Cimino, H], *Behind the Prison Bars in Germany: A Detailed Record of Six Months' Experiences in German Prisons and Detention Camps by a British Doctor who Has Just Been Released* (London: George Newnes, 1915).

Cohen, Israel, *The Ruhleben Prison Camp: A Record of Nineteen Months' Internment* (London: Methuen, 1917).

Dennett, Carl P, *Prisoners of the Great War: Authoritative Statement of Conditions in the Prison Camps of Germany* (Boston, MA: Houghton Mifflin, 1919).

Doegen, Wilhelm (ed), *Kriegsgefangene Völker: Band I: Der Kriegsgefangenen Haltung und Schicksal in Deutschland* (Berlin: Dietrich Reimer (Ernst Vohsen), 1919).

Durnford, H G, *The Tunnellers of Holzminden (With a Side-issue)* 2nd edn (Cambridge: Cambridge University Press, 1930).

Ellison, Wallace, *Escaped! Adventures in German Captivity* (Edinburgh: Blackwood, 1918).

Emden, Richard van, *Prisoners of the Kaiser: The Last POWs of the Great War* (Barnsley: Pen and Sword, 2009).

Eugster, A, *Berichte über Kriegsgefangenenlager in Deutschland und Frankreich: erstattet zuhanden des Internationalen Komitees vom Roten Kreuz in Genf: Januar bis Juni 1915* (Basel: Verlag Georg, 1915).

Evans, A J, *The Escaping Club* (London: John Lane the Bodley Head, 1921).

Hall, Malcolm, *In Enemy Hands: A British Territorial Soldier in Germany, 1915–1919* (Stroud: Tempus, 2002).

Harding, Geoffrey, *Escape Fever*, (London: John Hamilton, [1932?]).

Harrison, Major M C C, DSO, MC and Captain H A Cartwright MC, *Within Four Walls* (London: Edward Arnold, 1930).

Harvey, F W, *Comrades in Captivity: A Record of Life in Seven German Prison Camps* (London: Sidgwick and Jackson, 1920).

In the Hands of the Huns: Being the Reminiscences of a British Civil Prisoner of War, 1914–1915 (London: Simpkin Marshall Hamilton Kent, 1916).

Ketchum, J Davidson, *Ruhleben: A Prison Camp Society*, foreword and post-script by Robert B. Macleod (Toronto: University of Toronto Press, 1965).

Knight, Captain, *'Brother Bosch': An Airman's Escape from Germany* (London: Heinemann, 1919).

McCarthy, Daniel J, *The Prisoner of War in Germany: The Care and Treatment of the Prisoner of War, with a History of the Development of the Principle of Neutral Inspection and Control*, 3rd edn (London: Skeffington, n.d.).

Mahoney, Henry C (narrator), *Sixteen Months in Four German Prisons: Wesel, Sennelager, Klingelputz, Ruhleben*, chronicled by Frederick A Talbot (London: Sampson Low, Marston, 1917).

O'Sullivan Molony, W, *Prisoners and Captives* (London: Macmillan, 1933).

Otte, Klaus, *Lager Soltau: das Kriegsgefangenen- und Interniertenlager des Ersten Weltkriegs (1914–1921)* (Soltau: Mundschenk, 1999).

Page, Edward, *Escaping from Germany* (London: Andrew Melrose, 1919).

Powell, Joseph, and Francis Gribble, *The History of Ruhleben: A Record of British Organisation in a Prison Camp in Germany* (London: Collins, 1919).

Pyke, Geoffrey, *To Ruhleben – and Back: A Great Adventure in Three Phases* (London: Constable, 1916).

Sladen, Douglas (ed), *In Ruhleben: Letters from a Prisoner to his Mother: With an Account of the 'University' Life Classes, Sports, Food Accommodation etc., of the Internment Camp of British Prisoners* (London: Hurst and Blackett, 1917).

Stibbe, Matthew, *British Civilian Internees in Germany: The Ruhleben Camp 1914–18* (Manchester: Manchester University Press, 2008).

Thomas, Cecil, *They Also Served: The Experiences of a Private Soldier as Prisoner of War in German Camp and Coal Mine, 1916–1918*, foreword by Field-Marshal Lord Birdwood (London: Hurst and Blackett, n.d.).

Warburton, Ernest, *Behind Boche Bars* (London: John Lane the Bodley Head, 1920).

Warin, Ann (ed), *Dear Girl, I Escaped . . . : Experiences of the Great War 1914–1918* (Redcliffe, Bristol: Redcliffe Press, 1989).

Waugh, Alec, *The Prisoners of Mainz* (London: Chapman and Hall, 1919).

West, Alick, *One Man in his Time: An Autobiography* (London: Allen and Unwin, 1969).

Winchester, Barry, *Beyond the Tumult*, foreword by Group Captain Douglas Bader; introduction by Group Captain L G Nixon (Ret'd) (London: Allison and Busby, 1971).

Turkey

Armstrong, Harold,*Turkey in Travail: The Birth of a New Nation* (London: John Lane the Bodley Head, 1925).

Bishop, H C W, *A Kut Prisoner* (London: John Lane the Bodley Head, 1920).

Blackledge, W J, *The Legion of Marching Madmen* (London: Sampson Low, Marston, [1936?]).

[Bott, Alan], 'Contact', *Eastern Nights – and Flights: A Record of Oriental Adventure* (Edinburgh: William Blackwood, 1920).

Brown, James, *Turkish Days and Ways* (Sydney: Angus and Robertson, 1940).

Gariépy, Patrick, *British and Dominion Servicemen Captured at Gallipoli who Died in Captivity* (Eugene, OR: P Gariépy, 1999).

Gwatkin-Williams, Captain R S, *Prisoners of the Red Desert: Being a Full and True History of the Men of the 'Tara'*, introduction by the Duke of Westminster (London: Thornton Butterworth, [1919]).

Harvey, F A, *The Sufferings of the Kut Garrison during their March into Turkey as Prisoners of War: 1916–1917*, ed by J S Hewick (Ludgershall: Adjutants Press, 1923).

Hill, Group Captain C W, *The Spook and the Commandant* (London: Kimber, 1975).

Johnston, Captain M A B, RGA and Captain K D Yearsley, RE, *Four-Fifty Miles to Freedom* (London: Blackwood, 1919).

Keeling, E H, *Adventures in Turkey and Russia* (London: John Murray, 1924).

Long, Flight Sergeant P W, MM, *Other Ranks of Kut* (London: Williams and Norgate, 1938).

Lushington, R F, *A Prisoner with the Turks 1915–1918* (London: Simpkin, Marshall, Hamilton, Kent, 1923).

Neave, Dorina L, *Remembering Kut: 'Lest We Forget'* (London: Arthur Barker, 1937).

Sandes, Major E W C, MC, RE, *In Kut and Captivity: With the Sixth Indian Division* (London: John Murray, 1919).

Sandes, Major E W C, DSO, MC, RE, *Tales of Turkey* (London: John Murray, 1924).

Still, John, *A Prisoner in Turkey* (London: John Lane the Bodley Head, 1920).

Tetik, Ög.Alb. Ahmet, *Çanakkale muharebeleri'nin esirleri. İfadeler ve mektuplar: Prisoners of War at the Çanakkale Battles. Testimonies and Letters* trans by Yusuf Serdar Demirtas and Sema Demirtas (Ankara: Genelkurmay Basimevi, 2009).

Treatment of British Prisoners of War in Turkey (Delhi: Government Printing, n.d.).

Yeats-Brown, Francis, *Caught by the Turks* (London: Edward Arnold, 1919).

United Kingdom

Bird, J C, *Control of German Enemy Alien Civilians in Great Britain 1914–1918* (New York: Garland, 1986).

Bogenstätter, L von, and H Zimmermann, *Die Welt hinter Stacheldraht: Eine Chronik des englischen Kriegsgefangenlagers Handforth bei Manchester* (Munich: Kunst- und Verlagsanstalt Piloty und Loehle, 1921) [Contains roll of honour of men who died].

Braithwaite Thomas, Anna, et al (compilers), *St. Stephen's House: Friends' Emergency Work in England, 1914 to 1920* (London: Emergency Committee for the Assistance of Germans, Austrians and Hungarians in Distress, [192–?]).

Butt, Maggie, *Ally Pally Prison Camp* (Kingsbridge: Oversteps Books, 2011).

Chinchen, Barry, *Aliens, Internees and Prisoners of War in the UK, 1914–1920* (n.p.: n.pub., [2007]).

Cohen-Portheim, Paul, *Time Stood Still: My Internment in England 1914–1918* (London: Duckworth, 1931).

Cresswell, Yvonne M (ed), *Living with the Wire: Civilian Internment on the*

Isle of Man during the Two World Wars (Isle of Man: Manx National Heritage, Manx Museum and National Trust, 1994).

Deutsche Kriegsgefangene in Feindesland: England (Berlin: Vereinigung Wissenschaftlicher Verlager Walter de Gruyter, 1919).

Dewey, P E, *British Agriculture in the First World War* (London: Routledge, 1989).

Dove, Richard (ed), *'Totally Un-English'?: Britain's Internment of 'Enemy Aliens' in Two World Wars* (Amsterdam: Editions Rodolphi, 2005) [Yearbook of the Research Centre for German and Austrian Exile Studies, vol. 7, 2005].

Nicol, Nic (compiler), *Not Necessarily Behind Barbed Wire: Places of Internment in the United Kingdom of Great Britain and Ireland During the First World War [1919–1920]* (compiled for the Prisoners of War Internment Camp Project, 2010).

[Noschke, Richard], *An Insight into Civilian Internment in Britain during WWI: From the Diary of Richard Noschke and a Short Essay by Rudolf Rocker* (Maidenhead: Anglo-German Family History Society, 1998).

Plüschow, G, *My Escape from Donington Hall* (London: The Bodley Head, 1929).

Rintelen, Captain von [Franz Rintelen von Kleist],*The Dark Invader: Wartime Reminiscences of a German Naval Intelligence Officer*, 2nd rev edn (London: Lovat Dickson, 1933).

Sachsse and Cossman (eds), *Kriegsgefangen in Skipton: Leben und Geschichte deutscher Kreigsgefangener in einem englischen Lager* (Munich: Verlag von Ernst Reinhardt, 1920) [Contains roll of honour of men who died].

Sargeaunt, B E, *The Isle of Man and the Great War* (Douglas: Brown, [1920]).

Stoffa, P, *Round the World to Freedom: Being the Escapes and Adventures of Major Paul Stoffa (of the Hungarian Army)*, ed and trans by L Harta (London: John Lane the Bodley Head, 1933).

West, Margery, *Island at War* (Laxey: Western Books, 1986).

Appendix 6

LOCATIONS OF PRISON CAMPS IN GERMANY AND AUSTRIA

Information here is based on the 'new and revised edition' of Mrs Una Pope-Hennessy's *Map of the Main Prison Camps in Germany and Austria*, originally published by Nisbet in 1918 (republished by IWM in the early 1990s – these names appear in capitals). This has been supplemented, and in some cases corrected, by BRC&OSJ, *List of Internment Camps for British Prisoners of War in Enemy Countries* (January 1918), which contains details of working camps and is indicated by name in lower case, and *Kriegsgefangene Völker* by Wilhelm Doegen, published in Berlin in 1919, and other sources.

Adeleben – Attached to Hameln.

Ahlhorn – Oldenberg. Z. 209. Attached to Soltau.

AIX OR AACHEN – A very ancient town (pop 150,000) surrounded by gently sloping wooded hills. Once the favourite abode of Charlemagne, now a manufacturing city with over a hundred cloth factories and forty-five foundries, machine-shops, etc. There are nine hospitals in which British POWs have been quartered: Reifmuseum, Maschinenbauschule, Mariahilf, Luisen, Marien, Elisabeth and Garnison Hospitals, and Reserve Lazarets I and II. All British POWs going to England or Holland are assembled here before leaving Germany. 8th Army Corps.

Alfeld a/Leine – Hanover. Hospital. Attached to Hameln.

Allenstein – Attached to Hameln.

ALTDAMM – Pommern. Small town (pop 7,300) at the mouth of the Oder opposite Stettin. Three camps; capacity 15,000. Built on a sandy drill-ground amidst pine woods. A few naval and civilian POWs here. The centre of a large number of working gangs employed in the neighbourhood on estates, in forestry, factories, hotels, etc. 2nd Army Corps. Now called Dąbie, and a suburb of Szczecin (formerly Stettin) in Poland.

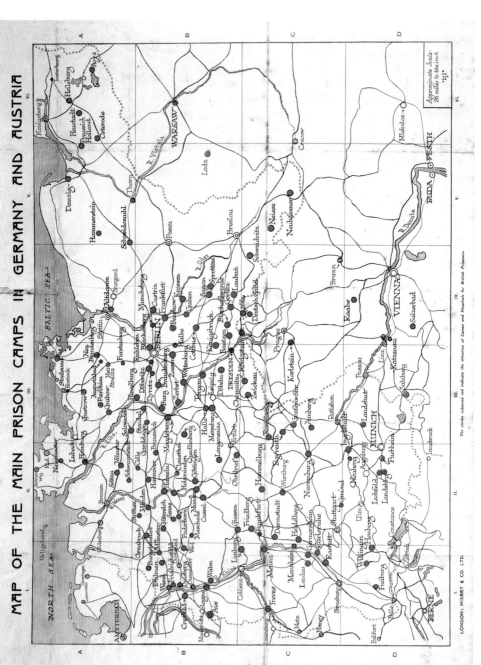

Mrs Pope-Hennessy's map, showing the principal POW camps in Germany and Austria (© IWM, K 28445).

Altenau – Attached to Hameln.

ALTENGRABOW – Also known as Grabow. A great working camp centre. Prisoners employed on estates, in forestry, on railway line between Berlin and Lübeck, in factories, etc. Camp consists of eight compounds of six barracks each. Formerly a military camp. 4th Army Corps.
www.reminiscene.co.uk/alb-hay.html
www.oucs.ox.ac.uk/ww1lit/gwa/document/9575/8303
www.oucs.ox.ac.uk/ww1lit/gwa/document/9572/8292?REC=1

Alt Glienicke – Bei Grünau. Attached to Döberitz.

Altona – Bei Hamburg, Schleswig-Holstein. Hospital.

AMBERG – An old town (pop 15,700) on the Vils, surrounded by a well-preserved wall and moat. The camp is built on rising ground near the new Bavarian Barracks on the outskirts of the city. Capacity 5,000. Many prisoners go out to work in surrounding country. 3rd Bavarian Army Corps.

Angermund – Attached to Friedrichsfeld.

Anholt – Westfalen.

Ansbach – Bayern.

Aplerbeck – Kreis Horde, Westfalen. Attached to Senne.

ARYS – Three-quarters of a mile from the town of Arys. East Prussia. Camp situated on undulating ground. Consists of fifty barracks. Prisoners are employed in building, agriculture, etc. NCOs who do not volunteer for work are quartered there. The accommodation is of the earth barrack type. Winter climate very severe. 20th Army Corps. Now called Orzysz, in Poland.

Aschaffenburg – Reserve Hospital.

Ascheberg – Westfalen.

Aselage – Attached to Hameln.

Asperg – Württemberg.

Aszód – Hungary. Civilian Camp.

Atzendorf – Magdeburg, Saxony.

Augsburg – Bayern.

AUGUSTABAD (also known as NEU BRANDENBURG) – Hotel compound near the little town of Neu Brandenburg (pop 12,300), which is enclosed by a wall 25ft high and ramparts. The Kurhaus is known as Lager A (100 officers), while the Villas Maria (35 officers) and Falkenberg (28 officers) form Lager B. Villa Undine contains offices for the German staff. Situated on the slope just above the Tollensee; fishing and bathing are allowed in this lake. All British officers have been moved from here. 9th Army Corps.

BAD BLENHORST – Eight miles from the station of Nienburg on the Weser, not far from Soltau. The camp is situated in a Kurhaus in a good-sized park, partially wooded; tennis-lawns and fishing-ponds; surrounded by the Lüneberger Heide. Officers Camp. 10th Army Corps.

BAD COLBERG – The sanatorium for thermal springs is now an officers' camp. Temporary buildings have been added. Surroundings attractive and healthy. 11th Army Corps.

Camp magazine (shared with Ströhen): *The Morning Walk* – souvenir issue held at IWM.

www.gordonjacob.org/pictures.html

Bad Ems – Hessen-Nassau. Hospital.

Badendorf – Post Zarpen, Schleswig-Holstein.

Bad Kissengen – Unterfranken, Bayern. Hospital.

Bad Lauterberg – Attached to Hameln.

Bad Orb – Frankfurt a/M, Hessen-Nassau.

Baistrup – Schleswig-Holstein.
The Joint Memorial in Tinglev Churchyard (Slesvig, Denmark): In Memory of British, French and Russian Soldiers who Died as Prisoners of War in the Camp at Bajstrup (n.p.: n.pub., n.d.).

Bamberg – Bayern. Hospital.

Barbara Hospital, Hamborn – Attached to Friedrichsfeld.

Barg – Post Sörup, Schleswig-Holstein. Attached to Güstrow.

Bargfeld – Bei Bargeteheide, Schleswig-Holstein. Attached to Güstrow.

Barmen – Rheinland. Attached to Münster.

Bartenstein – Ost Preussen. Attached to Heilsberg.

BAUTZEN – Saxony. A town (pop 32,800) situated on a height above the Spree. The prisoners are lodged in new artillery barracks completed just before the war. 12th Army Corps.

BAYREUTH – Famous as the shrine of Wagner's operas. Camp situated on the outskirts of the town. A military manoeuvring ground. Barracks of wood to accommodate 5,000. There is a hospital in the town in a large stone drill hall in the garrison compound. American prisoners here. 3rd Bavarian Army Corps.

Beckum – Westfalen. Attached to Münster.

Bedburg – Bei Cologne.

BEESKOW – Near Frankfurt a/d Oder. An officers' camp. Prisoners housed in the old castle of the local Bishop, built in the sixteenth century. The buildings form a good-sized court. 3rd Army Corps.

Beienrode – Hanover. Attached to Celle.

Bensheim – Hessen. Hospital.

Bergenhusen – Schleswig-Holstein. Attached to Güstrow.

Berger Damm – Nauen, Kreis Potsdam. Attached to Döberitz.

Berghof – Attached to Friedrichsfeld.

BERLIN – The capital of Prussia (pop 3,500,000), the third largest city in Europe. Several prison camps are established in the neighbourhood of Berlin, but none in the city itself. There is one large hospital. The Alexandrinenstrasse Lazaret, a special hospital for POWs established in the barracks of the 1st Guard Dragoons; these barracks are built around a yard, and four wooden huts have been added to the accommodation in the barrack-yard. There is also the Stadtvogtei, a prison to which British civilians from Ruhleben are sometimes sent. Guard Corps.

Bernau I/Mark – Bei Berlin.

Bernburg – Anholt.

Bersenbrück – Hanover.

BEUTHEN – Pop 67,700. The centre of the important Upper Silesian mining industry. There are two large lazarets here. British prisoners first sent here in the spring of 1918. 6th Army Corps. Now called Bytom, in Poland.

Bexten Listrup – Bei Salzbergen, Hanover. Z. 3054. Attached to Soltau.

Bielefeld – Westfalen. Hospital. 7th Army Corps. Attached to Minden.

BINGEN – On the Rhine (pop 12,000), the centre of a large wine trade, with good quays and embankments, and also a renowned technical college. British officers have recently been sent to this town. 18th Army Corps.

BISCHOFSWERDA – Saxony. A little town (pop 8,000). The officers' camp consists of new cavalry barracks situated some distance from the town on a hill near pine woods. Barracks not used before the war. For the moment abandoned. 12th Army Corps.

BLANKENBURG – An officers' camp six miles from Berlin, located in a three-storied sanatorium, well built, lighted and heated. Formerly a home for gentlewomen. Surrounded by well-kept grounds. Five British officers in July 1917. 3rd Army Corps.

Blumenthal – Attached to Celle.

Bochum – Bei Essen, Westfalen. Attached to Friedrichsfeld.

Bockelsessor Moor – Bei Dauenhof. Attached to Güstrow.

Boetzow – Bei Berlin.

Bohmte – Bei Osnabruck. Attached to Hameln.

Bokelah – Kreis Bremervorde. Z. X. Attached to Hameln.

Bonn – Rheinland. Hospital.

Borbeck – Bei Essen. Attached to Friedrichsfeld.

Börger – Kreis Hummling, bei Pappenburg. Attached to Hameln.

Borgholzhausen – Bei Bielefeld. Attached to Senne.

Bornim – Bei Berlin.

Borstel – Attached to Soltau.

BRANDENBURG – A town (pop 53,500) on the Havel, thirty-eight miles west south west of Berlin. The camp consists of an abandoned terracotta factory. Prisoners here are naval and Mercantile Marine. 3rd Army Corps.
   http://johnbradleyswar.co.uk/brandenburg.htm

Braunschweig.

Breisach – Alsace.

Breitenborn – Post Lieblos, Kreis Gelnhausen. Attached to Giessen.

BREMEN – An important city (pop 247,000) on both banks of the Weser; one of the chief commercial centres in north Germany and the headquarters of North German Lloyd. There is a newly built garrison hospital in which prisoners are treated, also working camp attached to Soltau. 9th Army Corps.

Brockhofe – Kreis Uelzen. Attached to Hameln.

Bromberg – Posen. Attached to Schneidermühl. Now called Bydgoszcz in Poland.

Buchholz – Attached to Soltau.

Buhnerbachgebiet – Attached to Hameln.

BURG – A town (pop 24,100) with cloth factories founded by Huguenots. Near Magdeburg. The officers' camp was an artillery mobilisation centre, and consists of wagon-sheds, stores and stables. Wooden huts have been added to these buildings and some 900 prisoners can be accommodated here. The exercise ground is limited. 4th Army Corps.

Burgdorf – Attached to Münster.

BURGSTEINFURT – Westfalen. There are no longer any British prisoners in this camp. 7th Army Corps.

Burtzbach – Bei Giessen, Hessen.

Busem – Schleswig-Holstein. Attached to Güstrow.

CARLSRUHE (also Karlsruhe) – The capital (pop 100,000) of the Grand Duchy of Baden. The streets spread out fan-wise from the Schloss. This town has become industrialised since 1870 and makes engines, railway carriages, furniture, plated goods, etc. There is an officers' camp to which the great number of newly captured British officers are sent. Camp opened in February 1917. It consists of wooden hutments erected in the grounds of the Schloss. POWs interrogated at Europa Hotel (Europäischer Hof). 14th Army Corps.

Cassebruch – Bei Hagen i/Bremen. Attached to Soltau.

CASSEL (also Niederzwehren) – This town (pop 153,000) is the headquarters of the 11th Army Corps. The camp is placed on a hill overlooking the Fulda Valley, one mile from Niederzwehren, a suburb of Cassel. Barracks of wood accommodating some 20,000. Prisoners employed in factories and work-shops. American prisoners here.

Castrop – Westfalen. POWs worked in coal mines of Graf Schwerien.

CELLE, Scheuen – Camp a few miles from the town of Celle on the Aller, 28 miles north east of Hanover. Attached to Hameln. A training centre for German reserves. On sandy soil near pine woods. Camp broken up in the autumn of 1916, but Reserve Lazaret I (St Joseph) reserved for eye cases. 10th Army Corps.

CELLE SCHLOSS – A camp for civilians and ex-officers at Celle town established in the old castle, which is picturesquely situated on a hill amongst fine grounds. It is a large building, formerly belonging to the King of Hanover. 10th Army Corps.

Charlottenburg – Bei Berlin.

CHEMNITZ – A large and important manufacturing town (pop 287,000) at the base of the Erzgebirge, Saxony. The camp is on a hill above the town in newly built artillery barracks – the Friedrich August Kaserne. Central steam heating throughout, as in some other Saxon camps. British prisoners brought back from Russian Poland were, for the most part, brought to this camp. Many are employed in neighbouring salt mines. 19th Army Corps.

CLAUSTHAL – The most important place in the Oberharz, and a mining centre. Country bleak and sterile. The mining output includes gold, silver, lead and copper. There is an officers' camp about two miles from the town, established in the Kurhaus Pfauenteich, 2,000 ft above sea-level, in the Hartz Mountains. It is built of wood with brick foundations. 10th Army Corps.

www.worcestershireregiment.com/wr.php?main=inc/whs_chance_7

COBLENZ – The capital of Rhenish Prussia (pop 55,000) in a beautiful position at the confluence of the Moselle and Rhine. The centre of the wine trade. There is a hospital lazaret here run by the Brothers of Mercy, in which prisoners are treated. 8th Army Corps.

COLOGNE – The largest town (pop 500,000) in Rhenish Prussia and one of the most important commercial places in Germany, with extensive harbour works and wharves on the Rhine. A first-class fortress. There is no general camp for prisoners here, but there are several hospitals. The majority of the British prisoners are treated either in the Garnison Lazaret I or the Kaiserin Augusta Schule Lazaret VI. There is also a prison for officers undergoing special punishment in the Schnurgasse, a massive old military prison. 8th Army Corps.

CONSTANCE – Pop 15,000. Situated on the lake of the same name. It is the place in which all officers and men for internment in Switzerland are concentrated.

Cordingen – Post Walsrode. Z. 3003. Attached to Soltau.

Cortemark – Westflandern. Hospital.

Coswig – Anholt.

COTTBUS – A busy town on the Spree (pop 48,600) containing wool, linen and yarn factories. 70 miles SE of Berlin. The camp is situated on rising ground on the outskirts of the town. The buildings radiate from a central guard tower. There is a YMCA hut. This is a coal-mining district, and the camp is under the same command as Merzdorf. 3rd Army Corps.

www.heimatsammlung-cottbus.de/seite11.htm

Courtrai – Westflandern. Hospital.

CREFELD – An important railway centre (pop 130,000) containing the chief velvet and silk factories in Germany. Rheinland. Has now been abandoned as a British officers' camp [in May 1917?] Located in former cavalry barracks. There is a lazaret for men here. 7th Army Corps.

Crefeld Magazine, May 1917.

Prisoners' Pie: L'Assiette sans beurre, nos. 1–3, June, July, October 1916; Christmas issue.

Crossen a/d Oder.
http://homepage.ntlworld.com/bandl.danby/CrossenPOWCamp.pdf

CÜSTRIN – A strongly fortified town (pop 17,600) at the confluence of the Warthe and the Oder. Two of the forts forming part of the fortress surrounding the town are arranged to accommodate officers – Fort Gorgast and Fort Zorndorf. 3rd Army Corps.

CZERSK – Small town on the Danzig–Schneidemühl Railway in West Prussia. Near Dirschau. A camp for Russians to which British prisoners have recently been sent. 17th Army Corps.

Dachau – Bayern.

Dahlenburg – Hanover. Attached to Soltau.

Daldorf – Schleswig-Holstein. Attached to Parchim.

Dankersen – Bei Minden, Westfalen.

DANZIG, Troyl – Capital of West Prussia (pop 170,000). Headquarters of 17th Army Corps. One of the most important commercial towns in North Germany. The prisoners here are housed in barges four deep and four in length, moored to a flat stretch of land on the bank of the Vistula River opposite the city of Danzig. Some of these barges contain 100–500 men. The holds are lit by electricity. The administration, kitchen, store-houses, etc. of the camp are on land. There is a YMCA hut. Now called Gdansk, in Poland.
www.irishbrigade.eu/camps/danzig.html

Darkehmen – Ost Preussen.

DARMSTADT – Capital of the Grand Duchy of Hesse (pop 87,000). The camp is 4 miles from the town and consists of brick buildings on the cavalry exercise ground. There are a large number of working commandos attached to this camp; there is also a camp hospital in which 6 Catholic Sisters work. There is a lazaret in the town. American prisoners here. 18th Army Corps.

Dätgen – Post Nortorf, Schleswig-Holstein. Attached to Parchim.

Deinstedt – Hanover.

Delecke – Kreis Soest. Attached to Senne.

Delligsen – Kreis Gandersheim. Attached to Hameln.

Dettingen – Attached to Stuttgart.

DEUTSCH GABEL – A camp on the confines of Bohemia and Saxony for Merchant Seamen. Under Austrian administration. Now called Jablonné v Podještědí, in the Czech Republic.

Deutz – Rheinland. Hospital. 8th Army Corps.

Diebach – Attached to Hammelburg.

Diedenhofen – Lorraine. Now called Thionville.

Diepholz – Hanover. Z. 3032. Attached to Soltau.

Dieuze – Lorraine.

Dillingen – Bayern.

Dinslaken – Rheinland.

Dirschau – Bei Danzig, Westpreussen.

Dobbertin – Attached to Güstrow.

DÖBELN – Saxony. A small town (pop 19,600). There is an officers camp here established in brick built barracks about a mile from the station. 19th Army Corps.

DÖBERITZ – A large camp 8 miles from Berlin in which prisoners of the Naval Division captured at Antwerp in 1914 were imprisoned. It is described as the Aldershot of Berlin and is close to an important military training centre. There is a YMCA hut here. Guard Corps.
  The Link: A Souvenir Book Published by British Prisoners of War Interned at Doeberitz, Germany, 1914–17 edited by A E Barker, J Power and C A Tooke.
  Döberitz Gazette – March 1916; *The New Gefangener*, April 1916; *Gazette de Döberitz*, August 1916; *Deberitskaya Gazeta.*
  www.doberitz.com/index.html [truncated website still under construction which features images and transcripts from the magazine]

Dorfmark – Hanover. Attached to Hameln.

Dorlaun – Hospital. Attached to Münster I.

Dorsten – Bei Recklinghausen, Westfalen. Attached to Dülmen.

DORTMUND – The largest city in Westphalia (pop 229,000) and the centre of an important mining district. There is a modern hospital for prisoners on the outskirts of the town administered by Catholic Brothers of Mercy. There is also a working camp. Men are housed in large brick buildings and are engaged in mining and in iron foundries. 7th Army Corps.

Drensteinfurt – Bei Münster. Attached to Münster I.

Drosendorf (a/d Thaya) – Merchant Seamen interned here. Austria-Hungary.

Drossenbach – Attached to Heuberg.

Duderstadt – Bei Göttingen, Hanover.

DUISBURG – An ancient town which has become a large manufacturing city (pop 229,000). One of the chief depots of the Ruhr coal traffic, and one of the finest river ports in Germany. There is an assembly camp for prisoners here, and it is the centre of many working commandos. Attached to Friedrichsfeld. 7th Army Corps.

Duisburg-Meiderich – Attached to Friedrichsfeld.

DÜLMEN – A small town (pop 7,500) with a castle surrounded by estates of the Duke of Croy-Dülmen, the centre of numerous working commandos. There is a large assembly camp placed on high heather ground 5 miles from the town. The barracks are good. 7th Army Corps.
  http://heimatblaetter.heimatverein-duelmen.de/hefte/2-2002/mein_krie gsdienst_1915-1918/index.html
  http://heimatblaetter.heimatverein-duelmen.de/hefte/2-2000/ausgrabu ngen/index.html

Durlach – Baden.

DÜSSELDORF – A centre on the Lower Rhine (pop 380,000) of great industrial importance. A great land port. There is a garrison lazaret newly built on the outskirts of the town in which prisoners are treated. They also work in the town. Attached to Friedrichsfeld. 7th Army Corps.

Duvensee – Lauenburg. Attached to Güstrow.

DYROTZ – 7 miles from Döberitz, near Berlin. Prisoners are housed in newly erected, well-ventilated barracks. There is a recreation hut built by the men themselves out of British funds. Guard Corps.

Ebersdorf – Attached to Chemnitz.

Edemannswich – Post Wöhrden, Schleswig-Holstein. Attached to Güstrow.

Edemissen – Attached to Hameln.

Edewecht – Oldenburg. Z. 209. Attached to Soltau.

Edewechtmoor – Z. 3012. Attached to Soltau.

Ehlerschausen – Bei Otze.

Ehrenbreitstein – Bei Coblenz, Rheinland.

Eichstätt – Bayern.

Eidelstedt – Attached to Güstrow.

Einbeck – Attached to Hameln.

Eisdorf – Bei Halle a/d Saale. Attached to Merseberg.

Eisenach – Weimar.

Eisleben – Saxony.

Elberfeld – Rheinland. Hospital. 7th Army Corps.

Elbing – Attached to Preussisch Holland.

Elbingerode – Bei Blankenburg, a/Harz. Attached to Hameln.

Ellerbek – Kreis Pinneberg. Attached to Soltau.

Ellwangen – Württemberg. (Officers).

Emmerich – Rheinland.

Emmertal – Kirchohsen. Attached to Hameln.

Emsdetten – Attached to Münster I.

Eppendorf – Lazaret III, Hamburg. Attached to Parchim.

ERFURT – Thüringen. Attached to Langensalza. A very ancient town on the Gera (pop 111,500). The prisoners' barracks here are built in the exercise ground in the town. Tented camp until October 1914 when wooden huts were erected. Capacity 15,000. 7th Army Corps.

ERLANGEN – A university town (pop 15,814). Hospital for officers. 3rd Bavarian Army Corps.

Eschede – Hanover. Attached to Hameln.

Eschershausen – Bei Holzminden. Attached to Hameln.

Eschwege – Bei Cassel, Hessen-Nassau.

Essen – Rheinland. Hospital. 26 British POWs reported to be interned at main station in Essen, and living at Bachstrasse 20A (October 1918).

Etelsenmoor – Achim, bei Bremen. Attached to Soltau.

Eupen – Rheinland.

EUTIN – An old town (pop 6,200) on a lake in Holstein. Officers' camp. 9th Army Corps.

www.bg-eutin.de/ausstellung-eutin-1-weltkrieg-ehrenmal/eutin-1914-
1918/1917-offiziersgefangenenlager-in-eutin

Ewald – Buer Resse, Westfalen.

Fallingbostel – Hanover.

Flensburg – Schleswig-Holstein. Hospital. Attached to Güstrow.

Frameries – Bei Mons, Belgium. Hospital.

FRANKFURT A/M (am Main) – Important commercial city (pop 410,000)
on the Main with large Jewish colony. There are several hospitals here in
which British officers have been treated. Reserve Lazaret II and H 65 are
the principal ones. 18th Army Corps.

FRANKFURT A/O (am Oder) – Brandenburg. Pop 68,200. Formerly the
seat of a university (1506–1811). The camp lies on a high sloping plain 4
miles from the town, with lovely views. There is a YMCA hut. Formerly
the site of the Grube Vaterland coal-mining works. Capacity 18,000. 3rd
Army Corps.

Freden a/d Leine – Attached to Hameln.

FREIBURG – A beautifully situated town (pop 80,000) with views of the
surrounding country. The officers' camp is in the old university building
in the town, built around a quadrangle with trees in it. 14th Army Corps.
   The Freiburg Review, 2 typescript and duplicated issues dated 1 and 15
July 1917.
   Also various issues from 1918.

Freistätt – Post Varrell. Attached to Soltau.

Fresenburg – Bei Bad-Odesloe. Attached to Güstrow.

FRIEDBERG – Hessen. Pop 9,500. Once a free imperial city. It is twenty-five
miles north of Frankfurt am Main, within sight of Nauheim. Officer prisoners are quartered in stone barracks completed on outbreak of war.
Situated on extreme outskirts of town. There is a row of little gardens for
the use of the interned, but no trees. 18th Army Corps.
   *The Friedberg and Clausthal Daily Mail Year Book for 1925: The Only Reliable
Handbook for ex-K.G.'s* – Listing of ex-POWs in camp if they wished to
remain in touch, together with current address. Useful for obituaries of
those who have died, and there are some letters updating on situation, and
reporting annual reunion dinner. Also including list of men for whom
addresses are sought – held at Suffolk Record Office in Bury St Edmunds
– as are issues for 1927 and 1928.

Friedrichenhof – Bei Marienfeld, Berlin.

FRIEDRICHSFELD – Sixty miles north of Cologne near Wesel. Capacity 35,000. There is an open space in the centre of the camp for football and tennis; also gardens with flower-beds between the barracks; large vegetable gardens and potato field run by the prisoners. It is the centre of many working commandos, mining and otherwise. It is also a postal station for a large number of prisoners who have never been in the camp itself. 7th Army Corps.

The Optimist – four handwritten and cyclostyled issues between March and May 1916.

http://keswick-at-war.yolasite.com/prisoner-of-war.php

http://members.kingston.net/hfraser/genealogy/macintosh/GeoLawson.htm

Friedrichshall – Attached to Hameln.

Friedrichshausen – Attached to Hameln.

Friedrichstadt – Schleswig-Holstein.

Fuchsberg – Bei Königsberg, Ost Preussen.

Fuhlenhagen – Bei Schwarzenbek, Lauenberg, Schleswig-Holstein.

Fühlsbüttel – Hamburg 7. Hospital. Attached to Parchim.

Furstenau – Attached to Hameln.

FÜRSTENBERG – Mecklenburg-Strelitz. A small town fifty miles north of Berlin. The officer prisoners are quartered in a well-known summer hotel or Erholungsheim, with a good view over the surrounding country and lake, a mile from the town. It has a glass verandah and the grounds are considerable. Walks are permitted. Close to the main road. 70 British officers and 14 orderlies in July 1917. 9th Army Corps.

Furstenfeldbruck – Oberbayern. Hospital.

Gamsen-Kastorf – Hanover. Attached to Soltau.

Gandersheim – Braunschweig. Attached to Hameln.

GARDELEGEN – Altmark. An old town with dilapidated walls (pop 8,500) near Stendal on the line Hanover–Berlin. A large camp, to which prisoners have been sent since September 1914. The centre of many working commandos. 4th Army Corps.

Geestemunde – Prison.

Gelsenkirchen – Bei Essen. Hospital. Attached to Hameln.

Gemünden – Unterfranken. Attached to Hammelburg.

Gera – Reuss, Thüringen. Hospital.

GERMERSHEIM – Pop 6,000. Situated at the confluence of the Gneich and Rhine. The camp is a mile from the town, which contains eleven hospitals. 2nd Bavarian Army Corps.

Getschenkrug – Attached to Friedrichsfeld.

Gettorf – Attached to Güstrow.

Ghent – East Flanders. Hospital.

GIESSEN – Chief town in Upper Hesse, on the Lahn (pop 31,000), the seat of a university. The prisoners' camp stands on a hill a mile and a half above the town flanked on one side by main highway and on the other by pine-woods, surrounded by a high board fence. Barracks are raised two to three feet from the ground. Library, good prisoner of war band and YMCA hut. A great many Canadians concentrated here at one time. American prisoners here. 18th Army Corps.
   Kriegsgefangenen-Lager Giessen (Mannheim: Druckerei Dr Haas, [191–?]) [Illustrated volume].
   www.curme.co.uk/bro1.htm
   www.worcestershireregiment.com/www.worcestershireregiment.com/pow_england.php
   www.bbc.co.uk/schools/worldwarone/survivor/memoir01.shtml

Gilten – Bei Schwarmstedt, Hanover. Z. 3258. Attached to Soltau.

Glashütte – Attached to Güstrow.

GLEIWITZ – Pop 66,900. Situated in a mining and manufacturing district of Silesia. British prisoners sent there after March, 1918. Accommodation in cavalry barracks. 6th Army Corps. Now called Gliwice in Poland.

Gmünd – Württemberg.

Gmünden – Austria-Hungary. Civilian Camp.

GNADENFREI – A Moravian Colony in Silesia, near Neisse. Officers' camp situated in a school for boys belonging to a religious brotherhood. 6th Army Corps.

Goldap – Attached to Heilsberg.

Goldman – Attached to Dülmen.

Golmbach – Attached to Hameln.

Golzern a/d Mulde – Saxony. (Main Camp).

Gorden – Hospital. Attached to Brandenburg.

GÖRLITZ – Schlesien. A busy town (pop 85,800) with extensive cloth and machinery factories on the Neisse. The camp, with a capacity of 14,000, is situated near the town. It is liable to become muddy, and plank walks and roads have been made throughout the enclosure. 5th Army Corps.

Gorries – Bei Schwerin. Attached to Parchim.

Gosloh – Bei Uchte, Hanover. Z. 3034. Attached to Soltau.

GÖTTINGEN – Hanover. Old university town (pop 37,500). The prison camp is situated on the side of a hill on the outskirts of Göttingen. Main Camp. British prisoners sent away from here November, 1916. Library. Classes and lectures held in the camp under Professor Stange of the University. 11th Army Corps.
   The Wooden City: A Journal for British Prisoners of War, complete run from 1 July 1915 to October 1916 – contains a nominal roll and includes lists of men leaving the camp to be exchanged.
   Le Camp de Göttingen, February 1915–January 1917 – French magazine, but IWM bound volume contains the programme (in English, French and German) celebrating the opening of the YMCA hut.

GRAFENWÖHR – In Bavaria. Lazaret on the outskirts of the town near the new military drill ground; also camp for prisoners. Buildings modern with stucco walls and tiled roofs. Bavarian Corps.

Grafteniederung – Post Bohmte. Z. 3009. Attached to Hameln.

Gratz – Merchant Seamen interned here. Austria-Hungary.

GRAUDENZ – A strong fortress town (pop 40,300) on the Polish frontier, picturesquely situated on the right bank of the Vistula. British officers have been sent there since March, 1918. It was used as a prison in the war of 1870. American prisoners here. 17th Army Corps. Now called Grudziadz in Poland.
   The Vistula Daily Bulletin, issues between 29 October and 20 November 1918.
   Also three issues of *The Vistula Weekly Newspaper* from 1918.

Grefrath – Bei Crefeld, Rheinland.

GRIESHEIM – A village ten minutes by rail from Frankfurt a/M. Officers are quartered in school buildings. 18th Army Corps.

Groeppelingen – Attached to Güstrow.

Grossau – Merchant Seamen interned here. Austria-Hungary.

Grossdraxdorf – Endschutz, Saxe-Weimar. Attached to Langensalza.

Grosselsade – Attached to Hameln.

Grossenwedermoor – Post Schneverdingen. Z. 3036. Attached to Soltau.

Grosses Moor – Kreis Hunteburg. Z. 3104. Attached to Soltau.

Gross Hauslingen – Attached to Holzminden.

Gross Lichterfeld – Bei Berlin.

Gross Wusterwitz – Saxony. Attached to Altengrabow.

Gross Zeithen – Bei Berlin.

GUBEN – Pop 387,300. Brandenburg. Pleasantly situated on the Neisse, with extensive cloth and hat factories. As at Krossen, the prison camp is arranged round a central guard tower with barracks radiating from it. It is five miles from the city. 3rd Army Corps.

Gustersen – Bei Dransfeld. Attached to Soltau.

GÜSTROW – A cathedral town in Mecklenburg (pop 17,800) with an old ducal castle. The prison camp is situated in pine-woods three miles from the town. It consists of wooden barracks holding some 25,000 men. The camp carries on its register over 50,000 names, which proves that it is a centre for a great number of working commandos. 9th Army Corps.

GÜTERSLOH – Westfalen. A silk and cotton centre (pop 18,300). The officers' camp consists of brick buildings originally erected for a sanatorium. Situated in pine-wood district on sandy soil. Never before occupied. Large exercise ground, hockey, football and tennis. 7th Army Corps.
The Gütersloh Monthly Magazine: Being Echoes from Exile, January 1916–March 1917 – beautiful hand-made magazine with original artworks and typescript pages. Has listing of camp members occupying positions such as Hon Sec British Ping Pong Club (Captain Keppel) and editor of monthly magazine (Captain Grant-Dalton). October 1916 issue contains nominal roll.
Daily Budget and *The Warren* also produced, but no copies held at IWM.

Hademstorf – Attached to Soltau.

Hagen – Westfalen. Hospital. 7th Army Corps. Attached to Senne.

Hahnoefersand – Attached to Güstrow.

Hainholz – Bei Hanover. Attached to Holzminden.

Haistrup – Schleswig-Holstein.

Hakenmoor – Bremen. Z. 3033. Attached to Soltau.

Halbe – Brandenburg. Main Camp.

Halberstadt – Hospital.

HALLE – On the Saale (pop 180,500), with a university of great repute. It is an industrial place of some importance with manufactures of machinery, sugar and starch. The prison camp for officers is a disused factory in the manufacturing district. Built around three sides of a square. Exercise ground, 100 by 50 yards. Disused in 1917, now once more in use. 4th Army Corps.

Hallein – Salzburg, Austria-Hungary. Civilian Camp.

Halverde – Westfalen. Attached to Münster.

Hamborn – Attached to Friedrichsfeld.

HAMBURG – The second city of Germany (pop 932,000), one of the most important commercial centres in the world. There are two hospitals in which prisoners are treated. Reserve Lazaret 7, a ward of the central prison at Fühlsbüttel, near the city. Reserve Lazaret 3 at the Eppendorfer Krankenhaus. Veedel, a marine lazaret. 9th Army Corps. Hamburg III (Eppendorf). Attached to Parchim. Hamburg VII (Fühlsbüttel).

HAMELN – Pop 22,100. On the Weser near the influx of the Hamel. An old town. The salmon fishing here is important. The prison camp is placed on low ground with wooded hills behind it. It is a mile from Hameln town, and the parent camp of many working camps. It consists of 100 barracks, all of the same type, radiating from a central point. Theatre and YMCA hall. 10th Army Corps.
  Hameln: Tas de Blagues, issues 9, 12,13, 16, 20, 22–32, 34–8 – 6 May 1916–18 November 1916. French handwritten and drawn newsletter, but early issues do feature some English columns (principally sports).

Hamm – Westfalen. Attached to Minden.

HAMMELBURG – Unterfranken. An ancient town in Bavaria, picturesquely placed on a height of 2,500 feet on the right bank of the Saale. There is an assembly camp for British POWs two miles from the town. The camp enclosure is situated on sloping ground on the highest extremity of a large treeless military reservation extending for several miles. American prisoners here. 2nd Bavarian Army Corps.

HAMMERSTEIN – A small town near Neu Stettin in West Prussia. The centre of many working commandos. 17th Army Corps. Now called Czarne, in Poland.

Hammoor – Bargteheide, Schleswig-Holstein. Attached to Güstrow.

Hanau – Hessen-Nassau.

Hanigsen – Bei Burgdorf, Hanover. Attached to Hameln.

HANOVER – Capital of the Prussian province of Hanover (pop 302,000). Headquarters of the 10th Army Corps. Industrial centre for machinery, iron, indiarubber goods, textiles and ledgers. Prisoners are treated at Lazaret 5 in the Royal War Schools, a two-storied building, also at the Garrison Lazaret. There are several working camps here attached to Hameln.

Harburg a/Elbe – Hanover. Attached to Münster.

Haseldorf – Via Utersen. Attached to Parchim.

HAVELBERG – Small town (pop 6,200) with Romanesque cathedral. Near it is placed the camp for civilian prisoners, which consists of hutments surrounded by high wire netting. There are 4,500 of all nationalities there. Prisoners from Ruhleben are occasionally sent to this camp. Nearly 400 British Indians are on the register. 3rd Army Corps.

Heide – Attached to Güstrow.

HEIDELBERG – A university town (pop 56,000) at the confluence of the Neckar and Rhine. The officers are quartered in large new barracks never before occupied, four miles from town. Three tennis courts and small exercise ground. Recreation room and electric light. Billiard table. Practically a transit camp for officers going or hoping to go, to Switzerland. 14th Army Corps.

Heidemühl – Westpreussen.

HEILBRONN – Württemberg. An important commercial and manufacturing place (pop 40,000) charmingly situated on both banks of the Neckar. The camp is attached to Stuttgart.

HEILSBURG – East Prussia. A big camp on the outskirts of the town divided by a chaussee, the camp proper being on one side and the lazaret on the other. Consists of fifty earth huts. Centre of commandos engaged in agriculture and in rebuilding the devastated town of Goldap and other places. 1st Army Corps. Now called Lidzbark Warmiński in Poland.

Helmstedt – Braunschweig. Attached to Hameln.

Helzerade (or Helzerode?) – Bei Weldekappel. Attached to Langensalza.

Hemme – Bei Heide. Attached to Güstrow.

Herberger – Kreis Bersenbruck, Hanover. Attached to Hameln.

Herford – Attached to Senne.

Herne – Attached to Münster.

Herschbach – Hessen-Nassau. Attached to Limburg.

Hervest – Bei Dorsten, Westfalen. Attached to Dülmen.

Herzlake – Attached to Hameln.

HESEPE (see Hameln) – A small village with few inhabitants. Surrounding country flat, wooded and fertile. On the open sandy plain near the village there is a compound of three wooden barracks for officers. American prisoners here. 10th Army Corps.

Hestenmoor – Bei Gamsen, Gifhorn, Hanover. Z. 3010. Attached to Soltau.

HEUBERG – This camp is situated on high ground above the Danube, and was formerly a large exercise ground. It is twenty-five miles from Sigmaringen and 3,000 feet above sea level. Ten blocks each containing ten barracks. 14th Army Corps.

HEUSTADT – A centre of working commandos in East Prussia.

Hildesheim – Hanover. Attached to Soltau.

Hochst.

Hofgeismar – Hessen-Nassau. Hospital.

Hohensalza – Attached to Altdamm.

Hohen-schönhausen – Berlin. Attached to Döberitz.

Hohenzollern Park – Magdeburg, Saxony.

Hoisbüttel – Bei Wohdorf. Attached to Güstrow.

Holebüll – Kreis Apenrade. Attached to Güstrow.

Holhausem Schloss.

Hollenstedt – Attached to Hameln.

Holzkirchen – Bei Munich.

HOLZMINDEN – A town (pop 10,200) containing a modern school of engineering. Up till 1917 this camp was for French civilian prisoners of war, male and female. Since 1917 a British officers' camp has been established here. 10th Army Corps.
  The Occasional Review, no. 1, 28 August 1918.
  http://holzminden-camp.com

Hörde – Bei Dortmund. Attached to Münster II.

Hostrup – Post Satrup. Attached to Parchim.

Höxter – Westfalen. Hospital.

Huckingen – Bei Düsseldorf. Attached to Münster III.

Huddestorf – Attached to Hameln.

Huels – Attached to Münster II.

Hulseberg – Kreis Osterholz, Scharmbeck. Attached to Soltau.

Illman – Post Kautzen, Nieder Oesterreich. Austria-Hungary. Civilian Camp.

INGOLSTADT – A fortified town on the Danube and the scene of previous fighting. The town (pop 19,000) was besieged by Gustavus Adolphus in 1632, and by Moreau in 1800. The camp is situated in a flying field on the edge of the town. It is of the barrack type, with a capacity for 4,000 POWs. There are two hospitals in the town. In the surrounding fortifications, ie, in Fortresses 8, 9 and 10, officers are imprisoned. Prince Karl is the name of the best of these forts, which is situated on a dry part of the hill. 3rd Bavarian Army Corps.

Jarplund – Via Flensburg. Attached to Güstrow.

Jena – Saxe-Weimar. Hospital.

Johannisburg – Hessen-Nassau.

Johannisthal – Stettin, Pomern. Attached to Altdamm.

JÜLICH (see Aix) – A town (pop 6,000) near the Dutch Frontier. Seventeen miles from Aix/Aachen. Many British prisoners have been treated in hospital here. Attached to Limburg. 8th Army Corps.

Kaiserhof – near Prague. Austria-Hungary. Civilian Camp.

Kaiserlautern – Bayern. Hospital. Bavarian Corps.

KALISCH – In West Prussia. A camp for Russian and Roumanian prisoners, to which British prisoners were sent in April, 1918. Now called Kalisz, in Poland.

Kamstigall – Bei Pillau, East Prussia. 500 POWs still there 25 November 1918. Probably now in Russia – Pillau appears to be Baltiysk.

Karlsruhe – see Carlsruhe.

KARLSTEIN – In Lower Austria. A village with a medieval castle, erected in 1348 by the Emperor Charles, standing on a height. An internment station for civilians.

Kastorf – see Gamsen-Kastorf.

Kattenvenne – Westfalen. Attached to Münster.

KATTOWITZ – A thriving industrial town (pop 43,200). Chief seat of the coal trade of Upper Silesia. A camp for Russian and Roumanian prisoners, to which British prisoners were sent in April 1918. Now called Katowice in Poland.

Katzdangen – Attached to Friedrichsfeld.

KATZENAU – A concentration camp near Vienna for civilians of all nationalities.

Kautzen – near Dobersberg. Austria-Hungary. Civilian Camp.

KEMPTEN – Schwaben, Bayern. A free town (pop 14,800) of the Empire until 1803. It is picturesquely placed on the Iller, and consists of two portions – the Altstadt on the river, and the Neustadt on the hill. British prisoners are quartered on the hill. British prisoners are quartered in the hospital here. 13th Army Corps.

Kirchberg (a/d Wild) – Lower Austria. Civilian Camp.

Kirchboitzen.

Kleine Bahn – Lingen Berg, Hanover. Attached to Hameln.

Königsberg – Bayern.

KÖNIGSBRÜCK – Saxony. A camp of wooden hutments situated on sandy soil amidst pine-woods a short distance from the town. Capacity 15,000. 12th Army Corps.

Königsmoor – Kreis Harburg a/Elbe. Z. 3015. Attached to Soltau.

KÖNIGSTEIN – A fortress high above the Elbe near the Saxo-Bohemia Frontier. Beautiful position. Officers. 12th Army Corps.

Koprivnica – Merchant Seamen interned here. Austria-Hungary. Probably now in Croatia.

Koscielez – Attached to Schneidemühl.

Kratze – Attached to Giessen.

Kreis Neustadt – Hanover.

Krems (a/d Donau) – Austria-Hungary. Civilian Camp.

KREUZNACH – A small town on the Saarbrücken–Metz line. The prisoners are in a civilian hospital five or six stories high, holding some 600 wounded. British first heard of here in 1918. 18th Army Corps.

KRONACH (see ROSENBERG)

Kröpelin – Attached to Güstrow.

Kroppleshagen – Bei Hamburg. Attached to Güstrow.

KROSSEN – Also known as Crossen. A town on the Oder above Frankfurt. Near the town is a large camp radiating from a circular space in the centre of which is a large mound surmounted by a tower. Round this mound are placed three field-pieces which would control the camp in case of mutiny. The compounds radiate off from this centre like the spokes of a wheel. There is a YMCA hut here and workshops for bootmaking, etc. The camp is well spoken of. 3rd Army Corps.

LAHR – An industrial town (pop 14,000) three miles from Offenburg. British prisoners were first sent here in 1917. Officers camp.

Laibach – Merchant Seamen interned here. Austria-Hungary.

LAMSDORF – In Silesia. Kreis Falkenberg. A centre for working commandos. 6th Army Corps.

Lamstedt – Neuhaus a/Oste, Hamburg. Attached to Soltau.

LANDAU – A small town (pop 3,200) with large breweries on the right bank of the Isar. The camp is on the outskirts of the town amid views of the Hartz and Vosges Mountains. A wine-growing country. 2nd Bavarian Army Corps.

LANDSBERG – An old town (pop 6,500) in the valley of the Lech. The church contains wonderful stained glass. There is a lazaret here in which prisoners are treated. 1st Bavarian Army Corps.

LANDSHUT – An old-fashioned town (pop 19,000) with wide streets and gabled houses on the Isar. An old castle rises above the town. American prisoners here. Officers' camp. 1st Bavarian Army Corps.

Langelsheim – Attached to Hameln.

Langendreer – Westfalen. Attached to Münster.

Langenhagen – Attached to Hameln.

Langenmoor – Post Edewecht, Oldenburg. Z. 3009. Attached to Soltau.

LANGENSALZA – Thüringen. A busy town (pop 12,600) containing cloth and cotton factories. The camp was opened in 1914, and consists of hutments, each holding 250 men. Capacity 10,000. Centre of numerous working commandos. American prisoners here. 11th Army Corps.

LAUBAN – Town (pop 15,500) with sixteenth century Rathaus, on Silesian Mountain Railway. The centre of many working camps and locomotive works. Attached to Sagan. 5th Army Corps. Now called Luban, in Poland.

Lauenberg – Pommern. Now called Lebork, in Poland.

LECHFELD – The camp is situated in the valley of the Lech one mile from the village. It is a compound of wooden and brick barracks placed on the exercise ground of the Artillery and Flying Corps. Three hours by rail from Munich. Capacity 10,500. 1st Bavarian Army Corps.

Ledeghem – Westfalen. Hospital.

Leese – Bei Stolzenau. Attached to Hameln.

Lehrte – Attached to Hameln.

LEIPZIG – One of the most important commercial towns in Germany (pop 586,700). The centre of the publishing and book trade and the seat of an ancient university. Prisoners are treated in hospitals here.

Lengerich – Ostfriesland. Attached to Münster.

Lethmate – Westfalen.

Leuna – Attached to Merseburg.

Libau – Now Liepaja, in Latvia. One of locations in Courland reprisal.

Lichtenau – Bayern.

Lichtenberg – Bei Berlin.

Lichtenhorst – Neustadt, Hanover. Z. IX. Attached to Soltau.

Liebstadt – Ostpreussen.

LIMBURG – An old cathedral town on the Lahn (pop 10,500) of some importance in the Middle Ages. The prison camp near the town is celebrated as the place in which Irish prisoners were concentrated at Christmas, 1914, for the purpose of recruiting for the Irish Brigade. Now the centre of a number of invalid working camps and hospitals in occupied territory; also the head camp for a certain number of men working in occupied territory. Capacity 12,000. Limestone barracks. American prisoners here. 8th Army Corps.
   www.irishbrigade.eu/camps/limburg.html
   www.dublin-fusiliers.com/Pows/irish-pows-limburg.html

Lindau – Bayern.

Linden – Bei Hanover. Attached to Hameln.

Lingen – Attached to Hameln.

Lippstadt – Westfalen. Attached to Senne.

Lochnits (?) – Attached to Hameln.

Lossen – Schleisien. Now called Łosiów, in Poland.

Lübben – Hospital.

LÜBECK – A busy commercial and industrial city (pop 101,000). A land port fourteen miles from the sea. Exports wine, timber and tar. Working gangs of prisoners employed here at the docks, etc. There is also a reserve lazaret here for prisoners, next to a large German hospital. Attached to Güstrow. 9th Army Corps.

Lucherberg – Kreis Düren, Rheinland.

LUDWIGSBURG – A dull modern town (pop 20,000) and a Württemburg military depot. The large prison camp is two miles from the station on high ground. A good view is obtainable; the air dry and bracing. There are gravel paths, vegetable gardens and flower-beds in the camps. Lazaret. 13th Army Corps.

LUDWIGSHAFEN – A town (pop 70,000) on the opposite bank of the Rhine to Mannheim. Famous for its chemical works. Officers have been quartered here since 1917. Recently abandoned.

Lügumkloster – Schleswig-Holstein. Attached to Parchim.

Lunderborg, – Bei Lunden. Attached to Parchim.

Lundun – Bei Friedrichstadt, Schleswig-Holstein. Attached to Parchim.

Lüneberg – Hanover. Attached to Soltau.

MAGDEBURG – Capital of the Prussian province of Saxony (pop 280,000). Headquarters of the 4th Army Corps. The camp is situated on low ground near the Elbe. Officers are imprisoned in the citadel, an island in the river consisting of the Wagon Haus, railway storehouse and Scharnhorst, the semi-circular part of an old fortress. There is also a lazaret here for men which was formerly a theatre and dance hall.

MAINZ – A fortified cathedral town (pop 110,000) on the Rhine. The barracks are partly new and partly of historic age. They are placed round a large recreation ground situated on a hill in the middle of the town over-looking the valley of the Rhine, and command extensive views. There are sometimes as many as 700 officers here. 18th Army Corps.

The Queue: A Monthly Magazine Published for and by the Officers Temporarily Domiciled in the Citadel, Mainz Germany, July, August–September, October–November 1918 [complete run – contains nominal roll].

Maizieres – Bei Metz, Lorraine. Hospital.

Malmedy – Rheinland. Hospital.

MANNHEIM – A town (pop 200,000) on the right bank of the Rhine, connected by a bridge with Ludwigshafen. The prison camp is situated on sandy soil near a big manoeuvring field two miles from Mannheim. Barracks laid out for 10,000 prisoners. 17,000 POWs there in August 1917, only 87 of whom were British. Wooden huts and other buildings. In February 1917, it was used as a clearing or exchange camp for British POWs going to Switzerland and England. There is a clock-tower in the centre of the camp, also a library and reading hall. Gardening in the open spaces. 14th Army Corps.

Marburg a/Lahn – Hessen, Nassau. Hospital.

Marga Grube – Senftenberg. Attached to Döberitz.

MARIENBURG – A centre for working commandos in East Prussia.

Marke – Bei Berlin.

Markl – Austria-Hungary. Civilian Camp.

Marquard-Satzkorn – Attached to Döberitz.

Mattierzoll – Kreis Wolfenbüttel. Attached to Hameln.

Mecklenburg – Mecklenburg Schwerin. Attached to Güstrow.

Mecklingen – Bei Bremen. Attached to Hameln.

Meiningen – Thüringen. Hospital.

Melk – Austria-Hungary. Civilian Camp.

Memeln – Attached to Hameln.

Menden – Westfalen.

Mengede – Attached to Münster I.

Menin – Belgium. Hospital.

Mergentheim – Württemburg. Hospital.

MERSEBURG – An ancient cathedral town on the Saale (pop 21,000). The prison camp consists of eight compounds of three barracks each, divided by wire. Capacity 25,000. It is placed on the Infantry drill ground a short distance from the town, and is an assembly camp from which men are drafted out to working camps. 4th Army Corps.
   www.kingscollections.org/servingsoldier/index.php?id=711

MERZDORF – Three miles from COTTBUS. Prisoners attempting to escape have been frequently sent to this camp. 3rd Army Corps.

MESCHEDE – Westfalen. An ancient town (pop 3,400) with an early Gothic church. Camp of wooden hutments situated on a hill near railway station just outside the town. Beautifully situated and healthy. Capacity 10,000. American prisoners here. 7th Army Corps.

Meseburg – Kreis Osterburg. Altmark. Attached to Wittenberg.

METZ – Cathedral city, the capital of German Lorraine (pop 68,000) and a first-class fortress. Headquarters of the 16th Army Corps. British officers and men in hospital here (St Clement's).

Meynesburg – Post Blumenthal.

Milesdorf – Bei Hamburg. Attached to Güstrow.

MINDEN – Old cathedral town (pop 26,500) lying on both banks of the Weser, forty miles from Hanover. The camp is three miles from the town and is surrounded by farms. It consists of a big square with six blocks of huts. Capacity 18,000. Many NCOs were concentrated here at one time. 7th Army Corps.

Misburg – Attached to Hameln.

Mitau – Now Jelgava, in Latvia. One of locations in Courland reprisal.

Moers – Westfalen. Attached to Friedrichsfeld.

Mohrungen – Ost Preussen.

Mückenberg – Sachsen. 1 and 3. Attached to Wittenberg.

Mückenberg – Sachsen. 2. Attached to Döberitz.

Müggenberg – Hanover. Attached to Hameln.

Mülheim a/Ruhr – Rheinland. Hospital. Attached to Friedrichsfeld.

MÜNCHEBERG – Between Berlin and Cüstrin. The prison camp, four acres in extent, is in the town and is surrounded on three sides by houses. American prisoners here. 3rd Army Corps.

MÜNDEN – Hanover. A pleasant, old-fashioned little town (pop 11,500) on the banks of the Weser. The prison is a factory building, formerly the Union Oil Works. It is built of brick and is a mile from the town. It has contained as many as 600 officers at a time. New barracks were constructed in 1917. There is also a lazaret here. 11th Army Corps.

MUNICH – The capital of Bavaria (pop 596,000). A large war school in the Mars Platz is used as a hospital, and there is a hospital known as Lazaret B. 1st Bavarian Army Corps.

MÜNSTER (Westfalen) – Capital (pop 91,000) of Westphalia, a cathedral city and the seat of a university and headquarters of the 7th Army Corps. It is on the banks of the Dortmund–Ems Canal. There are four prison camps in the neighbourhood, known as Münster I, II, III and IV. Münster I (Hauspital) is some distance from the city, in open country. The camp is placed on clay soil and is liable to become very muddy. There is a YMCA hut and a large lazaret. Münster II (Rennbahn) is on the racecourse, the grandstand of which is used for administrative purposes, Catholic chapel and theatre. Münster III is a block of brick barracks, built for German troops. Many prisoners are engaged in coal-mining in Camps II and III. Münster IV is said to be reserved for Russian prisoners. Bergkaserne Lazaret.

The Münster Church Times, various issues between February 1917 and March 1918. Originally *The Rennbahn Church Times*, issues between July and December 1916 – and the remit appears to have been enlarged to expand beyond Münster II. The magazine is primarily a religious publication, but has interest beyond this, including some details of arrivals and departures from Rennbahn.

The Rennbahn Review: A Journal for British Prisoners of War, nos. 2 (January 1917), 4 (June 1918) and 5 (October 1918) held at IWM. *Camp III Gazette* is contained inside.

Souvenir of Captivity: August 1917 (featuring empty pages at the back for POWs to sign autographs).

http://pw20c.mcmaster.ca/case-study/letters-german-soldier-first-world-war-otto-hartmann

MUNSTER (Hanover) – Camp near Soltau on the Lüneberger Heide. It has been in use since 1914. 10th Army Corps.

Münsterlager – Hanover. Hospital. Attached to Hameln.

NEISSE – Schlesien. A pleasant town (pop 30,000) with a military academy. The camp is in the centre of the town and consists of barracks and parade ground. The riding ring is used as a chapel. There are also two-storied log huts built on the parade ground. Officers' camp. 6th Army Corps.

Neubeckum – Attached to Senne.

NEUBERG – Small town (pop 2,900) which is a great ironworks centre in Lower Bavaria. Lazaret. Bavarian Corps.

NEUHAMMER – On the Queis. The clearing camp for Upper Silesia. Register contains 100,000 men, many of whom have never been to the parent camp, but go straight to working camps under its administration. 6th Army Corps. Now called Swietoszów, in Poland.

Neuhaus – Bei Paderborn. Hospital. Attached to Senne.

Neuhausen – Attached to Friedrichsfeld.

NEUMÜNSTER – Town (pop 34,700) in Holstein with considerable cloth factories. Prisoners employed in the vicinity. Attached to Güstrow. 9th Army Corps.

NEUNKIRCHEN – Small town on the railway near Saarbrucken. The officers are quartered in the house of Catholic monks. 21st Army Corps.

Neu-rahlstadt – Bei Hamburg.

Neu-ruppin – Brandenburg. Hospital. Attached to Zossen.

Neustadt in Hartz.

Neustadt (see Kreis Neustadt).

Neu-St. Jurgen – Kreis Osterholz. Attached to Hameln.

Neustrelitz.

Neu-Welzow – Brandenburg. Attached to Döberitz.

Niederbartau – Attached to Friedrichsfeld.

Nieder-Bockhorst – Bei Neumünster. Attached to Güstrow.

Nieder-Ochtenhausen – Bei Bremervorde. Attached to Soltau.

Niederschönweide – Berlin. Attached to Müncheberg.

Niederzwehren – Bei Cassel. 11th Army Corps.

Nienburg a/d Weser – Hanover. Attached to Münster.

Nienhagen – Post Dobbertin. Attached to Güstrow.

Norddeich – Attached to Güstrow.

Norden – Ost Friesland, Hanover. Hospital.

Norderstapel – Kreis Schleswig. Attached to Güstrow.

Nord Kampen. – Bei Kirchboitzen. Attached to Soltau.

Nordstemmen – Attached to Hameln.

Nortorf – Kreis Neumünster. Attached to Güstrow.

Nossen – Bei Dresden, Sachsen.

NUREMBERG – Ancient town (pop 130,000) in Bavaria. The large camp is three miles from the town on the side of a hill, and was the old training ground of the Nuremberg Garrison. The barracks form the sides of a quadrangle. There is a reserve Lazaret, in which prisoners are treated in Nuremberg in the grounds of the Artillery Barracks. 3rd Bavarian Army Corps.

Nutschau – Bad Odesloe. Attached to Güstrow.

Ober-Beuna – Attached to Merseburg.

Obercassel – Bei Düsseldorf.

Oberhausen – Bei Essen. Hospital. 7th Army Corps.

Oberhollabrunn – Austria-Hungary. Civilian Camp.

Obertz – Attached to Hameln.

Ohligs – Düsseldorf. Hospital.

OHRDRUF – Thüringen. Camp built on a hill near the permanent practice ground of German troops. Clay soil. Capacity 15,000. Lazaret on hill near barracks. Attached to Langensalza. American prisoners here. 11th Army Corps.

Ohrtermersch – Attached to Hameln.

Oldenburg – Hospital. 10th Army Corps.

Oldesloe – Schleswig-Holstein.

Oldisleben – Weimar. Attached to Langensalza.

Olvite – Attached to Hameln.

Oppeln – Schlesien. Hospital. Now called Opole, in Poland.

Oranienburg – Bei Berlin. Attached to Döberitz.

OSNABRÜCK – Cathedral town (pop 65,000) on the Hase, and the centre of extensive ironworks. The prisoners are quartered in Artillery barracks. Officers Camp. The riding school is used as a concert room and there are tennis-courts in the yard. 10th Army Corps.

Ostenhohen – Schwarmstedt. Attached to Soltau.

Ostenholzer Moor – Kreis Schwarmstedt. Z. 3265. Attached to Soltau.

OSTERODE – Kreis Allenstein, Ostpreussen. Barracks inside enclosure of locomotive works. Under the administration of Preussisch Holland. Prisoners are allowed to attend religious service in town on Sundays. 20th Army Corps. Now called Ostróda, in Poland.

Osterterp – Kreis Apenrade, Schleswig-Holstein. Attached to Güstrow.

Over – Bei Harburg a/d Elbe.

PADERBORN – Ancient cathedral town (pop 29,400). No camp, but British prisoners have been treated in several lazarets, including Bruderhaus, Kaiserhof and St Vincents. Attached to Senne. 7th Army Corps.

PARCHIM – Town (pop 10,600) on the Elbe. The prison camp resembles another Mecklenburg camp – Güstrow. Capacity 25,000. Both Güstrow and Parchim are used as distributing camps. Parchim Camp is built on a former cavalry drill ground, and is situated on sandy soil amidst pine-woods in an enclosure three miles in circumference. It is three miles from the station. At times there are 45,000 men on the register, some of them working in occupied territory. Large library here. 9th Army Corps.

Parnewinkel – Kreis Bremervorde.

Pecheloh – Bei Verzmold. Attached to Minden.

Peine – Attached to Hameln.

PFORZHEIM – Pop 27,200. Centre of large manufactures of gold and silver articles. Officers sent here early in 1918. Situated in school building in Holzgarten Strasse. 14th Army Corps.
    NAM has an unnamed magazine from here dated October 1918.
    www.users.zetnet.co.uk/dms/past/ww1/pforzheim1.html

Pillkallem – Attached to Heilsberg. Now called Dobrowolsk, in Russia.

Pinneburg – Attached to Soltau.

Potsdam – Brandenburg. Hospital.

Pötzdorf – Osterode, Ostpreussen. Attached to Preussisch Holland.

Pressburg (also known as Porsony) – Austria-Hungary. Civilian Camp.

PREUSSISCH HOLLAND – In East Prussia. The camp is situated on a sloping hill. A rail-track divides the main camp from the guards' barrack. It is well planned and well constructed. Capacity 15,000, though at times carrying over 35,000 names on its register. A very severe winter climate. 20th Army Corps. Now called Pasłek, in Poland.

PUCHHEIM – Thirteen miles from Munich. The prisoners' compound was a flying field. Stucco wall now surrounds the camp. Capacity 12,000. 1st Bavarian Army Corps.

Quakenbrück – Kreis Bersenbrück. Attached to Hameln.

QUEDLINBURG – Saxony. Old town (pop 28,000) with walls, towers, moats and interesting timber houses. Noted now for its nurseries and cloth factories. The prison camp is near the railroad two and a half miles from the town. It consists of eight compounds of six barracks each. Capable of accommodating 1,500 men apiece. 4th Army Corps.
    www.camp-de-quedlinburg.fr

RAABS – An internment camp for civilians in Austria.

Radewege – Bei Brielow. Attached to Döberitz.

RASTATT – Town in Baden (pop 14,000). There is a civilian prisoners' camp here, where French women and children are interned. During 1918 it has been used as a military transit camp for numbers of British prisoners, both officers and men. Some of the prisoners are housed in the casemates of the old fortress. American prisoners here. 14th Army Corps.

Ratingen – Rheinland. Attached to Münster.

RATISBON (REGENSBURG) – Old town on the Danube in which there are hospitals in which prisoners are treated. Bavarian Corps.

Ravensburg – Württemberg.

Recklinghausen – Westfalen. Hospital. 7th Army Corps.

Regensburg – Bayern.

Reinsdorf – Bei Wittenberg, Sachsen. Attached to Merseburg.

Rekum – Kreis Blumenthal, Hanover.

Remscheid – Rheinland. Hospital. 7th Army Corps.

Rendsburg – Schleswig-Holstein. Attached to Güstrow.

Rennbahn – see Münster II.

Renzel – Bei Quickborn, Schleswig-Holstein.

Rethemer Moor – Post Rethem. Z. VII. Attached to Soltau.

Rethen a/Leine – Attached to Hameln.

Rheda – Attached to Senne.

Rheinbach – Bei Bonn. Officers Camp.

Rinkerode – Attached to Münster II.

Rochenburg – Attached to Giessen.

Ronnenberg – Kreis Hanover. Attached to Hameln.

ROSENBERG – The fortress of Rosenberg is situated on a hill above the town of Kronach. Officers are concentrated in two wings of this high citadel. Attached to Hameln. 18th Army Corps.

Rosenheim – Bayern.

Rosenthal – Hessen-Nassau. Hospital.

Rostock – Mecklenburg-Schwerin. Hospital.

Rothenditmold – Bei Cassel.

Rothenfeld – Braunschweig.

Rothenuffeln – Westfalen. Attached to Minden.

Rubeland – Bei Blankenburg.

Rudolstadt i/Schwarzburg – Thüringen.

RUHLEBEN – Six miles from Berlin. A civilian camp situated on a race-course, formerly used as a trotting track. Four thousand five hundred civilians were concentrated here in stables and lofts on the racecourse. The number has now been reduced by exchange to 2,500. YMCA hut.

In Ruhleben Camp, 6 June 1915, 27 June 1915, 11 July 1915, August 1915, 15 August 1915, 29 August 1915, 12 September 1915, September 1915, October 1915, Christmas no. 1915 [also supplement to no. 1, and issue dedicated to Ruhleben by-election, July 1915].

The Ruhleben Camp Magazine, March 1916, April 1916, May 1916, August 1916, Christmas 1916, June 1917.

Ruhleben Camp News, nos. 1–3, January–15 February 1915.

Ruhleben Daily News, 3 April 1917, 7 July 1917, 8–16 November 1918.

Prisoners' Pie, 1916 (New Year issue).

L'Eco: Foglio Istruttivo Settimanale, incomplete run from 1916–1918.

Messagero: Foglio Istruttivo Settimanale, incomplete run of 1916 issues.

La Vie Française: de Ruhleben, vol. 1, nos. 1–3, April–July 1916.

http://ruhleben.tripod.com

Ruhlsdorf – Bei Teltow, Berlin. Attached to Müncheberg.

Rühme – Braunschweig. Attached to Hameln.

Saal – Pommern.

SAARBRÜCKEN – Officers' camp at a railway junction near Metz. The prisoners are housed in a well-built school building. Lazaret. 21st Army Corps.

SAARLOUIS – Officers' camp on the railway-line near Saarbrücken. 21st Army Corps.

Sachsenburg – Bei Schwerin.

SAGAN – Schlesien. A busy little town on the Bober (pop 15,100). The prison camp is of the usual barrack type, built of wood on stone foundations. Capacity 6,000. Five miles from the town on a flat, sandy plain surrounded by forests. 5th Army Corps. Now called Zagan, in Poland.

Salzdetfurt – Kreis Marienburg. Attached to Hameln.

Salzerbad – Merchant Seamen interned here. Austria-Hungary.

Salzerhelden – Attached to Hameln.

SALZWEDEL – Pop 14,400. This large camp of wooden huts is thirty-five miles from Stendal. 10th Army Corps.

Sammallager – Mons-en-Baroenil.

Sangerhausen – Sachsen. Hospital.

Sarstedt – Kreis Hildesheim, Hanover. Attached to Hameln.

Scharnhorst – Bei Dortmund. Attached to Münster.

Schenefeld – Attached to Parchim.

Schiffdorf – Bei Geestemunde, bei Bremen. Attached to Parchim.

Schoningen – Attached to Hameln.

SCHNEIDEMUEHL – Posen. Pop 26,100. An important railway junction. The camp is placed three miles from the city on higher ground. It is situated on sandy soil surrounded by woods. Capacity 40,000–50,000. The centre of many working camps. Barracks are of the earth variety. 2nd Army Corps. Now called Piła, in Poland.
The British Times: The Official Organ of The British Help Committee, issues 1–9, 1 February–1 October 1918. Very informative about the work of a British Help Committee.

Schönebeck – Bei Magdeburg.

Schöneberg – Bei Berlin. Attached to Müncheberg.

Schönewald – Brandenburg.

Schöningen – Helmstedt. Attached to Hameln.

Schuhwiese – Bei Reinfeld. Attached to Güstrow.

Schvelsen – Bei Hamburg. Attached to Güstrow.

Schwaneberger Moor – Attached to Soltau.

SCHWARMSTEDT – Officers' camp near Hanover. Wooden huts, and originally a camp for privates, before housing Roumanian officers. 408 officers moved here from Crefeld in May 1917 (because of that camp's proximity to border and threat of escape). Now abandoned. 10th Army Corps.

Schwegermoor – Harburg, Hanover.

Schweicheln – Bei Herford. Attached to Minden.

SCHWEIDNITZ – Schlesien. Prettily situated town (pop 31,300) on the Weistritz. It was used as a place of internment in 1870. The building in which the officers are interned was once a lazaret and consists of usual brick barracks. A church is in the garden of about an acre. Half a mile from station and two hours by train from Breslau. 6th Army Corps. Now called Swidnica, in Poland.

The Barb Magazine, vol. 1, no. 1 [dated October 1918 although material encompasses the Armistice]. Dating is odd, as there are two issues of *The Barb Magazine* produced at Schweidnitz following on from its production at Trier – IWM has July 1918 issue but not May 1918.

www.bbc.co.uk/northernireland/yourplaceandmine/topics/war/A7505 48.shtml

Schweinau – Bei Nürnberg.

Schwelm – Westfalen. Hospital. Attached to Münster.

Seddin – Attached to Döberitz.

Seesen – Attached to Hameln.

Segeberg – Attached to Güstrow.

Semsdorf – Bad Odesloe, Schleswig.

Senftenberg – Brandenburg. Attached to Zossen.

SENNELAGER (Senne I, II and III) – Large camp near Paderborn, Westphalia, fifty miles south west of Hanover. Situated on open sandy country of heather, pine and bogland. Used as a summer training camp for soldiers. The camp is divided into three separate portions. There is a YMCA hut at Senne III. At one time there was a fourth camp reserved for civilians where English fishermen were interned. Near Lippspringe, a health resort six miles from Senne, a shooting gallery and assembly hall have been turned into sanatorium for prisoners. 7th Army Corps.

www.wfa-dorsetswilts.org.uk/articles/sennelager.htm

Sickingmühl – Westfalen. Attached to Dülmen.

Siegburg – Bei Bonn.

Siegen – Westfalen. Attached to Giessen.

Sielow – Bei Cottbus. Main Camp.

SKALMIERSCHÜTZ – Posen. Five miles from Ostrovo on the Polish Frontier. It is a very large camp for Russians and Roumanians, to which British prisoners were sent in March 1918. American prisoners here. 5th Army Corps. Now called Skalmierzyce, in Poland.

Soest – Westfalen. Attached to Senne.

SOLTAU – Hanover. Little town (pop 5,200) on the Stendal–Bremen line. Centre for working commandos and is said to accommodate 30,000 men, but sometimes it carries 50,000 on its register. 10th Army Corps.

Sommerfeld – Bei Berlin.

Sondershausen – Schwarzburg, Thüringen.

SPANDAU – Town (pop 85,000) at the confluence of the Spree and the Havel, close to Berlin. Prisoners are treated in Reserve Lazaret II. Men work in the chemical factory here. 3rd Army Corps.

Springhirsch – Schleswig-Holstein. 1464 POWs in 1918.

SPROTTAU – Schlesien. The prison camp is three miles from the station, on a sandy plain. It is a working-camp centre. Close by is a lazaret of forty barracks for tubercular prisoners. 5th Army Corps. Now called Szprotawa, in Poland.
   Kriegsgefangenen-Lager Sprottau: Teil 2 – postcard book with twenty-eight picture postcards.

Stade – Hanover.

Staden – Hessen.

Stadtvogtei – Dircksenstrasse, Berlin. Prison.

Stalluponen – Ostpreussen. Attached to Heilsberg. Now called Nesterov, in Russia.

Stamin – Ostpreussen. Attached to Preussisch Holland.

Stampfmühle – Bei Rendsburg. Attached to Parchim.

STARGARD – Pommern. Old town (pop 27,500) surrounded by a well-preserved wall with handsome towers and gateway. British prisoners are treated in the hospitals here. There is also a camp with basket-weaving workshops, etc. Attached to Altdamm. 2nd Army Corps. Now called Stargard Szczecinski, in Poland.

Staumuhle – Westfalen. Attached to Senne II.

Steinheim – Attached to Senne.

Steinhorst – Hanover. Z. 3035. Attached to Soltau.

Steinwärder – Bei Hamburg. Attached to Güstrow.

STENDAL – Saxony. Cathedral town (pop 27,200) on the Uchte, founded in the twelfth century. The prison camp is one mile north east of the city and is situated on sandy soil. Capacity 15,000. The centre of a number of working camps. 4th Army Corps.

Sterkrade – Rheinland. Attached to Münster.

STETTIN – Capital of Pomerania (pop 236,000). Headquarters of the 2nd Corps. Commercial and manufacturing town of great importance on the banks of the Oder. Officers and men treated in sanatorium. Prisoners employed in the town. Attached to Altdamm. Now called Szczecin, in Poland.

Steyerberg – Bei Stolzenau. Attached to Hameln.

Stiderdorf – Bei Peine. Attached to Hameln.

STRALKOWO (also Stralkovo) – Attached to Friedrichsfeld. Town on the Polish Frontier. Kreis Kosten, Posen. The prison camp is three miles from station. Russians and Romanians have been here for some time, but British prisoners were only sent here in March 1918. 5th Army Corps. Now called Strzalkowo, in Poland.

STRALSUND – Town (pop 34,000) lies opposite the island of Rügen, where a number of prisoners are employed. Prisoners treated in the hospital here. 2nd Army Corps.

A Prisoners-of-War Library: [Being the History of the British Officers' Library, Stralsund, Germany] by Luxmoore Newcombe and John H E Winston (Aberdeen: University Press, 1919) [fifteen-page article].

STRASSBURG – Capital of Alsace (pop 170,000). Headquarters of the 15th Army Corps and the seat of a university, and a strongly fortified town. It contains tobacco factories, breweries, engine works, foundries and tanneries. Officer prisoners have been sent here.

Strelitz – Mecklenburg-Strelitz. Attached to Güstrow.

Strodthagen – Kreis Einbeck, Post Edmissen. Attached to Soltau.

STRÖHEN – Kreis Sulingen. Officers' camp now abandoned. 430 officers in July 1917. Wooden huts. Attached to Hameln. 10th Army Corps.

Camp magazine (shared with Bad Colberg): *The Morning Walk*, souvenir issue held at IWM.

Ströhen Nord – Hanover. Attached to Hameln.

Ströker Moor – Kreis Sulingen, Hanover. Attached to Hameln.

STUTTGART – Capital of Wurtemburg (pop 286,000). One camp in the city in an abandoned factory building. Another camp is in a disused factory on a slope overlooking the town, three miles from Stuttgart. 13th Army Corps.

Süd Edewechtermoor – Oldenburg. Attached to Soltau.

Suderhastedt – Schleswig-Holstein. Attached to Güstrow.

Süderstapel – Attached to Güstrow.

Süder-Zollhaus – Post Janneby, Schleswig-Holstein. Attached to Güstrow.

Sulingen – Bei Diepholz, Hanover. Attached to Soltau.

Sydow – Attached to Merseburg.

Tangstedt – Bei Hamburg. Attached to Güstrow.

Tauberbischofsheim – Baden.

Tegel – Bei Berlin. Attached to Döberitz.
FO 383/271 at TNA – contains inspection report on Borsig Factory at Tegel, and names of fifty-three British POWs working there in August 1917.

Teltow – Bei Berlin. Attached to Müncheberg.

Teufelsmoor – Bei Bremen, Hanover. Attached to Hameln.

Tingleff – Schleswig-Holstein. Attached to Güstrow.

THORN – Old fortified town (pop 47,000) on the Vistula. Prisoners are treated in the hospitals here. 2nd Army Corps. Now called Torun, in Poland.

Tollmingkehmen – Attached to Heilsberg.

Tonnenheide – Kreis Lübbecke, Westfalen. Attached to Minden.

Tönningstedt – Schleswig-Holstein. Attached to Güstrow.

TORGAU – Town (pop 15,000) on the Elbe. Officers are interned in the Brückenkopf Barracks and in Fort Zinna. The barracks are old and built close to the river. 4th Army Corps.

Tostedt – Kreis Harburg, Hanover. Attached to Münster.

Trakehnen – Attached to Heilsberg.

TREVES (or TRIER) – Said to be the oldest town (pop 45,000) in Germany. It has a famous cathedral, and the walls of the town are of red sandstone, and it is placed amongst vine-clad hills. Officer prisoners are treated in the Reserve Lazaret IV (Horn Kaserne). 8th Army Corps.
The Barb, 17 November 1917 (first issue) to 9 March 1918 (which carries announcement that all British POWs from Trier will be moving to either Holzminden or Schweidnitz). IWM has one issue from Schweidnitz dated 30 July 1918. Issue 12 is not held (issued at Schweidnitz on 27 May 1918). Includes directory of room numbers with officers in each room, caricatures,

and Christmas issue has photograph on the front, with list of names on front and continued inside.

Tübingen – Württemberg. Hospital.

Tüblanken – Attached to Heilsberg.

TUCHEL – Kreis Konitz. Camp in West Prussia for Russians and Romanians, to which British prisoners were sent in 1918. Hospital. American prisoners here. 7th Army Corps. Now called Tuchola, in Poland.

Tuttlingen – Württemberg. Hospital.

Uchter Moor – Post Uchte, Hanover. Z. 3010. Attached to Hameln.

Uelzen – Hanover. Attached to Soltau.

ULM – Old city on the Danube (pop 56,000). The prison camp is on the outskirts of the town and is of the usual barrack type. There is a garrison hospital on a hill overlooking the town, with a spacious garden.

Urach Moor – Württemberg.

Utersen – Bei Hamburg. Attached to Güstrow.

Vaale – Schleswig-Holstein.

Vacz – Austria-Hungary. Civilian Camp.

Vahle – Attached to Hameln.

Vahrenrode – Bei Spelle, Kreis Lingen, Oldenburg. Attached to Hameln.

Varel – Hanover. Attached to Soltau.

Vehnemoor – Oldenburg. Z. 6. Attached to Soltau.

Verden – Hanover. Hospital. 10th Army Corps. Attached to Hameln.

Verzmold – Attached to Minden.

VILLINGEN – An officers' camp in the Black Forest 2,500 ft above sea level, consisting of disused barracks built around a quadrangle. American prisoners here. 14th Army Corps.

Vintermoor – Via Recke, Westfalen. Attached to Hameln.

Vöhrenbach – Officers' camp in the Black Forest, 3,000 ft above sea level. 250 officers in March and April 1916, only seven of whom were British. In April 1916 British officers sent away and it became reprisal camp for French officers. Some British officers sent there in December 1916 pending transfer to Switzerland. 14th Army Corps.

Volmarstein – Bei Essen. Attached to Münster.

Volpke – Kreis Neuhaldensleben, Magdeburg. Attached to Soltau.

Vördenermoor – Bei Osnabrück, Hanover. Attached to Soltau.

Wagenfelder Moor – Kreis Sulingen. Attached to Soltau.

WAHMBECK (a/d Weser) – Port Bodenfelde, Hanover. A summer resort and an old-fashioned hotel for people of moderate means. The officers, who are mostly of the Merchant Service, are allowed to swim in the river. 10th Army Corps.

WAHN – Situated on rising ground twenty miles south east of Cologne. The camp, which was formerly the Wahner Heide Artillery practice camp, lies in open country and forms a sort of loosely jointed village. It carries 35,000 men on its register and was formerly a parent camp for working camps in the district. Barracks are set aside for prisoners who have tried to cross the frontier. 8th Army Corps.
    www.kopfwelten.org/kp/begegnung/wahn/#kopf

Wanheim – Attached to Friedrichsfeld.

Wansleben – Attached to Merseburg.

Warsaw (Main Camp).

Wasbek – Schleswig-Holstein. Attached to Parchim.

Watersdorf – Attached to Güstrow.

Wattenscheid – Bei Bochum, Westfalen.

Wedel – Bei Hamburg. Attached to Güstrow.

Wehlheiden – Attached to Cassel.

Weidenberstel – Attached to Güstrow.

WEILBURG – On the Lahn. Hessen. A little town (pop 3,700) with a castle situated on a rocky eminence. The officers' camp consists of a three-storied school-house in pretty surroundings. Garden plots are allotted to prisoners. Lawn-tennis courts. 18th Army Corps.

Weimar – Saxe-Weimar. Hospital.

WEINGARTEN – Forty-two kilometres from Heidelberg on the way to Karlsruhe. Officers' camp. 14th Army Corps.

Weissenborn – Attached to Langensalza.

Werben – Sachsen. Attached to Gardelegen.

WERL – Westfalen. Franciscan monastery built in 1913, an acre of ground in front and a cloister garden behind for RC officers. 7th Army Corps.

Werlte – Attached to Hameln.

Wermelskirchen.

WESEL – Fortress town (pop 22,500) situated at the confluence of the Rhine and Lippe. There is a prison used for officers here and two hospitals. 7th Army Corps.
www.kdg-wesel.de/index.php?id=1292

Wesselburen – Bei Heide. Attached to Güstrow.

Westerholt – Attached to Friedrichsfeld.

Westerloh – Westfalen.

Wetzlar – Bei Giessen, Hessen.

Wiedenbruck – Westfalen. Attached to Senne.

Wiesmoor – Ost Friesland, Hanover. Attached to Hameln.

Wietze – Steinforde. Attached to Hameln.

Wildemann – Bei Clausthal. Officers Camp. 10th Army Corps.

Wilhelmsburg – Austria-Hungary. Civilian Camp.

Windau – Russian Courland. Now Ventspils in Latvia. June 1916 – 335 British POWs sent to do harvesting work at Hofzumberge, Neu-Sessau, Klein Feldhpf [sic], Mosbuth, Griewen, Bludsen, Usingen, Klein-Platon, Klein-Berken, Dreimann, Wolfshof, Nauditten, Meiten and Aken. Germans claimed these were all more than 30km from firing line.

Winnert – Attached to Güstrow.

Wipperfurth – Bei Wahn.

Witten – Hospital. 7th Army Corps.

WITTENBERG – Town (pop 22,700) with a Luther Museum, fifty-nine miles south west of Berlin, on the Elbe. The prison camp is situated on a sandy plain ten and a half acres in extent, at a place called Klein Wittenberg, 2 miles from the city. It consists of eight sections or compounds. Capacity 13,000. 4th Army Corps.

Wolfenbüttel – Braunschweig.

Worms a/d Rhein – Hessen.

Wünsdorf – Bei Zossen.

WÜRZBURG – Cathedral town (pop 85,000) on the Main. The prison camp is of the usual barrack type, outside the town on the summit of a high hill.

In the town the Schiller Schule is requisitioned for a hospital. The citadel here is used as an officers' camp. 2nd Bavarian Army Corps.

Zarpen – Bei Lübeck, Schleswig-Holstein.

Zeithain – Sachsen.

ZERBST – Anhalt. An old town (pop 20,000) surrounded by walls, with a large Schloss and handsome gabled houses. The prison camp lies two miles north of the city at a moderate elevation. It carries 100,000 on its register, the majority of whom are engaged in industry and agriculture in the neighbourhood. The capacity of the prisoners' barracks on the Infantry drill ground is estimated at 15,000. 4th Army Corps.

Zipsendorf – Attached to Merseburg.

ZITTAU – A manufacturing town (pop 37,100). One of the principal cotton-spinning places in Saxony.

Zorndorf – Fort. Officers Camp. Attached to Cüstrin.

ZOSSEN – Twenty miles south of Berlin, with which it is connected by a military railway running parallel to the ordinary line. It is generally used as a camp for non-European prisoners. Guard Corps.
    www.irishbrigade.eu/camps/zossen.html

Zschornewitz – Bei Bitterfeld, Sachsen.

ZWEIBRÜCKEN – A small town (pop 13,700) twenty-two miles from Saarbrücken, to which British officers were first sent in 1916. 21st Army Corps.

ZWICKAU – Sachsen. Wood barracks. Capacity 10,000. Several acres of vegetable gardens inside the confines of the camp. Lazaret. 19th Army Corps.

Appendix 7

LIST OF TURKISH CAMPS

Based on BRC&OSJ, *List of Internment Camps for British Prisoners of War in Enemy Countries* (January 1918) and drawing on other sources. Numbers of Indian Army POWs taken from the India Office file F120/21: 'General Correspondence: Kut Prisoners of War'. Numbers of POWs in November 1918 taken from TNA FO 383/459 (British, Australian and New Zealand other ranks all included in term British).

Adana (also known as Andana?) – Hospital.

Ada Pazar (aka Ada-Bazar, Ade Bazar) (Men) – Opened 1917 or 1918. 9 British and 1 Indian POW – November 1918.

Afion-Kara-Hissar (aka Afion-Karah-Hissar, Afion Karahissar, Afium Kara Hissar, Efion Kara Hissar, Afieu Kara Hissal) – Located in Anatolia. Afion means 'opium' while Kara Hissar means 'black castle', referring to the ruins of the Byzantine castle which overlook the town. (Officers and Men, including 766 Indian Army (IA) in summer 1918). 105 British, 22 Australian, 1 New Zealand officer POWs – November 1918. 395 British and 770 Indian POWs – November 1918.

Officers accommodated in Upper Camp in former Armenian houses and Lower Camp near Constantinople Station. Men living in Armenian Church and surrounding buildings.

Railway hub where line from Constantinople united with branch from Smyrna and Konia and the East.

Hospital at Aleppo.

Magazine produced in UK: *The Afion Kara Hissar Gazette* – not held by IWM. Copies of this for 8 and 13 May 1916 at TNA in FO 383/227 – extracts from letters home, put together by Olive Pass. Sent to Sir Horace Rumbold because POWs were moved and confined to a church (as reprisal for the escape of three POWs), and representations made for more suitable accommodation and adequate access to fresh air and exercise.

Airan (Secteur Taurus Sud) (IA).

Aleppo.

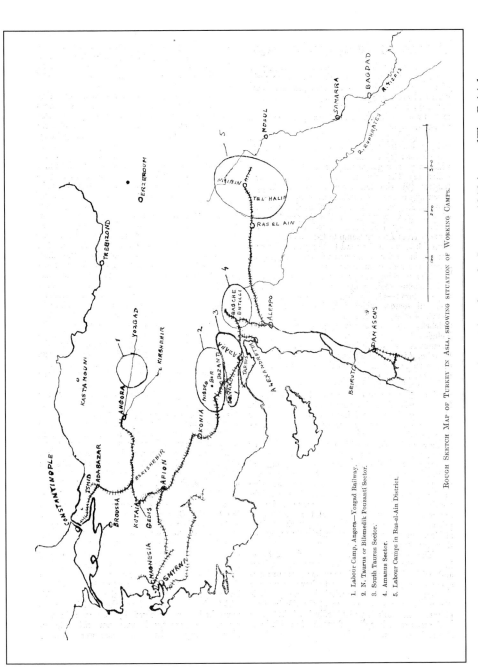

ROUGH SKETCH MAP OF TURKEY IN ASIA, SHOWING SITUATION OF WORKING CAMPS.

1. Labour Camp, Angora—Yozgad Railway.
2. N. Taurus or Bilemedik Pouzanti Sector.
3. South Taurus Sector.
4. Amanus Sector.
5. Labour Camps in Ras-el-Ain District.

Map showing the main POW camps and sectors in Turkey. Taken from the January 1918 issue of The British Prisoner of War (with kind permission of the British Red Cross Museum and Archives).

Amanus – 3 British officer POWs – November 1918.

Angora (aka Ancyra) (Officers and Men including IA) – Men often sent to work on Angora-Erzerum Light Railway. 238 British and 26 Indian POWs – November 1918.

Magazine (produced in UK for relatives of Royal Gloucestershire Hussars prisoners): *The Angora News* – not held by IWM.

Baghtché (aka Bagtche) (286 IA – Summer 1918) – Amanus Sector – 134 British and 2134 Indian POWs – November 1918. Amanus (5th Section: 228 IA, 14th Section: 471 IA – Summer 1918), Airan (292 IA – Summer 1918), Entelli (aka Entilli) (868 IA – Summer 1918), Sheher Dere, Tasch Durmas, Yarbaschi (aka Yarbachi) (202 IA – Summer 1918) (all working camps on the Baghdad Railway).

Belemedik (aka Bilémèdik and Kulu Maghara?) – In Taurus Mountains. 4 British officer POWs – November 1918.

Beychelin (aka Bey Shehir?) – Civilian camp – 15 in November 1918.

Binedjik (Euphrates) – 21 POWs – November 1918.

Bor by Nigdé (aka Bora, Bore) (IA) – Convalescent camp. 2 British officer POWs – November 1918. 118 British and 14 Indian POWs – November 1918.

Boudjak – South Taurus Sector – 5 British and 817 Indian POWs – November 1918. Adana, Boudjak (137 IA – Summer 1918), Dorak (aka Kelebek-Dorak?) (265 IA – Summer 1918) (all working camps on the Baghdad Railway). Hospital at Tarsus.

Bozanti (aka Pozanti, Pousanti, Pouzanti, Bozantika?) (IA) – North Taurus Sector – Apparently administered by Germans, it also functioned as Punishment camp. 868 British and 138 Indian POWs – November 1918. Bilémèdik (aka Belemedik, Kulu Maghara?) (113 IA – Summer 1918), Gelebek (aka Kelebek?) (IA), Hadji-Kiri (aka Adji Kiri, Ahji Keri, Hadjikéri, Hadjihiri), Kouchdjoula (aka Kouch Joular, Koutchdgoular, Koutchd Goular), Tasch Durmas (all working camps on Baghdad Railway).

Broussa (aka Brusa, Brousse) – Senior Officers Camp. 29 British and 1 New Zealand officer POWs – November 1918.

Magazine produced by relatives in UK: *Yozgad, Broussa and Constantinople Magazine* – contains nominal rolls of officers in the three camps, and extracts from letters home. Three issues held at IWM in Department of Documents (Major General Sir Ernest Walker papers – 76/128/1).

Also camp for men (419 IA – Summer 1918). 24 British and 424 Indian POWs – November 1918.

Changri (aka Chiangri, Chiangeri, Kiangheri, Khiangeri, Khiangherai, Chungri, Kengheri, Kangeri) (Officers and Men). Ceased use by the summer of 1918.

From Kastamuni to Kedos: Being a Record of Experiences of Prisoners of War in Turkey, 1916–1918, written by many hands and edited by C L Woolley, Capt RFA (Oxford: Blackwell, 1921) – contains nominal roll of officers and orderlies.

Constantinople – now Istanbul.

Camps at Pzamatia (aka Psamatia) – Established in 1917. Camp set up in a disused Armenian school and church in a suburb of Angora. San Stephano (aka Bayuk Tschekmedje San Stefano) – 134 British POWs – November 1918. Saraskerat – 17 British officer POWs – November 1918. 86 British and 51 Indian POWs – November 1918.

Hospitals at Zepion, Gaziler, Haida Pasha, Harbié, Gulkané, Maltepe, Mèteb-Arbeg, Zeyne-Kiamil.

Magazine produced by relatives in UK: *Yozgad, Broussa and Constantinople Magazine* – contains nominal rolls of officers in the three camps, and extracts from letters home. Three issues held at IWM in Department of Documents (Major General Sir Ernest Walker papers – 76/128/1).

Damascus

Hospitals at Bab Toulma, Hospital Chirurgical, Hamadiah.

Daridja [aka Gebizel?] – Cement work centre. Opened 1917 or 1918. 54 British and 49 Indian POWs – November 1918.

Denizli (aka Denizle, Karack Salamia?) – 50 IA – Summer 1918. 50 Indian POWs – November 1918.

Derbezie, near Ras-el-Ain.

Dorak – 1 British officer POW – November 1918.

Esherie (aka Eskéri).

Eski-Chehir (aka Eski-Shehir, Eski Chekir) – 102 Indian POWs here. Closed 1918 and POWs transferred to Broussa or Afion Kara Hissar.

Eski-Hissar – Cement work centre. Opened 1917 or 1918. 26 British and 17 Indian POWs – November 1918.

Ismidt (aka Ismid) – Opened 1917 or 1918. 5 British POWs – November 1918.

Kara-Pinar (IA).

Kastamuni (aka Kustamouni, Kastamouni, Castamouni, Kastamoni, Castamowni, Castamuni) – Nearest railway station at Ushak – about twelve hours journey. Opened following the Fall of Kut and ceased use by the summer of 1918.

Magazine produced in UK: *The Kastamuni Chronicle* (also *The Chronicle?*) IWM has one issue of *The 'Kronical': Kastamuni Kronical,* dated January 1918 – handwritten publication with lists of men and drawing on information received from letters and postcards from men in camps. Two civilians there in November 1918.

Magazines: *Mastik, Smoke* and *Ekmek* (produced by the orderlies probably in single issues, and unlikely to have survived).

From Kastamuni to Kedos: Being a Record of Experiences of Prisoners of War in Turkey, 1916–1918, written by many hands and edited by C L Woolley, Capt RFA (Oxford: Blackwell, 1921) – contains nominal roll of officers and orderlies.

Kedos (aka Gedis, Gediz or Ghedos) (IA) 101 British and 2 Australian officer POWs – November 1918.

Lived in three barracks on outskirts and private houses in the town.

Magazine produced in UK: *The Kedos Gazette* – not held by IWM.

From Kastamuni to Kedos: Being a Record of Experiences of Prisoners of War in Turkey, 1916–1918, written by many hands and edited by C L Woolley, Capt RFA (Oxford: Blackwell, 1921) – contains nominal roll of officers and orderlies.

Kedos (aka Koulah?) – 58 British and 2 Indian POWs – November 1918.

Kirchehir (aka Kirshehir).

Kir-Hut.

Konia – 237 IA – Summer 1918. 237 Indians – November 1918. Accommodation located in three hotels in the town.

Kutahya.

Magnesia, near Smyrna (Civilians and Merchant Marine) – 64 civilians – November 1918.

Crews of SS *Assiout* and SS *City of Khios.* Located in Greek Protestant school with large yard, good quality housing and high walls.

Mosul (aka Mossoul) – 237 IA – Summer 1918. 87 Indian POWs – November 1918.

Nevshehr (aka Nevchehir) (Civilian) – 12 civilians – November 1918.
Hospitals at Petit Arada and Djir-Djib-el-Kebir.

Noussaybin (aka Nissibin, Nisibin, Nicebin) – 71 IA – Summer 1918. 308 British and 70 Indian POWs in district in November 1918.

Oulache, near Sires.

Ras-el-Ain (aka Ras-el-Ein, Rasel Ein) – 4,032 IA – Summer 1918. 2 British officer POWs – November 1918. 39 British and 3979 Indian POWs – November 1918.

Scheker-Dere – reference to 8th Section in connection with IA. 214 IA – Summer 1918 Probably under Amanus sector on Baghdad Railway.

Serdji-Han (aka Serdjihan) – 20 British POWs – November 1918.
    Situated near Nisibin, between Ras-el-Ain and Mousoul.

Sivas (aka Sivan, Sebasteia) (IA).

Smyrna – 1 civilian – November 1918.

Tel Halif (aka Tel-Helif) near Ras-el-Ain.

Ulu-Kishla, near Bor by Nigdé.

Yozgad (aka Yuzgad, Yozgat) – Angora nearest railway station – about five days' journey away. Opened following the Fall of Kut (IA). 94 British and 1 Australian officer POWs – November 1918. 64 British and 3 Indian POWs – November 1918.

    Magazine produced by relatives in UK: *Yozgad, Broussa and Constantinople Magazine* – contains nominal rolls of officers in the three camps, and extracts from letters home. Three issues held at IWM in Department of Documents (Major General Sir Ernest Walker papers – 76/128/1).

Appendix 8

CAMPS AND PLACES OF INTERNMENT IN THE UNITED KINGDOM

Information gleaned from *List of Places of Internment* produced by the Prisoners of War Information Bureau, dated January 1919 and other sources. The name of the place is followed by the official abbreviation, and the postal address or county.

Abbess Roding (Agric Group attached to Chipping Ongar Agric Depot under Pattishall). Pa (Ch O) (Ao).
   The Old Rectory, Abbess Roding, Ongar, Essex.

Abbeydore (Agric Group attached to Leominster Agric Depot under Shrewsbury). Shrw (Lmr) (Ae).
   42, West Street, Leominster, Hereford.

Abergavenny (Agric Group attached to Leominster Agric Depot under Shrewsbury). Shrw (Lmr) (Aa).
   The Garage, Abergavenny, Monmouth.

Aberglasney (Agric Group attached to Brecon Agric Depot under Frongoch). Fg (Bre) (Ag).
   Aberglasney, Carmarthen, S Wales.

Aber Llowyn House (Agric Group attached to Brecon Agric Depot under Frongoch). Fg (Bre) (Ab).
   Aber Llowyn House, Llanfarian, Cardigan.

Addington Park Hospital. APH.
   Addington Park War Hospital, Croydon, Surrey.

Addlestone (Working Camp under Feltham). Fe (Adl). [Surrey.]

Aldborough (Agric Group attached to King's Lynn Agric Depot under Pattishall). Pa (KL) (Alh).
   Aldborough, Norwich, Norfolk.

Aldershot (*see under* Cambridge Hosp and Connaught Hosp).

Aldershot Isolation Hospital. AIH.

Alexandra Palace. Ax P.
Alexandra Palace, Wood Green, London N 22.

Alton (Working Camp under Dorchester). Dor (Alt). [Hants.]

Ambergate (Working Camp under Brocton). Bro (Am).
Crich Matlock, Ambergate, Derby.

Ampthill (Working Camp under Pattishall). Pa (Amp). [Beds.]

Arrington (Working Camp under Pattishall). Pa (Ar).
Kardwick Arms, Arrington, Cambridge.

Ashbourne (Agric Depot under Brocton). Bro (Ash). [Derby.]

Ashby-de-la-Zouch (Agric Group attached to Loughborough Agric Depot under Brocton). Bro (Lo) (As).
Queen's Head Hotel, Ashby-de-la-Zouch, Leicester.

Ashwell (Working Camp under Pattishall). Pa (Asw). [Herts.]

Atherstone (Working Camp under Dorchester). Dor (At). [Warwick.]

Auchterarder (Agric Depot under Stobs). Stbs (Au). [Perth.]

Axbridge (Agric Group attached to Long Ashton Agric Depot under Dorchester). Dor (LA) (Abg). [Somerset.]

Badsey Manor (Working Camp under Dorchester). Dor (Bad).
Badsey Manor, Badsey, Worcs.
www.badsey.net/past/pows.htm

Baldersby Park (Agric Group attached to Thirsk Agric Depot under Catterick). Cat (Th) (Bd).
Home Farm, Baldersby Park, Yorks.

Baldock (Working Camp under Pattishall). Pa (Bal).
Malting House, Baldock, Herts.

Balgowan (Agric Group attached to Auchterarder Agric Depot under Stobs). Stbs (Au) (Bw). [Perth.]

Banbury (Working Camp under Dorchester). Dor (Ba). [Oxon.]

Bandeath (*see under* Polmaise). [No entry in list.]

Barnstone (Agric Group attached to Plumtree Agric Depot under Brocton). Bro (Pl) (Bar).
Langor Hall, Barnstone, Notts.

Beachley. Bch.
Beachley, Chepstow, Monmouth.

Beaminster (Agric Group attached to Gillingham Agric Depot under Dorchester). Dor (Gil) (Bmr). [Dorset.]

Beauly (Working Camp under Stobs). Stbs (Be).
Beauly, Lentran, Inverness.

Beckenham (Working Camp under Feltham). Fe (Bek). [Kent.]

Bedford Military Hospital. Bed H.

Belmont Hospital (*see under* P/W Hospital, Belmont).

Belmont House (Agric Group attached to Chigwell Agric Depot under Pattishall). Pa (Chg) (Bn).
Belmont House, Chigwell, Essex.

Berkhampstead (Agric Group attached to Hemel Hempstead Agric Depot under Pattishall). Pa (Heml) (Bk). [Herts.]

Berkswell (Working Camp under Dorchester). Dor (Ber).
Berkswell, Hampton in Arden, Warwick.

Bethnal Green Military Hospital. BGH.
Military Hospital, Cambridge Road, Bethnal Green, London NE.

Billericay (Working Camp under Pattishall). Pa (Bill). [Essex.]

Billingford (Working Camp under Pattishall). Pa (Bf).
Billingford Maltings, near Diss, Norfolk.

Bilston (*see under* Ettingshall).

Binegar (Agric Group attached to Shepton Mallet Agric Depot under Dorchester). Dor (Sh M) (Bin). [Somerset.]

Birmingham Hospital. Bm H.
1st Southern General Hospital, Edgbaston, Birmingham.

Bishop Stortford (Working Camp under Pattishall). Pa (Bis).
Oak Hall, Bishop's Stortford, Herts.

Black Park (*see under* Langley Park).

Blaisdon (Agric Depot under Dorchester). Dor (Bla). [Gloucester.]

Blanches Banques. Jersey.
www.greatwarci.net/pow/index.htm

Blandford (Working Camp under Dorchester) (formerly a Parent Camp).
Dor (Bl). [Dorset.]

Bletchley (Agric Group attached to Leighton Buzzard Agric Depot under Pattishall). Pa (LB) (By).
Watling Street, Bletchley, Bucks.

Blunham (Working Camp under Pattishall). Pa (Bh). [Beds.]

Boddam (Working Camp under Stobs). Stbs (Bdm).
Boddam, near Peterhead, Aberdeen.

Bolsover Castle (Agric Group attached to Sheffield Agric Depot under Catterick). Cat (Shfd) (Bs). [Chesterfield.]

Boroughbridge (Agric Group attached to Thirsk Agric Depot under Catterick). Cat (Th) (Bor).
Boroughbridge, West Riding, Yorks.

Boston Dock (Civilian Working Camp under Brocton). Bro (Bos). [Lincs.]

Bovington (Working Camp under Dorchester). Dor (Bv). [Dorset.]

Bracebridge (Agric Depot under Brocton). Bro (Bbe). [Lincs.]

Brackley (Working Camp under Pattishall). Pa (Br). [Northants.]

Bradford Abbas (Agric Group attached to Gillingham Agric Depot under Dorchester). Dor (Gil) (Brd).
Bradford Abbas, near Yeovil, Somerset.

Braemore (Working Camp under Stobs). Stbs (Bra).
Braemore, Loch Doon, near Ullapool, Ross.

Brailes (Agric Group attached to Chipping Norton Agric Depot under Dorchester). Dor (CN) (Brl).
Springfield House, Brailes, Warwick.

Bramley. Brm.
Bramley, near Basingstoke, Hants.

Brampton (Agric Group attached to Huntingdon Agric Depot under Pattishall). Pa (Hu) (Brp). [Hunts.]

Braughing (Working Camp under Pattishall). Pa (Bru).
Oak Hall, Bishop Stortford, Herts.

Brecon (Agric Depot under Frongoch). Fg (Bre).
County Prison, Brecon, Wales.

Bretby Hall (Agric Group attached to Burton-on-Trent Agric Depot under Brocton). Bro (Brt) (Bry).
Bretby Hall, Burton-on-Trent, Staffs.

Brighton General Hospital. Brg H.
2nd Eastern General Hospital, Brighton, Sussex.

Brightwell (Agric Group attached to Cholsey Agric Depot under Dorchester). Dor (Cho) (Bri). [Berks.]

Brixworth (Working Camp under Pattishall). Pa (Brx). [Northants.]

Broad Marston (Working Camp under Dorchester). Dor (BM).
The Priory, Broad Marston, Warwick.

Brockenhurst (Working Camp under Dorchester). Dor (Brc). [Hants.]

Brocton Camp. Bro.
P/W Camp, Brocton, Staffs.
[*Deutsche Zeitung* – daily handwritten paper mainly concentrating on war news – 1918–1919, and one issue from 1917.]

Brocton Camp Hospital (*see under* P/W Hospital, Brocton).

Bromfield (Agric Group attached to Leominster Agric Depot under Shrewsbury). Shrw (Lmr) (Bfd).
42, West Street, Leominster, Hereford.

Bromyard (Agric Group attached to Leominster Agric Depot under Shrewsbury). Shrw (Lmr) (Byd).
42, West Street, Leominster, Hereford.

Brook House (*see under* Beaminster).

Brooker Hall (*see under* Hove).

Broome (Working Camp under Pattishall). Pa (Boo).
[No postal address given.]

Bucknall (Agric Group attached to Bracebridge Agric Depot under Brocton). Brp (Bbe) (Bc).
Tupholme Hall, Bucknall, Bardney, Lincs.

Bulford (Civilian Camp under Dorchester). Dor (Bu). [Wilts.]

Buntingford (Working Camp under Pattishall). Pa (Bg).
Hare Street, Buntingford, Herts.

Burbage (*see under* Stanley Moor).

Burnham Market (Working Camp under Pattishall). Pa (Burn). [Norfolk.]

Burton Hall (Agric Group attached to Bracebridge Agric Depot under Brocton). Bro (Bbe) (Bt). [Lincs.]

Burton-on-Trent (Working Camp under Brocton). Bro (Brt). [Staffs.]

Buxton (Peak Dale) (Agric Depot under Brocton). Bro (Pe D).
Peak Dale, Buxton, Derby *via* Stockport.

Caersws (Agric Group attached to Kerry Newtown Agric Depot under Frongoch). Fg (Ke N) (Csw). [Montgomery.]

Camberley (*see under* College Town).

Cambridge (Working Camp under Pattishall). Pa (Cam).
  Newmarket Road, Cambridge.

Cambridge Hospital, Aldershot. Ca H.

Cambridge Military Hospital, Cambridge. C M H.

Canning Town (*see under* West Ham).

Caolas-na-Con (Working Camp under Stobs). Stbs (Cs).
  Caolas-na-Con, near Kinlochleven, Argyll.

Cardiff, 3rd Western General Hospital. 3 W G H (C).

Carlton (Agric Group attached to Kelham Agric Depot under Brocton). Bro (Kel) (Ct).
  Carlton, near Kelham, Notts.

Carmarthen (Agric Depot under Frongoch). Fg (Crm). [Wales.]

Castle Bromwich (Working Camp under Dorchester). Dor (Ca B). [Near Birmingham.]

Castleside (*see under* Rowley).

Catterick (formerly a Working Camp under Brocton). Cat. [Yorks.]

Catterick Military Hospital. Ck M H. [Yorks.]

Cawood (Working Camp under Catterick). Cat (Caw).
  Fosters Flour Mills, Cawood, Selby, W Riding, Yorks.

Caxton (Working Camp under Pattishall). Pa (Cax). [Cambs.]

Caythorpe (Agric Group attached to Grantham Agric Depot under Brocton). Bro (Gr) (Cay). [Lincs.]

Chapel-en-le-Frith (Agric Group attached to Peak Dale Agric Depot under Brocton). Bro (Pe D) (Cf).
  Bank Hall, Chapel-en-le-Frith, Derby.

Chapel Oak (Agric Group attached to Evesham Agric Depot under Dorchester). Dor (Ev) (CO).
  Chapel Oak, Iron Cross, Salford Priors, Warwick.

Cheam (Working Camp under Feltham). Fe (Che). [Surrey.]

Chelmsford (Working Camp under Pattishall). Pa (Chfd). [Essex.]

Chelmsford Detention Barracks. CDB. [Essex.]

Chelsea Hospital. Chl H.
2nd London General Hospital, St Mark's College, Chelsea, London SW.

Cheltenham (Working Camp under Dorchester). Dor (Ch). [Gloucester.]

Cheriton Bishop (Working Camp under Dorchester). Dor (Ce). [Devon.]

Chesterton (Working Camp under Pattishall). Pa (Ches). [Cambridge.]

Chevington (Working Camp under Pattishall). Pa (Chv).
Chevington, Bury St Edmunds, Suffolk.

Chigwell (Working Camp under Pattishall). Pa (Chg).
Foxbarrow Farm, Chigwell Row, Essex.

Chippenham (Agric Group attached to Devizes Agric Depot under Dorchester). Dor (Dvz) (Chp). [Wilts.]

Chipping Norton (Working Camp under Dorchester). Dor (CN). [Oxon.]

Chipping Ongar (Agric Depot under Pattishall). Pa (Ch O). [Essex.]

Chisledon (Working Camp under Dorchester). Dor (Chi). [Wilts.]

Chisledon Military Hospital. Chs H. [Wilts.]

Cholsey (Agric Depot under Dorchester). Dor (Cho). [Devon.]

Churchdown (Working Camp under Dorchester). Dor (Cd). [Gloucester.]

Churt (Working Camp under Dorchester). Dor (Cu).
Churt, Farnham, Surrey.

Cilian Aeron (Agric Group attached to Carmarthen Agric Depot under Frongoch). Fg (Crm) (CA). [Cardigan.]

Cirencester (Working Camp under Dorchester). Dor (Cir). [Gloucester.]

City of London Military Hospital. CLH.
42, Clifden Road, Homerton, London NE.

Claydon (Agric Group attached to Haughley Agric Depot under Pattishall). Pa (Hgy) (Cn). [Suffolk.]

Clee Hill Dhu (Working Camp under Shrewsbury). Shrw (Cle). [Salop.]

Clent (Agric Group attached to Northfield Agric Depot under Dorchester). Dor (Nfd) (Cln). [Worcester.]

Cleobury Mortimer (Agric Group attached to Leominster Agric Depot under Shrewsbury). Shrw (Lmr) (Cb). [Salop.]

Codford (Civilian Working Camp under Dorchester). Dor (Cod). [Wilts.]

Colchester Hospital. Col H.
  Military Hospital, Colchester.

College Town (Working Camp under Dorchester). Dor (Cg).
  College Town, Camberley, Surrey.

Colsterdale (Officers). Ctd.
  Colsterdale, near Masham, Yorks.

Compton (Agric Depot under Dorchester). Dor (Cmp). [Berks.]

Coningsby (Agric Group attached to Bracebridge Agric Depot under Brocton). Bro (Bbe) (Con). [Lincs.]

Connaught Hospital. Con H.
  Connaught Hospital, Aldershot, Hants.

Consett (*see under* Rowley).

Conveth Mains (Working Camp under Stobs). Stbs (Cv).
  Conveth Mains, Laurencekirk, Kincardine.

Copt Hewick Hall (Agric Group attached to Thirsk Agric Depot under Catterick). Cat (Th) (Cp).
  Copt Hewick Hall, near Ripon, Yorks.

Corby (Civilian Working Camp under Pattishall). Pa (Cor).
  Corby, near Kettering, Northants.

Corfton Hall (Agric Group attached to Leominster Agric Depot under Shrewsbury). Shrw (Lmr) (Cof).
  42, West Street, Leominster, Hereford.

Cove (Working Camp under Dorchester). Dor (Cve).
  Cove, Farnborough, Hants.

Cranleigh (Working Camp under Pattishall). Pa (Crg). [Surrey.]

Crawford (Working Camp under Stobs). Stbs (Cra). [Lanark.]

Crichel (Working Camp under Dorchester). Dor (Ci).
  Crichel, Blandford, Dorset.

Crickhowell (Working Camp under Frongoch). Fg (Cri). [S Wales.]

Crondall (Working Camp under Dorchester). Dor (Cr). [Hants.]

Crowthorne War Hospital (formerly known as Broadmoor Military Hospital). Cr H.
  Crowthorne, War Hospital, Crowthorne, Berks.

Croxton (*see under* Warren Wood).

Croxton Park (Agric Depot under Brocton). Bro (Crx).
Croxton Park, Melton Mowbray, Leicester.

Cuddington (Working Camp under Handforth). Hfth (Cdg). [Cheshire.]

Cumnor (Agric Group attached to Cholsey Agric Depot under Dorchester).
Dor (Cho) (Cm). [Oxon.]

Dartford War Hospital. LDH. [Kent.]

Dawyck (Working Camp under Stobs). Stbs (Da).
Dawyck, Stobo, Peebles.

Deal Royal Marine Infirmary. DMI.

Deddington (Agric Group attached to Banbury Agric Depot under Dorchester). Dor (Ba) (Dd). [Oxon.]

Denby (Working Camp under Brocton). Bro (De). [near Derby.]

Denham Lodge (Agric Depot under Feltham). Fe (DL).
Denham Lodge, Uxbridge, Middlesex.

Devizes (Agric Depot under Dorchester). Dor (Dvz). [Wilts.]

Devonport Hospital. Dpt H.
Military Hospital, Devonport.

Digby (Agric Group attached to Grantham Agric Depot under Brocton). Bro (Gr) (Di). [Lincs.]

Dolyhir (Working Camp under Shrewsbury). Shrw (Doy).
Dolyhir, Kington, Hereford.

Donington Hall. Dgn.
Donington Hall, Castle Donington, Derby.

Dorchester. Dor.
Bilder aus dem 'P.O.W. Camp' Dorchester (London: Minister, 1919).
[*Deutsche Blatter* – not held by IWM. No. 3, 24 December 1916 – at SOF.]

Dorking (Working Camp under Feltham). Fe (Dok). [Surrey.]

Douglas. Doug. [Isle of Man.]
[*Camp Echo: Halbmonatsschrift für das Douglas Prisoner of War Camp* – not held by IWM. Nos. 3–7, March 1915–January 1916 – at British Library.]

Dover Military Hospital. Dv H. [Kent.]

Downham Hall (Working Camp under Pattishall). Pa (Dw).
Downham Hall, Brandon, Suffolk.

Drim Wood (Working Camp under Frongoch). Fg (Dr).
Drim Wood, Narberth, Pembroke, S Wales.

Droitwich (Working Camp under Dorchester). Dor (Dro). [Worcester.]

Drumbuach (Working Camp under Stobs). Stbs (Du). [Methven.]

Dulverton (Agric Depot under Dorchester). Dor (Dlv). [Somerset.]

Dunmow (Working Camp under Pattishall). Pa (Dun). [Essex.]

Dykebar War Hospital. Dy H. [Paisley.]

Eardiston (Working Camp under Dorchester). Dor (Ear).
Eardiston, Tenbury Wells.

Eartham (Working Camp under Pattishall). Pa (Ert).
Eartham, Slindon, near Chichester.

Easingwold (Agric Group attached to Thirsk Agric Depot under Catterick). Cat (Th) (Eas).
Easingwold, N Riding, Yorks.

Eastcote (name now changed to Pattishall).

Eastcote (Agric Group attached to Denham Lodge Agric Depot under Feltham). Fe (D L) (Es).
Eastcote, Pinner, Middlesex.

East Dereham (Working Group under Pattishall). Pa (E D). [Norfolk.]

Eastgate (Working Camp under Catterick). Cat (Ea).
Rosehill Farm, Eastgate, Co Durham.

East Grinstead (Working Camp under Pattishall). Pa (E G). [Sussex.]

East Leake (Agric Group attached to Loughborough Agric Depot under Brocton). Bro (Lo) (Ek).
East Leake, Loughborough, Leicester.

East Leeds War Hospital. L W H.
Harehills Road, Leeds.

Easton-on-the-Hill (Working Camp under Pattishall). Pa (Ean).
Easton-on-the-Hill, near Stamford, Northants.

East Preston (Working Camp under Pattishall). Pa (E P).
East Preston, Angmering, Sussex.

Edinburgh. Edin.
The Detention House, Edinburgh Castle.

Edinburgh Castle Hospital. ECH.

Castle Military Hospital, Edinburgh.

Eggesford (Agric Depot under Dorchester). Dor (Eg). [Devon.]

Ellesmere (Agric Group attached to Leominster Agric Depot under Shrewsbury). Shrw (Lmr) (Ee).
42, West Street, Leominster, Hereford.

Elton (Working Camp under Pattishall). Pa (El). [Hunts.]

Enfield (Working Camp under Feltham). Fe (En).
Clayhill Lodge, Enfield, Middlesex.

Epping (Working Camp under Pattishall). Pa (Epp). [Essex.]

Estuary Road (Working Camp under Pattishall). Pa (ER).
Estuary Road, King's Lynn, Norfolk.

Ettingshall (Working Camp under Brocton). Bro (Et).
Bilston, Staffs.

Etwall (Agric Group attached to Burton-on-Trent Agric Depot under Brocton). Bro (Brt) (Ew). [Derby.]

Evesham (Working Camp under Dorchester). Dor (Ev). [Worcester.]

Eye (Working Camp under Pattishall). Pa (Eye). [Suffolk.]

Falmouth Military Hospital. Fa H.

Fargo Rolleston Military Hospital. FRH.
Fargo Rolleston Military Hospital, Salisbury, Wilts.

Faringdon (Agric Group attached to Compton Agric Depot under Dorchester). Dor (Cmp) (Fdn).
Pidnell House, Faringdon, Berks.

Feltham. Fe. [Middlesex.]

Fladbury (Working Camp under Dorchester). Dor (Fla).
Craycombe House, Fladbury, Pershore, near Worcester.

Flax Bourton (*see under* Long Ashton).

Flowerdown (Working Camp under Dorchester). Dor (Fld). [Winchester.]

Folkingham (Agric Group attached to Sleaford Depot under Brocton). Bro (Sl) (Fl). [Lincs.]

Forgandenny (Agric Group attached to Auchterarder Agric Depot under Stobs). Stbs (Au) (Fa). [Perth.]

Forteviot (Agric Group attached to Auchterarder Agric Depot under Stobs). Stbs (Au) (Ft). [Perth.]

Fovant (Working Camp under Dorchester). Dor (Fo). [Wilts.]

Frampton-on-Severn (Working Camp under Dorchester). Dor (Fra). [Gloucester.]

Frith Hill. F Hi.
Headquarters, Blackdown, Surrey.

Frome (Working Camp under Dorchester). Dor (Fr).
Keyford, Frome, Somerset.

Frongoch. Fg.
Frongoch, near Bala, N Wales.

Fulham Military Hospital. Fu H.
St Dunstan's Road, Hammersmith, London W.

Gamlingay (Working Camp under Pattishall). Pa (Gg).
Gamlingay, Sandy, Beds.

German Hospital. Ger H.
German Hospital, Dalston, London NE.

Gillingham (Agric Depot under Dorchester). Dor (Gil). [Dorset.]

Gisburn (Agric Group attached to Pateley Bridge Agric Depot under Catterick). Cat (PB) (Gi).
Gisburn, West Riding, Yorks.

Glasgow. 3rd Scottish General Hospital. 3 SGH (G).

Glasgow. 4th Scottish General Hospital. 4 SGH (G).

Glatton (Working Camp under Pattishall). Pa (Glt). [Hunts.]

Glendevon (Working Camp under Stobs). Stbs (Gle).
Glendevon, Dollar, Clackmannan.

Glentham (Agric Group attached to Bracebridge Agric Depot under Brocton). Bro (Bbe) (Ce) [sic].
Glentham, Market Rasen, Lincs.

Gore Farm (Working Camp under Pattishall). Pa (Go).
Gore Farm, Dartford.

Grantham (Working Camp under Brocton). Bro (Gr).
Belton Park, Grantham, Lincs.

Grays (Working Camp under Pattishall). Pa (Ga).
The Wouldham Cement Co., Grays, Essex.

Great Baddow (Working Camp under Pattishall). Pa (G B). [Essex.]

Great Coggeshall (Agric Group attached to Halstead Agric Depot under Pattishall). Pa (Hst) (Gra). [Essex.]

Great Hale (Agric Group attached to Sleaford Agric Depot under Brocton). Bro (Sl) (Gh).
Great Hale, Heckington, Lincs.

Great Hampton (Working Camp under Dorchester). Dor (Gh). [Evesham.]

Great Offley (Working Camp under Pattishall). Pa (GO). [Herts.]

Great Ouseburn (Agric Group attached to Thirsk Agric Depot under Catterick). Cat (Th) (Gre). [Yorks.]

Great Witley (Working Camp under Dorchester). Dor (GW). [Worcester.]

Green Lane Farm (Agric Group attached to Pateley Bridge Agric Depot under Catterick). Cat (PB) (GF).
Green Lane Farm, near Doncaster, West Riding, Yorks.

Gringley-on-the-Hill (Agric Group attached to Retford Agric Depot under Brocton). Bro (Ret) (Gn).
Gringley-on-the-Hill, W Gainsborough, Lincs.

Guildford (*see under* Langton Priory).

Guilsborough (Working Camp under Pattishall). Pa (Gu). [Northants.]

Hackney Wick. Hny.
Hackney Wick, Gainsborough Road, London NE.

Hailsham (Working Camp under Pattishall). Pa (Hail). [Sussex.]

Halam (Agric Group attached to Kelham Agric Depot under Brocton). Bro (Kel) (Hl).
Halam, Southwell, Notts.

Halesworth (Working Camp under Pattishall). Pa (Has). [Suffolk.]

Hallatrow (Agric Group attached to Shepton Mallet Agric Depot under Dorchester). Dor (Sh M) (Hall). [Somerset.]

Halling (also known as Snodland) (Working Camp under Pattishall). Pa (Hlg).
Lee's Cement Works, Halling, Snodland, Kent.

Halstead (Working Camp under Pattishall). Pa (Hst). [Essex.]

Halton Park (Working Camp under Pattishall). Pa (Ha P).
Halton Park, Wendover, Bucks.

Hammersmith Military Hospital. HH.
Ducane Road, Shepherd's Bush, London W.

Handforth. Hfth.
Rubber Works, Handforth, Cheshire.

Harewood (Agric Group attached to Pateley Bridge Agric Depot under Catterick). Cat (PB) (Hd).
Harewood, West Riding, Yorks.

Harperley (Working Camp under Catterick). Cat (Har).
Harperley Station, Co Durham.

Hatfield (Working Camp under Pattishall). Pa (Hat). [Herts.]

Hatherleigh (Working Camp under Dorchester). Dor (Ht). [Devon.]

Hatherton (Working Camp under Handforth). Hfth (Han).
Hatherton, near Nantwich, Cheshire.

Hatley St George (Working Camp under Pattishall). Pa (Hs).
The Rectory, Hatley St George, Gamlingay, Sandy, Beds.

Haughley (Agric Depot under Pattishall). Pa (Hgy). [Suffolk.]

Haughton Lodge (Agric Group attached to Market Harborough Agric Depot under Brocton). Bro (MH2) (Hh).
Haughton Lodge, Market Harborough, Leicester.

Haverfordwest (Working Camp under Frongoch). Fg (Hf). [Pembroke.]

Hawkesbury (Working Camp under Dorchester). Dor (Hk). [Upton.]

Haywards Heath (Working Camp under Pattishall). Pa (Hy). [Sussex.]

Heacham (Working Camp under Pattishall). Pa (Hm). [Norfolk.]

Healeyfield (*see under* Rowley).

Hemel Hempstead (Agric Depot under Pattishall). Pa (Heml). [Herts.]

Hendon (*see under* Mill Hill).

Henfield (Working Camp under Pattishall). Pa (Hn). [Sussex.]

Hermitage (Working Camp under Frongoch). Fg (He C).
'The Hermitage', Crickhowell, Brecon.

Heveningham (Agric Group attached to Haughley Agric Depot under Pattishall). Pa (Hgy) (Hv).
Heveningham, Saxmundham, Suffolk.

Hogsthorpe (Agric Group attached to Wainfleet Agric Depot under Brocton).
Bro (Wai) (Hog). [Lincs.]

Holbeach (Agric Group attached to Wingland Agric Depot under Brocton). Bro (Wgl) (Hol). [Lincs.]

Hollowell (Working Camp under Pattishall). Pa (Hw).
Hollowell Grange, Creaton, Northants.

Holmbury (*see under* Shere).

Holyport (Officers). Hlt.
Holyport, near Bray, Maidenhead, Berks.

Honiton (Agric Group attached to Sidbury Agric Depot under Dorchester). Dor (Sd) (Ho). [Devon.]

Horsham (Working Camp under Pattishall). Pa (Hsm). [Sussex.]

Houghton Regis (Working Camp under Pattishall). Pa (Hi). [Beds.]

Hove (Working Camp under Pattishall). Pa (Hov).
Brooker Hall, Hove, Sussex.

Huntingdon (Working Camp under Pattishall). Pa (Hu). [Hunts.]

Hunton Bridge (Working Camp under Pattishall). Pa (Hb).
Hunton Bridge, King's Langley, Herts.

Hursley Park (Working Camp under Dorchester). Dor (Hur).
Hursley Park, Standon, Hursley, near Winchester.

Ilchester (Working Camp under Dorchester). Dor (Ih).
Ilchester, near Yeovil, Somerset.

Ilkeston (Agric Group attached to Barton-on-Trent Agric Depot under Brocton). Bro (Brt) (Il).
Oakwell Colliery Buildings, Ilkeston, Derby.

Illeston (Agric Group attached to Market Harborough Agric Depot under Brocton). Bro (MH 2) (Ie).
Illeston Grange, Market Harborough, Leicester.

Inverlaidnan (Working Camp under Stobs). Stbs (Ivl).
Inverlaidnan, Carr Bridge, Inverness.

Ipswich Military Hospital. Ip H.

Isleworth (Working Camp under Feltham). Fe (Isw). [Middlesex.]

Islington. Isl.
St Mary's Institute, Cornwallis Road, Islington, London N.
Hinter dem Stacheldraht – facsimile issue for 5 September 1915 held in Barry Chinchen's 'Aliens, Internees and Prisoners of War in the UK, 1914–1920' at IWM.

Itton (Agric Group attached to Leominster Agric Depot under Shrewsbury). Shrw (Lmr) (It).
Cottage Farm, Itton, near Chepstow, Monmouth.

Ivybridge (Working Camp under Dorchester). Dor (Iv).
Lee Mill, Ivybridge, Devon.

Iwerne Minster (Working Camp under Dorchester). Dor (Iw).
Iwerne Minster, near Blandford, Dorset.

Jersey. Jer.
Jersey, Channel Islands.

Justinhaugh (Working Camp under Stobs). Stbs (Ju).
Newmiln of Craigeassie, Justinhaugh.

Kedington (Working Camp under Pattishall). Pa (Kedn).
Kedington, near Haverhill, Suffolk.

Kegworth (Officers). Keg. [Derby.]

Kelham (No 3 Agric Depot under Brocton). Bro (Kel).
Kelham Brickfields, Kelham, Newark, Notts.

Kempshott Park (Agric Depot under Dorchester). Dor (KP).
Kempshott House, Kempshott Park, Basingstoke, Hants.

Kenilworth (Agric Depot under Dorchester). Dor (Ke). [Warwick.]

Kenninghall (Working Camp under Pattishall). Pa (Ken).
Kenninghall, East Harling, Norfolk.

Kerry Newtown (Agric Depot under Frongoch). Fg (Ke N). [Montgomery.]

Kettleburgh (Working Camp under Pattishall). Pa (Ket).
Kettleburgh, Wickham Market, Suffolk.

Keyston (Agric Group attached to Oundle Agric Depot under Pattishall). Pa (Ode) (Ky). [Hants.]

Kilburn (*see under* Denby).

Kimbolton (Working Camp under Pattishall). Pa (Kim).
The Stables, Kimbolton Castle, Kimbolton, Hunts.

King George's Hospital. Std H.
King George's Hospital, Stamford Street, London SE.

King George V Hospital, Dublin. GVH.

Kingsbridge (Agric Depot under Dorchester). Dor (Kg). [Devon.]

Kingsbury (Working Camp under Dorchester). Dor (Ks).

King's Lynn (Working Camp under Pattishall). Pa (KL).
St James's Hall, King's Lynn, Norfolk.

Kinlochleven (Working Camp under Stobs). Stbs (Ki). [Argyll.]

Kinmel Park Military Hospital. Km H.
Military Hospital, Kinmel Park, Denbigh.

Kintillo (Agric Group attached to Auchterarder Agric Depot under Stobs). Stbs (Aa) (Kl).
Kintillo, Bridge of Earn, Perth.

Knightwick (*see under* Martley).

Knockaloe. Kck.
Knockaloe, Peel, Isle of Man.
[*Quousque Tandem*, November 1915 and October 1916 issues – military camp.]
[*D.H.: Zivilgefangenen-Halbmonatsschrift*,15 May and 1 June 1917 issues – Knockaloe Aliens Camp.]
[*Knockaloe Lager Zeitung*, nos. 7–19, 10 May 1917–5 September 1918 – held at IWM as photocopies; vol. 2, nos. 3–10, 22 December 1916–4 July 1917 – at SOF – Camp IV Gazette published monthly – 600–700 circulation inside camp and 900 copies sent abroad.]
[*Knockaloe Lager-Echo*, vol. 1, nos. 1–12, vol. 2, nos. 1–7, 18 November 1916–2 October 1918 – Camp 3 – photocopies held by IWM. Some originals at SOF.]
[*Werden: Knockaloe Aliens' Detention Camp* – No. 1, Easter 1915 – not held by IWM – at SOF.]

Knutsford (Working Camp under Handforth). Hfth (Ku). [Cheshire.]

Ladbroke Hall (Working Camp under Dorchester). Dor (Lad).
Ladbroke Hall, Harbury, Southam, Warwick.

Lakenham (Working Camp under Pattishall). Pa (Lk).
Lakenham Mills, near Norwich, Norfolk.

Lambourne (Agric Group attached to Compton Agric Depot under Dorchester). Dor (Cmp) (Lmb). [Berks.]

Lampeter (Agric Group attached to Carmarthen Agric Depot under Frongoch). Fg (Crm) (Lam). [Cardigan.]

Lancaster Castle (Working Camp under Leigh). Lgh (La C). [Lancs.]

Lancing (Working Camp under Pattishall). Pa (Lc). [Sussex.]

Laneham (Agric Group attached to Retford Agric Depot under Brocton). Bro (Ret) (Lh).
Laneham, Retford, Notts.

Langley Park (Agric Group attached to Denham Lodge Agric Depot under Feltham). Fe (DL) (Lgy).
Langley Park, Iver Heath, Bucks.

Langton Priory (Working Camp under Pattishall). Pa (Gfd).
Langton Priory, Guildford, Surrey.

Larkhill (Working Camp under Dorchester). Dor (La).
Larkhill, Salisbury Plain, Wilts.

Lawford Heath (Working Camp under Dorchester). Dor (L Hth).
Lawford Heath, Rugby, Warwick.

Leasowe (Working Camp under Handforth). Hfth (Lea).
Leasowe Castle, near Birkenhead.

Ledbury (Agric Group attached to Leominster Agric Depot under Shrewsbury). Shrw (Lmr) (Ldy).
42, West Street, Leominster, Hereford.

Leicester Hospital. Les H.
No 5 Northern General Hospital, Leicester.

Leigh. Lgh. [Lancs.]

Leigh (Working Camp under Dorchester). Dor (Lei). [near Worcester.]

Leighterton (Working Camp under Dorchester). Dor (Lig).
Leighterton, Tetbury, Gloucester.

Leighton Buzzard (Working Camp under Pattishall). Pa (LB).
20, Market Square, Leighton Buzzard, Bedford.

Lentran (*see under* Beauly).

Leominster (Agric Depot under Shrewsbury). Shrw (Lmr). [Hereford.]

Lewes (Working Camp under Pattishall). Pa (Le).
North Street, Lewes, Sussex.

Lewisham Military Hospital. LH.
Military Hospital, Lewisham, London SE13.

Leystone Farm (Agric Group attached to Auchterarder Agric Depot under Stobs). Stbs (Au) (Ly). [Perth.]

Libury Hall. Lib.
Libury Hall, Ware, Herts.

Lincoln Hospital. Li H.
4th Northern General Hospital, Lincoln.

Linton (Working Camp under Pattishall). Pa (Lin). [Cambs.]

Little Balbrogie (Working Camp under Stobs). Stbs (Lt). [Ardler.]

Littleport (Working Camp under Pattishall). Pa (Lp).
Littleport, near Ely, Cambs.

Liverpool Hospital. Lpl H.
1st Western General Hospital, Fazakerley, Liverpool.

Llanafon (Agric Group attached to Brecon Agric Depot under Frongoch). Fg (Ty) (Lf).
Grogwynion House, Llanafon, near Aberystwyth.

Llanbedr (Agric Group attached to Towyn Depot under Frongoch). Fg (Ty) (Lla).
Penyalt Hall, Llanbedr, Merioneth.

Llandebie (Agric Group attached to Brecon Agric Depot under Frongoch). Fg (Bre) (Llb).
Lime Farm Bldings., Llandebie, Camarthen.

Llandinabo (Agric Group attached to Leominster Agric Depot under Shrewsbury). Shrw (Lmr) (Lb).
42, West Street, Leominster, Hereford.

Llanerchymedd (Agric Group attached to Penmaenmawr Agric Depot under Frongoch). Fg (Pen) (Ll).
The Workhouse, Llanerchymedd, Anglesea.

Llanmartin (Agric Group attached to Leominster Agric Depot under Shrewsbury). Shrw (Lmr) (Llan).
42, West Street, Leominster, Hereford.

Long Ashton (also known as Flax Bourton) (Agric Depot under Dorchester). Dor (LA). [Bristol.]

Long Clawson (Agric Group attached to Croxton Park Agric Depot under Brocton). Bro (Crx) (LC).
The Hall, Long Clawson, Leicester.

Loughborough (Agric Depot under Brocton). Bro (Lo).
The Workhouse, Loughborough, Leicester.

Machynlleth (Agric Group attached to Towyn Agric Depot under Frongoch). Fg (Ty) (Mc). [Montgomery.]

Magdalen Camp Military Hospital. MCMH.
Military Hospital, Magdalen Camp, Winchester.

Maldon (Working Camp under Pattishall). Pa (Mal). [Essex.]

Manchester Hospital. Mn H.
Nell Lane Military Hospital, West Didsbury, Manchester.

Marcham (Working Camp under Dorchester). Dor (Ma). [Berks.]

Market Harborough (No 2 Agric Depot under Brocton). Bro (MH2).
No 2 Agric Depot, Market Harborough, Leicester.

Market Harborough (Agric Group attached to No 2 Agric Depot Market Harborough under Brocton). Bro (MH2) (MH). [Leicester.]

Marks Tey (Working Camp under Pattishall). Pa (MT). [Essex.]

Marshmoor (Working Camp under Pattishall). Pa (Msh).
Marshmoor Sidings, North Mimms, Herts.

Martlesham (Working Camp under Pattishall). Pa (Mar).
Martlesham Heath, Woodbridge, Suffolk.

Martley (formerly at Knightwick) (Working Camp under Dorchester). Dor (Mrt). [Worcester.]

Mayland (Working Camp under Pattishall). Pa (May).
Mayland, Maldon, Essex.

Melchbourne (Working Camp under Pattishall). Pa (Me). [Beds.]

Meldreth (Working Camp under Pattishall). Pa (Mel).
Meldreth, near Royston, Cambs.

Midhurst (Working Camp under Pattishall). Pa (Mid). [Sussex.]

Mildenhall (Working Camp under Pattishall). Pa (Mil). [Suffolk.]

Mile End Military Hospital. MEH.
Bancroft Road, London E.

Millbank Hospital. Mil H.
Queen Alexandra Hospital, Grosvenor Road, London, SW.

Milldown (Working Camp under Dorchester). Dor (Mi). [Dorset.]

Mill Hill (Working Camp under Pattishall). Pa (M Hl). [Middlesex.]

Milnthorpe (Agric Group attached to Stainton Sidings Agric Depot under Leigh). Lgh (St S) (Ml). [Westmorland.]

Monkspath (Working Camp under Dorchester). Dor (Mpa). [Warwick.]

Morton (Agric Group attached to Sleaford Agric Depot under Brocton).
Bro (Sl) (Mo). [Lincs.]

Mundford (Working Camp under Pattishall). Pa (Mun).
   West Tofts, Mundford, Norfolk.

Napsbury War Hospital. Np H.
   Napsbury War Hospital, St Albans.

Narborough (Agric Group attached to Loughborough Agric Depot under
Brocton). Bro (Lo) (Nb).
   The Workhouse, Narborough, Leicester.

Neptune Hall (*see under* Towyn).

Netheravon Aerodrome (Civilian Working Camp under Dorchester). Dor
(Na).
   The Aerodrome, Netheravon, Wilts.

Nethy Bridge (*see under* Seafield). [Not on list.]

Netley Hospital. Net H.
   Royal Victoria Hospital, Netley.

Newcastle Hospital. 1 NGH (N).
   1st Northern General Hospital, Newcastle.

Newlandside (identical with Stanhope) (Working Camp under Catterick).
Cat (Sta).
   Newlandside, Stanhope, Co Durham.

Newport Hospital. 3 WGH (N).
   3rd Western General Hospital, Newport.

Newport Pagnell (Working Camp under Pattishall). Pa (N Pl).
   Headquarters, Westbury House, Newport Pagnell, Bucks.

Newton Abbot (Working Camp under Dorchester). Dor (NA).
   The Institute, Newton Abbot, Devon.

Nocton (Agric Group attached to Grantham Agric Depot under Brocton).
Bro (Gr) (Nn). [Lincs.]

Norfolk War Hospital (*see under* Thorpe).

Normanton (Agric Group attached to Uppingham Agric Depot under
Brocton). Bro (Up) (Nm).
   Normanton, Stamford, Lincs.

Normanton Hall (Agric Group attached to Loughborough Agric Depot
under Brocton). Bro (Lo) (N Ha).
   The Workhouse, Loughborough, Leicester.

Northallerton (Agric Group attached to Thirsk Agric Depot under Catterick). Cat (Th) (Nr).
Northallerton, East Riding, Yorks.

Northfield (Working Camp under Dorchester). Dor (Nfd). [Worcester.]

North Kilworth (Agric Group attached to Market Harborough No 2 Agric Depot under Brocton). Bro (MH2) (NK).
The Hawthorns, North Kilworth, Leicester.

North Leach (Working Camp under Dorchester). Dor (No L). [Gloucester.]

North Lew (Working Camp under Dorchester). Dor (NL). [Devon.]

Northolt (Agric Group attached to Denham Lodge Agric Depot under Feltham). Fe (DL) (Nh).
The Needles, Northolt, Middlesex.

North Ripon. Ni.
No 8, North Camp, Ripon, Yorks.

Norton Barracks Military Hospital. NMH.
Military Hospital, Norton Barracks, Worcester.

Norton Cuckney (Agric Group attached to Retford Agric Depot under Brocton). Bro (Ret) (No).
Norton Cuckney, Mansfield, Notts.

Ockendon (Working Camp under Pattishall). Pa (Ock).
South Ockendon, Romford, Essex.

Offchurch Bury (Agric Group attached to Ladbroke Hall Agric Depot under Dorchester). Dor (Lad) (Of). [Warwick.]

Orfordness (Working Camp under Pattishall). Pa (Ofd). [Suffolk.]

Osbournby (Agric Group attached to Sleaford Agric Depot under Brocton). Bro (Sl) (Ob).

Oswestry. Osw.
Eastern Camp, Park Hall, Oswestry, Salop.

Oswestry (Officers). Ow.
Officers P/W Camp, Park Hall, Oswestry, Salop.

Oswestry, P/W Hospital. O P H.
P/W Hospital, Park Hall Camp, Oswestry, Salop.

Oswestry, Park Hall Hospital. P H H. [Salop.]

Oswestry, Western Camp. Oe.
Western Camp, Park Hall, Oswestry, Salop.

Otley (Agric Group attached to Wetherby Agric Depot under Catterick). Cat (Wet) (Ot).
  Otley, West Riding, Yorks.

Oundle (Agric Depot under Pattishall). Pa (Ode). [Northants.]

Oxted (Working Camp under Pattishall). Pa (Ox). [Surrey.]

Panshanger (Working Camp under Pattishall). Pa (Pan). [Herts.]

Papplewick (Agric Group attached to Plumtree Agric Depot under Brocton). Bro (Pl) (Pp). [Notts.]

Partney (Agric Group attached to Wainfleet Agric Depot under Brocton). Bro (Wai) (Py). [Lincs.]

Pateley Bridge (Agric Group attached to Wetherby Agric Depot under Catterick). Cat (Wet) (P B).
  Pateley Bridge, West Riding, Yorks.

Pattishall (formerly known as Eastcote). Pa.
  Pattishall, near Towcester, Northants.

Peak Dale (*see under* Buxton).

Peasmarsh (Working Camp under Pattishall). Pa (Pea).
  Peasmarsh, Rye, Sussex.

Penarth (Working Camp under Frongoch). Fg (Pr).
  Penarth, Glamorgan, South Wales.

Penmaenmawr (Working Camp under Frongoch). Fg (Pen). [Carnarvon.]

Penshurst (Working Camp under Pattishall). Pa (Pst). [Kent.]

Penycoed Castle (*see under* Llanmartin).

Peopleton (Working Camp under Dorchester). Dor (Peo).
  Peopleton, Pershore, Worcester.

Perham Down (Working Camp under Dorchester). Dor (Prm).
  Perham Down, Salisbury Plain.

Pershore (Agric Depot under Dorchester). Dor (Per). [Worcester.]

Pinchbeck Road (No 16 Agric Depot under Brocton). Bro (Pi R).
  Pinchbeck Road, Spalding, Lincs.

Plumtree (Agric Depot under Brocton). Bro (Pl). [Notts.]

Podington (Working Camp under Pattishall). Pa (Po).
  Podington, near Wellingborough, Northants.

Port Clarence (Working Camp under Brocton). Bro (Po C).
Port Clarence, Middlesbrough, Yorks.

Port Talbot (Working Camp under Frongoch). Fg (Po T). [Glamorgan.]

Portsmouth Hospital. P H.
5th Southern General Hospital, Portsmouth.

Potter's Bar (Working Camp under Feltham). Fe (P Ba). [Middlesex.]

Potton (Working Camp under Pattishall). Pa (Pot). [Beds.]

Purfleet Military Hospital. P M H.

P/W Hospital, Belmont. Bel H.
P/W Hospital, Belmont, near Sutton, Surrey.

P/W Hospital, Brocton. B W H.
P/W Hospital, Brocton Camp, Staffs.

Raasay (Working Camp under Stobs). Stbs (Ra). [Kyle.]

Radford (Civilian Working Camp under Dorchester). Dor (Rad).
Radford, near Coventry, Warwick.

Ragdale Hall (Agric Group attached to Loughborough Agric Depot under Brocton). Bro (Lo) (Rd). [Leicester.]

Rainham (Working Camp under Pattishall). Pa (Rai). [Essex.]

Ramsbury (Working Camp under Dorchester). Dor (Ram).
Barney Farm, Ramsbury, Wilts.

Ranskill (Agric Group attached to Retford Agric Depot under Brocton). Bro (Ret) (Rn).
The Maltings, Ranskill, Notts.

Reading War Hospital. R W H.

Redhill (Working Camp under Pattishall). Pa (Rdh). [Surrey.]

Redmires (Officers' Camp). Re.
Redmires, Sheffield, Yorks.

Retford (Agric Depot under Brocton). Bro (Ret). [Notts.]

Rhoose (Working Camp under Frongoch). Fg (Rh).
Kemey's Hotel, Rhoose, near Cardiff.

Richmond Military Hospital. RH.
Grove Road, Richmond, Surrey.

Rickmansworth (Working Camp under Pattishall). Pa (Rk). [Herts.]

Riding Mill (*also known as* Slaley) (Working Camp under Catterick). Cat (Rid).
  Slaley P O, Riding Mill, Northumberland.

Rippingale (Agric Group attached to Sleaford Agric Depot under Brocton). Bro (Sl) (Rip). [Lincs.]

Rippingale Fen (Agric Group attached to Sleaford Agric Depot under Brocton). Bro (Sl) (Rip). [Lincs.]

Robertsbridge (Working Camp under Pattishall). Pa (Robs). [Sussex.]

Rochford (Working Camp under Pattishall). Pa (Rch). [Essex.]

Rochford (Working Camp under Dorchester). Dor (Rhd).
  Rochford House, Tenbury Wells, Worcester.

Rockland All Saints (Working Camp under Pattishall). Pa (Roc).
  Rockland, Attleborough, Norfolk.

Romsey (Working Camp under Dorchester). Dor (Ro). [Hants.]

Ross-on-Wye (Civilian Working Camp under Shrewsbury). Shrw (RW). [Hereford.]

Rosyth (Working Camp under Stobs). Stbs (Ros).
  Inverkeithing, Rosyth, Fife.

Rothwell (Working Camp under Pattishall). Pa (Rot).
  Rothwell, Kettering, Northants.

Rowley (Working Camp under Catterick). Cat (Rwl).
  Healeyfield, Castleside, near Consett, Co Durham.

Rowrah (Working Camp under Leigh). Lgh (Row). [Cumberland.]

Rumshott (Working Camp under Pattishall). Pa (Rm).
  Rumshott Wood, Sevenoaks, Kent.

Rushden (Working Camp under Pattishall). Pa (Rus).
  Rushden House, Rushden, Northants.

Ruthin (Agric Group attached to Carmarthen Agric Depot under Frongoch). Fg (Crm) (Ru).
  Bathafarm Hall, Ruthin, Denbigh.

Ruthwell (Working Camp under Stobs). Stbs (Rut).
  Ironhurst, Ruthwell, Dumfries.

Saffron Walden (Working Camp under Pattishall). Pa (Sf W).
  The Union, Saffron Walden, Essex.

St Albans (Working Camp under Pattishall). Pa (SA). [Herts.]

Saltram (Working Camp under Dorchester). Dor (Sa).
Saltram, Woodford, Plympton, Devon.

Sandgate (Working Camp under Pattishall). Pa (San).
'Sandgate', Storrington, Sussex.

Sandhill Park (Officers) (*see under* Taunton).

Sandhill Park (Working Camp under Dorchester). Dor (SP).
Sandhill Park, near Taunton, Somerset.

Sawley (Working Camp under Catterick). Cat (Sy). [Yorks.]

Semer (Agric Group attached to Haughley Agric Depot under Pattishall).
Pa (Hgy) (Sem).
Haughley, Suffolk.

Send (Working Camp under Feltham). Fe (Sen).
Boughton Hall, Send, Surrey.

Sheffield Hospital. 3 MGH (Sh).
3rd Northern General Hospital, Sheffield.

Shelsley Walsh (Working Camp under Dorchester). Dor (Sh W).
[Worcester.]

Shepton Mallet (Agric Depot under Dorchester). Dor (Sh M). [Somerset.]

Shere (Working Camp under Pattishall). Pa (She).
Holmbury St Mary, Shere, Surrey.

Shirehampton (Working Camp under Dorchester). Dor (Sh). [near Bristol.]

Shotley. Shy.
HM Training Establishment, Shotley, Harwich.

Shotley. SSQ.
Naval Sick Quarters, Shotley, Harwich.

Shouldham (Working Camp under Pattishall). Pa (Shm). [Norfolk.]

Shrewsbury. Shrw.
Abbey Wood, Shrewsbury.

Sidbury (Working Camp under Dorchester). Dor (Sd). [Devon.]

Sinnington (Agric Group attached to Sproxton Moor Agric Depot under
Catterick). Cat (Sp M). (Sin).
Sinnington, North Riding, Yorks.

Skipton Officers' Camp. Skp. [Yorks.]

Slaley (*see under* Riding Mill).

Sleaford (Working Camp under Brocton). Bro (Sl).
The Union, Sleaford, Lincs.

Slough (Working Camp under Feltham). Fe (Slo). [Bucks.]

Snettisham (*see under* Heacham).

Snodland (*see under* Halling).

Soberton (Agric Depot under Dorchester). Dor (Sob). [Hants.]

Soho Pool (Working Camp under Dorchester). Dor (Soh). [near Birmingham.]

Somerby Hall (Agric Group attached to Bracebridge Agric Depot under Brocton). Bro (Bbe) (So).
Somerby Hall, Gainsborough, Lincs.

Somerford Hall (Agric Group attached to Ettingshall Agric Depot under Bro). Bro (Et) (Sm).
Somerford Hall, Breewood [sic], Staffs.

Southampton. Spn.
Skating Rink Receiving Depot; Bevois Mount Receiving Depot, Southampton.

South Brent (Agric Depot under Dorchester). Dor (Su).
Coronation Hall, South Brent, Devon.

South Cleatham (Agric Group attached to Port Clarence Agric Depot under Catterick). Cat (Po C) (Sc). [Middlesbro.]

Southill Park (Working Camp under Pattishall). Pa (So P). [Beds.]

South Molton (Agric Group attached to Dulverton Agric Depot under Dorchester). Dor (Dlv) (SM). [Devon.]

Spalding. Spg.
The Union, Spalding, Lincs.

Spalding Agricultural Depot (*see under* Pinchbeck Rd).

Stainby (Working Camp under Brocton). Bro (Stby).
Stainby, Grantham, Lincs.

Stainton Sidings (Working Camp under Leigh). Lgh (St S).
Stainton Sidings, Dalton-in-Furness.

Stanford-le-Hope (Working Camp under Pattishall). Pa (Stn). [Essex.]

Stanley Moor (Working Camp under Brocton). Bro (St M).
Stanley Moor, Ladmanlow, Burbage, Buxton.

Stanstead (Working Camp under Pattishall). Pa (Std).
Oak Hall, Bishop's Stortford, Herts.

Starcross (Working Camp under Dorchester). Dor (Sr). [Devon.]

Steeple Bumpstead (Working Camp under Pattishall). Pa (Stg).
Steeple Bumpstead, near Haverhill, Sussex.

Steyning (Working Camp under Pattishall). Pa (Stg). [Sussex.]

Stobs. Stbs.
Stobs, Hawick, Scotland.
[*Stobsiade: Zeitung des deutschen Kriegsgefangenen-Lagers STOBS in Schottland* – incomplete run from 1915–1919.]
www.nls.uk/blogs/500years/index.cfm/2008/9/24/Exhibition-Tours-and
-German-Prisoners-of-War.
www.scotlandsplaces.gov.uk/search_item/index.php?service=RCAHM
S&id=86444.

Stobs P/W Hospital. Ss H.
P/W Hospital, Stobs, Hawick, Roxburgh.

Stoke Edith (Agric Group attached to Leominster Agric Depot under Shrewsbury). Shrw (Lmr) (SE).
42, West Street, Leominster, Hereford.

Stoke Green (Agric Group attached to Denham Lodge Agric Depot under Feltham). Fe (DL) (SG). [Bucks.]

Stone (Agric Group attached to Ashbourne Agric Depot under Brocton). Bro (Ash) (St). [Staffs.]

Stoulton (Agric Group attached to Pershore Agric Depot under Dorchester). Dor (Per) (Sn).
Stoulton, Whittington, Worcester.

Stowell (Agric Group attached to Gillingham Agric Depot under Dorchester). Dor (Gill) (Sto). [Somerset.]

Stow Park (Agric Group attached to Bracebridge Agric Depot under Brocton). Bro (Bbe) (St P). [Lincs.]

Stratford-on-Avon (Working Camp under Dorchester). Dor (Str).
Shottery, Stratford-on-Avon.

Sudbury (Agric Group attached to Burton-on-Trent Agric Depot under Brocton). Bro (Brt) (Sb). [Derby.]

Sutton Bonington [Notts.] – closed 1918.
www.nottingham.ac.uk/shared/shared_exchange/pdf/Exchange_june0
7_Page_21.pdf

www.nottingham.ac.uk/biosciences/schoolinformation/history.aspx

Sutton Bridge (*see under* Wingland).

Sutton Veny (Working Camp under Dorchester). Dor (Su V). [Wilts.]

Sutton Veny Military Hospital. SVH. [Wilts.]

Swanage (Working Camp under Dorchester). Dor (Sw). [Dorset.]

Tadcaster (Agric Group attached to Wetherby Agric Depot under Catterick). Cat (Wet) (Td).
The Workhouse, Tadcaster, W R Yorks.

Talgarth (Agric Group attached to Brecon Agric Depot under Frongoch). Fg (Bre) (Tal).
Fregunter Park, Talgarth, Brecknock.

Taplow Canadian Hospital. TCH.

Tarrylaw (Agric Group attached to Auchterarder Agric Depot under Stobs). Stbs (Au) (Tr).
Tarrylaw Farm, near Balbeggie, Perth.

Taunton (Officers). Tt.
Sandhill Park Officers' Camp, Taunton.

Temple Brener (Agric Group attached to Grantham Agric Depot under Brocton). Bro (Gr) (Tm). [No postal address given]

Tempsford (Working Camp under Pattishall). Pa (Tpf). [Beds.]

Tendring (Working Camp under Pattishall). Pa (Ten). [Essex.]

Tenterden (Agric Depot under Pattishall). Pa (Tet). [Kent.]

Thing Hall (Agric Group attached to Leominster Agric Depot under Shrewsbury). Shrw (Lmr) (Tn).
42, West Street, Leominster, Hereford.

Thirsk (Agric Depot under Catterick). Cat (Th).
Thirsk, North Riding, Yorks.

Thornbury (Working Camp under Dorchester). Dor (Thn). [Gloucester.]

Thorpe, Norfolk War Hospital. TWH.
The Norfolk War Hospital, Thorpe, Norwich.

Thorpe Satchville (Agric Group attached to Croxton Park Agric Depot under Brocton). Bro (Crx) (Tv).
Thorpe Satchville, near Melton Mowbray, Leicester.

Timberland (Agric Group attached to Grantham Agric Depot under Brocton). Bro (Gr) (Tb).
The Maltings, Timberland, Lincs.

Tiverton (Agric Group attached to Dulverton Agric Depot under Dorchester). Dor (Dlv) (Ti). [Devon.]

Tockwith (Agric Group attached to Pateley Bridge Agric Depot under Catterick). Cat (PB) (Tok).
Tockwith, near York, Yorks.

Toddington (Working Camp under Dorchester). Dor (To).
Toddington, Winchcombe, Gloucester.

Tooting Military Hospital. T H.
Church Lane, Tooting, London SW.

Tovil (Working Camp under Pattishall). Pa (Tov). [Kent.]

Towyn (Agric Depot under Frongoch). Fg (Ty).
Neptune Hall, Towyn, Merioneth.

Trawsfynydd (Working Camp under Frongoch). Fg (Trf). [Merioneth.]

Turvey (Working Camp under Pattishall). Pa (Tur). [Beds.]

Tutnall and Cobley (Working Camp under Dorchester). Dor (Tut).
Tutnall, Bromsgrove, Worcester.

Tuxford (Agric Group attached to Kelham Agric Depot under Brocton). Bro (Kel) (Tu). [Notts.]

Twyford (Working Camp under Dorchester). Dor (Tw).
Know Hill, Twyford, Berks.

Uckfield (Working Camp under Pattishall). Pa (Uk). [Sussex.]

Upavon (Working Camp under Dorchester). Dor (Upv). [Wilts.]

Uppingham (Working Camp under Brocton). Bro (Up). [Rutland.]

Upton (Working Camp under Pattishall). Pa (Upt).
The Vicarage, Upton, Northants.

Upton-on-Severn (Agric Group attached to Leigh Court Agric Depot under Dorchester). Dor (Lei) (Up S). [Worcester.]

Upware (Working Camp under Pattishall). Pa (Uw).
Upware, Wicken, Cambs.

Usk (Agric Group attached to Leominster Agric Depot under Shrewsbury). Shrw (Lmr) (Us).
42, West Street, Leominster, Hereford.

Uttoxeter (Agric Group attached to Ashbourne Agric Depot under Brocton). Bro (Ash) (Ut). [Staffs.]

Waddesdon (Working Camp under Pattishall). Pa (Wd). [Bucks.]

Wainfleet (Agric Depot under Brocton). Bro (Wai). [Lincs.]

Wakefield Officers' Camp. Wf.
Lofthouse Park, Wakefield.

Wakerley (Working Camp under Pattishall). Pa (Wa).
Wakerley, Stamford, Northants.

Walsham-le-Willows (Working Camp under Pattishall). Pa (Wal) [Suffolk.]

Wandsworth Hospital. Wds H.
3rd London General Hospital, Wandsworth, London SW.

Wantage (Agric Group attached to Compton Agric Depot under Dorchester). Dor (Cmp) (Wg). [Berks.]

Warmsworth Hall (Agric Depot under Catterick). Cat (War). [Doncaster.]

Warren Wood (Working Camp under Pattishall). Pa (WW).
Warren Wood, Croxton, Thetford, Norfolk.

Watlington (Agric Group under attached to Cholsey Agric Depot under Dorchester). Dor (Cho) (Wt).
Watlington, Brightwell, Oxon.

Wellesbourne (Agric Depot under Dorchester). Dor (Wel).
Holly Lodge, Wellesbourne, Warwick.

Welshpool (Agric Group attached to Kerry Newtown Agric Depot under Frongoch). Fg (Ke N) (Wsh).
The Horse Repository, Welshpool, Montgomery.

Wem (Agric Group attached to Leominster Agric Depot under Shrewsbury). Shrw (Lmr) (Wem).
42, West Street, Leominster, Hereford.

Weobly (Agric Group attached to Leominster Agric Depot under Shrewsbury). Shrw (Lmr) (Weo).
42, West Street, Leominster, Hereford.

West Ham (Working Camp under Pattishall). Pa (Weh).
Abbey Mills, Manor Road, West Ham, E 15.

West Mersea (Working Camp under Pattishall). Pa (Ws). [Colchester.]

Weston-on-the-Green (Working Camp under Dorchester). Dor (Wn). Weston-on-the-Green, near Bicester, Oxon.

Wetherby (Agric Depot under Catterick). Cat (Wet). The Brewery, Wetherby, West Riding, Yorks.

Whitwell (Agric Group attached to Kenninghall Agric Depot under Pattishall). Pa (Ken) (Whi). [Norfolk.]

Wicken (*see under* Upware).

Wigmore (Agric Group attached to Ross-on-Wye Agric Depot under Shrewsbury). Shrw (RW) (Wig). [Hereford.]

Wilby (Agric Group attached to Haughley Agric Depot under Pattishall). Pa (Hgy) (Wil). [Suffolk.]

Willington (Agric Group attached to Burton-on-Trent Agric Depot under Brocton). Bro (Brt) (Wl). [Staffs.]

Wimborne (Working Camp under Dorchester). Dor (Wmb). [Dorset.]

Winchcomb (Agric Group attached to Toddington Agric Depot under Dorchester). Dor (To) (Wm). [Gloucester.]

Winchester, Magdalen Camp Hospital (*see under* Magdalen Camp).

Wingland (Working Camp under Brocton). Bro (Wgl). Wingland, Sutton Bridge, Wisbech, Lincs.

Winwich (Working Camp under Pattishall). Pa (Win). [Northants.]

Wisborough Green (Working Camp under Pattishall). Pa (Wis). [Sussex.]

Withern (Agric Group attached to Wainfleet Agric Depot under Brocton). Bro (Wai) (Wih). Withern, near Alford, Lincs.

Witney (Working Camp under Dorchester). Dor (Wit). [Oxon.]

Woburn (Working Camp under Pattishall). Pa (Wo). [Beds.]

Woking Detention Barracks. WDB.

Womenswould (Working Camp under Pattishall). Pa (We). [Canterbury.]

Woodborough (Agric Group attached to Plumtree Agric Depot under Brocton). Bro (Pl) (Wb). [Notts.]

Woodham Ferrers (Working Camp under Pattishall). Pa (Wod Fr). Woodham Lodge, Woodham Ferrers, Bicknacre, Essex.

Woodstock (Working Camp under Dorchester). Dor (Wds). Drill Hall, Woodstock, Oxon.

Wookey (Agric Group attached to Shepton Mallet Agric Depot under Dorchester). Dor (Sh M) (Wk). [Somerset.]

Woolwich Hospital. Wch H.
Royal Herbert Hospital, Woolwich, London SE.

Wootton Bassett (Agric Group attached to Devizes Agric Depot under Dorchester). Dor (Dvz) (WB).
Corner House, Wootton Bassett, Wilts.

Worcester, Norton Barracks Hospital (*see under* Norton Barracks).

Worthy Down (Working Camp under Dorchester). Dor (WD). [Winchester.]

Wrotham (Agric Group attached to Halling Agric Depot under Pattishall). Pa (Hlg) (Wro).
Bayldon House, Kingsdown, Wrotham, Sevenoaks, Kent.

Wrottesley (Agric Group attached to Ettingshall Agric Depot under Brocton). Bro (Et) (Wr).
Wrottesley Hall, Wrottesley, near Codsall, Staffs.

Wymondham (Agric Group attached to Croxton Park Agric Depot under Brocton). Bro (Crx) (Wy). [Leicester.]

Yardley Gobion (Working Camp under Pattishall). Pa (Yg).
Yardley Gobion, Stoney Stratford, Bucks.

Yatesbury (Working Camp under Dorchester). Dor (Yby).
Yatesbury, Calne, Wilts.

INDEX